Played in Liverpool

Charting the heritage of a city at play

Played in Liverpool
© English Heritage 2007

English Heritage
is the government's statutory
advisor on all aspects of the
historic environment

3 Chepstow Street
Manchester M1 5FW
www.english-heritage.org.uk

Design by Doug Cheeseman

Production by Jackie Spreckley
Maps by Mark Fenton
For image credits see page 190

Malavan Media is a creative
consultancy responsible
for the Played in Britain series
www.playedinbritain.co.uk

Printed by Zrinski, Croatia
ISBN: 978 185074 9905
Product code: 51080

Played in Liverpool

Charting the heritage of a city at play

Ray Physick

Editor Simon Inglis

Frank Sugg, whose shop on Lord Street was a Liverpool landmark for much of the 20th century, was one of sport's greatest all rounders. Wisden Cricketer of the Year in 1890, he represented England at cricket, football and baseball (at Shiel Park in 1899), was a batsman for Derbyshire and Lancashire, played club football for Sheffield Wednesday, Derby, Burnley, Bolton and Everton, was an accomplished marksman, long distance swimmer and weightlifter, and also played bowls and billiards to a high level. Sugg died in Waterloo in 1933. The city's other main sports outfitters belonged to another former Everton player, Jack Sharp (*see page 112*).

Page Two Many a Liverpudlian honed his football skills on the streets, a tradition that carried on into the 1960s at St Andrew's Gardens, a council housing estate better known as the Bullring, on Copperas Hill (to the rear of Lime Street Station). Designed by John Hughes, the flats were famously dismissed by George Orwell as 'slums in the air' when they opened in 1935. Since refurbished, they are now used as student accommodation.

Page One Racing at Aintree in October 2006, home of the world famous Grand National steeplechase (*see Chapter Three*).

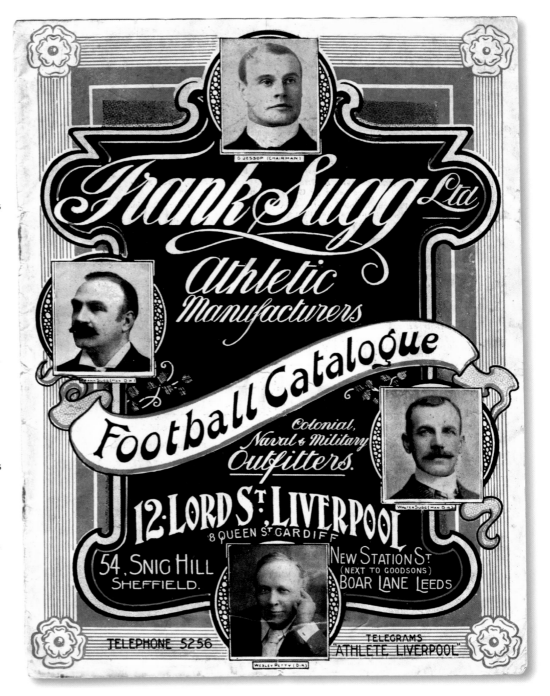

Contents

Foreword

by Councillor Warren Bradley, Leader of Liverpool City Council

Liverpool is famous the world over for its sporting legends and institutions. Although football is the dominant force in the city, Liverpool has an equally rich tradition in sports such as athletics, swimming, gymnastics and boxing.

The city has also been at the forefront of sporting innovation, even staging its own 'Olympic Festivals' during the 1860s. The experience of staging these events helped guide Pierre de Coubertin when it came to creating the first modern Olympiad in 1896.

Besides Everton FC being a founder member of the Football League, the City Engineer John Brodie invented football nets. The city also boasts the world's oldest open rugby club and the world's most famous steeplechase.

The Victorian passion for organisation has bequeathed the city an enviable roll call of sporting cathedrals, from Aintree to Anfield and from the Royal Liverpool at Hoylake to Royal Birkdale near Southport (venues of the 2006 and 2008 Open Golf Championships).

The Aigburth ground of Liverpool Cricket Club, shortly to celebrate its 200th anniversary, was described as one of the finest in Britain by no less an authority than Sir Donald Bradman.

With such inspirational venues to perform at, participation levels are huge, and the city can point to home-grown success stories in almost every field of play – most recently Beth Tweddle in gymnastics, Stephen Parry in swimming and Liverpool FC in the UEFA Champions League.

Sport is also fundamental to the renaissance of Liverpool's fortunes. The city is investing millions in facilities, not least a new 50m pool and a new indoor arena on the waterfront.

A European Capital of Culture sports strategy has also been created – the first of its kind – its focus being to attract high profile, international events and to support grassroots sports. Accordingly, the city will be staging the European Senior Boxing championships in February 2008 which act as Olympic qualifiers for Beijing.

Natural assets like the River Mersey are also being used to host major events, such as the Honda Power Boats Championships and the Clipper Round-the-World Yacht Race.

Our public parks are also a major resource. Calderstones Park, for example, stages the annual Liverpool International Tennis Tournament, which showcases current and legendary players. Besides attracting stars such as Navratilova and Borg, more than 4,000 local youngsters are coached throughout the week.

Youth participation is a big priority. Our Sports Development programme is one of the UK's largest. Over the past decade more than £40m has been invested in council sporting facilities, creating the UK's first publicly funded family gym along the way, in a bid to tackle youth obesity.

In short, Liverpool is committed to ensuring that one of the legacies of 2008 is a city in which sporting excellence and an active lifestyle continues to be an intrinsic part of our cultural DNA.

A member of the City of Liverpool Gymnastics Club and a student at John Moores University, Beth Tweddle won Britain's first ever gold medal in gymnastics at the World Championships in Denmark in 2006. But as we learn in Chapter Twelve, Tweddle is part of a long and proud gymnastics tradition in the city, dating back to the 1850s and to the Liverpool Olympic Festivals of the 1860s and 1890s.

◀ As might be expected in an area with strong maritime links, bells form a common feature on the local sporting scene. Shown here are the bells of four of the region's oldest clubs. **Birkenhead Park Cricket Club** (*top left*), formed in 1846 and are based in the oldest pavilion on Merseyside. In the clubhouse of the **Royal Liverpool Golf Club**, formed at Hoylake in 1869, this 1847 bell (*top right*) dates back to when the golf course was a racecourse, run by the Liverpool Hunt Club. The **Northern Cricket Club**, Crosby, formed in 1859, and call time in their clubhouse with a bell that commemorates the club's move to Waterloo Park in 1879 (*lower left*). Older than all these is the **Royal Mersey Yacht Club** (*lower right*), formed in 1844, although the bell in their committee room in Rock Ferry is more recent.

Chapter One

Played in Liverpool

Watching over the greens of the Royal Liverpool Golf Club in Hoylake is a carved representation of a liver bird, the symbol of Liverpool. The liver bird appears also on the badges of the Liverpool Ramblers FC (formed 1882), Liverpool FC, who chose it for their emblem in 1901, the Royal Mersey Yacht Club (formed 1844) and the Mersey Rowing Club (1854). And yet no-one knows what a liver bird really is. Our heritage is littered with such anomalies, and in this respect, sport is no different.

Popular culture, as well as High Art, played a key role in Liverpool's selection as European Capital of Culture for 2008. But while for most non-Liverpudlians the most obvious manifestations of popular culture in the city appear to have been The Beatles, followed closely by football, both reflect only a limited range of Liverpool's creative and sporting energies.

By charting the heritage of the city at play, Played in Liverpool seeks partly to redress that perception.

It also seeks, by drawing attention to the buildings and places of sport most associated with that heritage, to show how Liverpool's diverse range of sporting activities reflects the character of the city as a whole.

This book is divided into four sections. Following this chapter's summary of sporting history in Liverpool we focus on five areas, or clusters of sporting venues: the River Mersey, Aintree, and three public parks (Birkenhead, Stanley and Sefton). Most cities have such clusters. Finding out how and why they came about can provide

insights that help to understand the city's character as a whole.

This is followed by chapters on three sports related enterprises: the manufacture of billiards equipment, the invention of goal nets and the creation of the football pools industry.

There then follows nine chapters, each concerned with a specific building type, or sport that is characteristic of Liverpool and its surrounding areas.

As the map on page 23 shows, these areas include parts of the neighbouring boroughs of Knowsley, Sefton and the Wirral.

Any significant examples that lie just outside these boundaries, such as in St Helens and Chester, will be covered in future thematic studies being prepared as part of the series (see Links).

Early 'sport' in Liverpool

On 2 November 1565, William Bothill, the son of a mariner, was apprenticed to Oliver Garnet, a master tailor. The terms of his indentures were typical for the period. Bothill was forbidden from playing 'cardes, dice, bowlis [or]

other unlawful gammes,' these to include tennis, football and quoits.

Until well into the 19th century, the word 'sport' referred mainly to bloodsports (primarily hunting, the preserve of the rich), and to gambling (the folly of all men).

Tennis, football and quoits were, meanwhile, classed as games, which, according to edicts from the Common Council of Liverpool, were liable to lead to excessive drinking and gambling, and to the neglect of archery practice by men of a military age. In April 1573 the town's mayor even commanded that 'the wandrers and turners with the hobie horse' (that is, acrobats and tumblers) be 'punished in the stocks at the High Cross'.

Following the restoration of the monarchy in 1660 a more relaxed attitude towards sports and pastimes set in, with horse races drawing large crowds to the sands at Crosby (see page 34) and annual Wakes providing a high point in the calendar. Most celebrated were the West Derby Wakes. Cockfights and bare knuckle fights formed part of their attraction, but the

Joseph Strutt sums up the *Played in Britain* ethos in his seminal study of 1801, *The Sports and Pastimes of the People of England*.

In order to form a just estimation of the character of any particular people, it is absolutely necessary to investigate the Sports and Pastimes most generally prevalent among them.

main event was bull baiting, with the climax being the parade of the bull's corpse through the streets on the final day.

Liverpool's Common Council did not merely sanction bull baiting but encouraged it too, by resolving that 'no men should kill a bull until it had been set to fight for its life to amuse the people'.

Hence in 1672 two Liverpool merchants were brought before the Portmoot (or court), accused of allowing their dogs to kill a bull prematurely. (Apart from the amusement provided, the beef, it was argued, tasted better if the bull had been baited before slaughter).

A bull baiting did constitute 'sport' of a kind, however, in that dog owners competed to see whose animal could hang onto the chained bull for the longest, usually by clamping its teeth onto the bull's nose. The winner would receive a collar.

In his diary of July 1712, Bryan Blundell, the founder of the Bluecoat School, offers this description: 'I Baited a Large Bull in ye Bottom of my New Marl-pit in the Great Morehey... there was 8 or 9 Doggs played ye first Bait and onely two ye 3rd Bait...I gave a Collar to be played for but no Dogg could get it to Rich.'

Thomas Troughton's *History of Liverpool* in 1810 recalled that bull baiting in the 1760s was still attracting 'the most elegant ladies and gentlemen in the town.'

Presumably this was also true of a bull baiting staged to celebrate the opening of the Queen's Dock, in 1796.

In common with most towns at this time, Liverpool also had its own 'bearward', whose duty it was to oversee the ceremonial baiting of bears. These baits took place each October at the White Cross

(at the junction of modern day Old Hall Street and Tithebarn Street), in order to celebrate the election of the town's mayor.

Baiting was finally banned in 1835, followed by cockfighting in 1849. But this did not stop the landed gentry or the merchant classes from enjoying their own, rather more exclusive bloodsports.

The earliest reference to fox hunting in the Liverpool area is 1657, when a hunt took place within the former Royal Park of Toxteth, on the site of today's Sefton Park. In 1746 the Common Council donated £5 to the hunt.

Originally the pack was kennelled at the foot of Richmond Row (near to modern day Scotland Road), but as the town grew in the late 18th century the kennels were moved, first to the North Shore, then to Allerton, and finally to the Royal Hotel, Hoylake (where horse racing, then golf later became established). One report in the *Liverpool Courier* of 1809 describes a fox hunt running past Allerton Hall and through Toxteth Park.

Another sport to gain popularity among the elite in the late 18th century was archery. Exclusive societies appeared all over England at this time, of which one, the Mersey Bowmen, set up an archery lodge in Cazneau Street in 1781. Next door to this were indoor tennis courts. Lawn tennis had yet to be invented, but when it did emerge in the 1870s the Mersey Bowmen took that up too, and are playing it to this day, at their base in Sefton Park. They are, as a result, Liverpool's oldest surviving sports club.

Not far behind them is the Childwall Quoiting Club, which may have been in existence in 1795, but was certainly competing in 1811 (see page 16). »

▲ This red sandstone monolith has stood on the corner of **Archerfield Road** and **Booker Avenue**, West Allerton, since 1928, having been originally excavated in 1910, as the plaque records, from a spot 198 feet away, in a field known as Stone Hey. Because the stone is marked by a series of deep vertical grooves, it has been suggested that it was used by archers to sharpen their arrows. Hence it is known locally as the **Robin Hood Stone**.

Certainly there is evidence that archery butts (or targets) were sited in nearby Booker's Field during the period from the 14th to the 16th centuries, when the area formed part of the Royal Park of Toxteth and archery practice was compulsory for all males of a military age. However it is also possible the grooves are natural and that the stone once formed part of a Bronze Age tomb, along with six others now sited in Calderstones Park.

Following the introduction of gunpowder in the late 16th century, archery developed from a military necessity into a leisure pursuit. In Liverpool this led to the formation of the **Mersey Bowmen** in 1781 (see page 76).

Thomas Weltor, at Wallentroat near Northwich, in Cheshire.

Liverpool COCKING.

THE great COCK Match, betwixt the Gentlemen of Cheshire and Lancashire, will be Fought at the new Cock-Pit near the Infirmary, for five and one Hundred; to weigh the 26th Instant, and to fight on Monday the 28th, Tuesday 29 and Wednesday 30th.

BAILEY and } Feeders.
HOULERHEAD }

WHEREAS an Advertisement was inserted in this Paper of the ...

▲ In Liverpool, as in many other English cities, one of the earliest popular 'sports' to require purpose-built venues was **cockfighting**.

The first reference to such a venue in Liverpool appears in 1567, when, on his election as mayor, William Secum ordered that a 'handsome' cockpit be erected 'for further and greater repair of gentlemen and others' between Moor Street and Drury Lane. Over a century later, in 1688, the Moor Street cockpit is described as being built of stone and consisting of three bays with brick outbuildings.

In subsequent years the pit was also referred to as the Cockpit Yard Theatre, and was said to measure 50 x 20 feet, with a gallery and benches surrounding the stage. The building was demolished in the early 19th century, when a corn warehouse was erected on the site.

Meanwhile, as this weekly notice from the *Williamson's Liverpool Advertiser* of March 1756 shows, a new cockpit arose near the recently completed Infirmary (on the site of the present day St. George's Hall). This may well have been the Shaw's Brow cockpit, the remains of which were discovered in 1868 while the land was being cleared

to build the Walker Art Gallery. According to James Picton's *Memorials of Liverpool* the pit had a sunken area 'with tiers of benches round, cut in the rock...'

In 1785 another cockpit opened on what would subsequently be called Cockspur Street. But according to James Stonehouse in *The Streets of Liverpool* (1869) this closed around 1788–90 and in 1807 was converted, rather bizarrely, into the Presbyterian Chapel of St Andrew's (*below*). It was then demolished to make way for houses in the 1820s.

A second cockpit to have been converted into a place of worship, in 1847, was on Warbreck Moor, Aintree – subsequently rebuilt as St Peter's in 1876 – close to the present day racecourse. Other pits

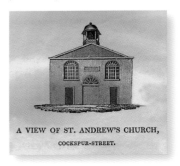

A VIEW OF ST. ANDREW'S CHURCH, COCKSPUR-STREET.

are recorded on Crosby Green and at Old Swan, where champion cocks from Liverpool, Knowsley and Prescot are known to have fought.

Cockfighting played a key role in both the social and organisational development of British sport.

Firstly, cockpits brought together all classes of gamblers, from aristocrats to artisans, in close proximity. One such enthusiast was the tenth Earl of Derby, who was said to have asked for a cockfight to be staged in his bedroom as he lay on his deathbed in 1736.

Secondly, cockfighting was the first sport, pre-dating even cricket, in which regular matches, usually called 'mains', were organised between county representatives.

As may also be seen in the match advertised here, between the Gentlemen of Cheshire and Lancashire, the stakes were high. Indeed Liverpool's last recorded main, in 1830, was between cocks owned by Lord Derby and John Gillivier, for a stake of £5,000.

Cockfighting was eventually banned in Britain in 1849, but the word 'main' lives on in crown green bowling (*see page 123*), where the betting is as keen, but the action rather less bloody.

>> **Early 19th century sport**
Growing urbanisation in the 19th century brought great change to Liverpool. In 1790 the population was 56,000. By 1841 this had increased to 223,000, a significant proportion of whom lived in cramped, airless courts, and who would soon be joined by thousands of Irish immigrants, fleeing from famine. Disease was endemic. Liverpool's death rate was the highest in Britain.

Yet at the same time, enriched by the slave trade (until its abolition in 1807), and by the port's rapidly expanding trade with America and the West Indies, Liverpool's merchant classes had more time than ever to indulge in recreation.

These parallel developments are reflected in the work of John Foster Junior, Corporation Surveyor from 1824–35. While mostly occupied with the usual range of civic buildings (including the Royal Infirmary, Custom House and various churches and cemeteries), in 1828 Foster designed Britain's first municipal swimming baths on the Pierhead (*see page 168*), followed by the first grandstand at Aintree racecourse the year after (*page 38*).

The completion of the Liverpool to Manchester railway in 1830 would further extend the town's social and trading links, connecting Aintree to the network nine years later.

One source of information concerning sporting life during this period is a publication called *Life in London*, later renamed *Bethell's Life in London and Liverpool Sporting Register*.

Published, despite its name, in Liverpool, between November 1824 and October 1827, this weekly journal focused particularly on the then vibrant and bloody world of bare knuckle pugilism. Detailed reports were carried of open-air prizefights on Wallasey Pool and at Chester, watched by thousands of 'sportsmen' from all levels of Liverpool society. There are also acounts of sparring matches, then largely the preserve of gentlemen, at such Liverpool venues as Sewell's Rooms, the Golden Lion, and the Houghton Assembly Rooms on Hood Street.

Cockfighting, still popular, was another favourite topic, as were field sports, such as angling, shooting and fox hunting.

In October 1825 the journal reported that badger baiting with dogs had also caught on, because 'few creatures defend themselves better, or bite with greater keenness than the badger.'

Further insight into the darker side of Liverpool sport comes from the 19th century journalist Hugh Shimmin. He described a number of pubs where boxing matches were held in what he called 'milling cribs'. Only one such pub is identified however, the Crane Beerhouse in Preston Street.

Although illegal, dog fighting was another big draw. A typical dog pit, we learn from Shimmins, measured 2–3 yards square and 30 inches high, lined either by tin or zinc, and made so that it could be dismantled at a moment's notice. In the centre of the pit was a scratch mark. Whichever owner won the toss would haul his dog to this mark (hence he was 'up to scratch'), for battle to commence. A typical purse for the winner's owner was £10. The loser would be lucky to escape with his life.

Dog fights were highly organised. To avoid detection, they were occasionally scheduled as early as 5 am, even on Sunday mornings. Venues, usually back rooms in pubs, were changed regularly. There were also dog fighting clubs, with subscriptions costing 2d or 3d per week. One club declared 'that any member neglecting to attend every Tuesday evening, at seven o'clock and bring his dog with, shall be fined 3d.'

Such clandestine sporting activity was partially phased out as a result of the 1853 Suppression of Betting Houses Act. But it undoubtedly continued well into the 20th century, with reports as recently as 2006 suggesting that pit bull terriers were still being bred in Liverpool for dog fighting.

But it was not only bloodsports on offer in Georgian Liverpool.

We have already noted the formation of the Mersey Bowmen in 1781. It was at their grounds in Cazneau Street where the newly organised sport of cricket appeared in the late 18th century, leading to the formation of the Liverpool Cricket Club at Mosslake Fields in 1811 (*see Chapter Eleven*). By the 1850s there would be approximately 20 other cricket clubs, though all were at that stage the preserve of the middle classes.

Two factors prevented working class participation.

Firstly and most obviously, Liverpool workers had no free time during the week, and were yet to gain a half day holiday on Saturdays. (The playing of sport on Sunday was of course still taboo for all classes, as were most other amusements. As an iron merchant told a Select Committee on Drunkenness in 1834, on Sundays in Liverpool 'all the public houses are open, and all the public walks, cemeteries, zoological gardens and botanical gardens, where people might amuse themselves innocently, are closed.')

Secondly, working class Liverpudlians enjoyed little access to open space.

Parliament first investigated the paucity of urban public space by setting up a Select Committee on Public Walks in 1833. Liverpool had just two recognised public walks at this time: on George's Pier, alongside the public baths, and at St James' Mount, which, according to the journal *Porcupine*, had degenerated into a 'blackened grass plot' owing to pollution.

This deficiency was only partially eased when the general public was allowed entry to the recently opened Botanical Gardens in Edge Lane for two days a week, in 1840. But as the town's first medical officer, Doctor WH Duncan, warned a Royal Commission in 1845, a 'deficiency of fresh air and of exercise' was proving to be a major cause of disease and ill-health.

It was to address these concerns that Liverpool Corporation, and its counterpart in Birkenhead, took the first steps towards providing public parks.

Liverpool's first park was Princes Park, opened in 1843–44. But this was a private venture. The land was purchased by a wealthy merchant and philanthropist, Richard Vaughan Yates, while the park's layout was funded by the sale of housing around its borders (a model borrowed from London's Regent's Park). Moreover, while public access was permitted to parts of the park, only private clubs were allowed to play cricket.

A similar approach was taken at Birkenhead Park across the Mersey (*see Chapter Four*). Although financed by the public purse – the first British park to have been funded this way, via an Act of Parliament – when opened in 1846 a section was already enclosed for the use of a private cricket club.

Meanwhile, in Liverpool the Corporation purchased　》》

BETHELL'S LIFE IN LONDON,
AND
LIVERPOOL SPORTING REGISTER.

Vol. II.—No. 59.　　SATURDAY, JANUARY 7, 1826.　　Price Two-pence. In the Country, Two-pence Halfpenny

Born in Tuebrook in 1829, Charles Melly was a cotton merchant, philanthropist and town councillor, best remembered for introducing drinking fountains to Liverpool (several of which survive). He was also active in helping to provide public seating, and in his capacity as chairman of the Parks Committee played a lead role in the creation of Sefton Park (*see Chapter Six*). But Melly was also a great promoter of physical fitness and the early Olympic movement in Britain, a contribution which surely deserves more recognition than the simple plaque to his memory in the Unitarian Church on Ullet Road. Or is this lack of a larger memorial because he was said to have taken his own life, in a fit of depression in 1888?

›› Wavertree Hall, adjacent to the Botanic Gardens, intending to build a new gaol on the site. However it was later decided not to proceed, and in 1856 the land was laid out to provide what would effectively become the first public park to serve a working class area.

Even then, as later chapters will relate, Wavertree Park was still too small to cope with demand, and also too far from the bulk of poorer districts in the north.

At the same time as pressure was building on the issue of public open space, Liverpool's middle classes were busy embracing a new ethos of 'rational' sport.

In 1844 Lewis Huguenin – a man almost certainly of Continental extraction – opened the town's first gymnasium, on Cook Street. This was followed in the late 1850s by one of Huguenin's pupils, John Hulley, setting up a gymnasium in the Rotunda, a building on Bold Street previously used for billiards. As discussed in Chapter Fifteen, the colourful and eccentric Hulley would later join with the philanthropist, Charles Melly (*see left*) to establish the much grander Liverpool Gymnasium, in 1865, and in doing so, help provide the basis for Liverpool's longheld enthusiasm for gymnastics.

One factor behind this trend was a growing belief that urban life stifled men's natural need for physical activity, especially in light of the British army's perceived failures during the Crimean War of 1854–56 and the Indian Mutiny of 1857-59. This worry, combined with the supposed threat of invasion by Napoleon III's France, prompted thousands of patriots to join volunteer units for rifle drill and physical training.

But Melly was not only concerned for the fitness of the middle classes. Inspired by the open-air gymnasiums he had seen at Primrose Hill, London, and at Peel Park, Salford, Melly identified a patch of spare land in the Smithdown Road area.

'If the council accede to my request,' he wrote in 1857, 'I propose to turn this piece of waste ground into a public playground, where vaulting bars, parallel bars, see-saws, swings and the various instruments of gymnastic exercises, would find their place... I believe that if the young men and elder men had an opportunity of exercising their muscles in some recognised way during their leisure hours, it would be a benefit to themselves and to Society at large; and there can be no doubt that such a playground would have the beneficial effect of clearing... the adjoining streets of the children that now throng them.'

Melly emphasised that the public had to respect the facilities. In a circular handed out at the opening, he stated, 'This playground... is placed under your care... it will be for you to protect (the poles, ropes, ladders and chains) from wilful damage... Let good humour and good temper prevail. Let there be no quarrelling among yourselves and allow no stone-throwing or fighting among your younger members. It rests with you whether the first attempt at free outdoor amusement in our town be a success or a failure.'

In fact the playground was an instant success. As a survey in the *Northern Daily Times* found, in June 1858, a month after it opened, nearly 7,000 people had made use of the facilities, many of them staying for several hours at a time.

Much encouraged, Melly went on to finance three further playgrounds, at Wavertree Park (in 1860), Mill Street, Toxteth (1861), and Kirkdale (1862). At each one he paid for keepers and gymnastic instructors to be on hand. Melly also lobbied for the playgrounds to remain open on Sundays, but had to back down following opposition from local residents.

As it transpired, none of Melly's playgrounds would survive beyond 1874. But by this time three major public parks had opened, all of which had playgrounds of their own and a range of other recreational facilities.

But before we move on to those developments, Messrs Hulley and Melly had more grandiose plans for their home town.

The Liverpool Olympics

As London prepares to stage the Olympic Games in 2012, it should be noted that Liverpool first staged a version of the games in 1862. Indeed there were six Liverpool 'Olympic Festivals' from 1862–67, followed by two later 'Grecian Games' in 1892 and 1894.

True, these were hardly international events on the scale of the 1896 Games and their successors. Nevertheless, they formed an integral part of a British-based movement which, following the establishment of the Much Wenlock Olympian Games in 1850, and of gymnasiums in London, Birmingham and Manchester, would offer critical succour to the Frenchman Pierre de Coubertin in his efforts to revive the Olympic movement.

The organisers of Liverpool's prototypical Olympics were the Liverpool Athletics Club, formed in January 1862 by John Hulley and Charles Melly. Indeed it was Hulley who is credited with choosing the club's motto, *Mens Sana in Corpore Sano* – a healthy mind in a healthy body – the phrase that would become inexorably linked with the emerging Victorian ethos of Muscular Christianity, and which would be proudly displayed on a banner attached to the grandstand at the first Liverpool Olympic Festival, staged on the Mount Vernon military parade ground on 14 June 1862.

In wintry conditions, an estimated 7–10,000 spectators watched a series of 22 events, mostly of the track and field variety that would become standard fare at Victorian athletics meetings, but also including sword fighting, Indian club exercises and throwing a cricket ball. And if at times the crowds proved rather too boisterous and the organisation was not always efficient, the *Daily Post* seemed in no doubt. 'That physical exercise is necessary to health is a lesson nature daily teaches. Men whose gymnasium is, as it were, the World – the soldier, the sailor, the open air labourer – are those who, generally speaking, enjoy the luxury of good bodily condition, and upon those whose manly power the safety of the nation in times of emergency must mainly depend.'

Melly himself was sure that this was just the beginning.

Speaking when the medals were awarded at a ceremony later in 1862 (five gold, 22 silver and 23 bronze), he declared, 'I believe this Athletic Club is only the beginning of a movement which will soon become general, not in Liverpool or Manchester only, but throughout the kingdom.'

The following year's festival proved more popular, attracting an estimated 12–15,000 to Mount Vernon, this time stewarded more effectively by a large contingent of police, and entrants from much

further afield than in 1862. The organisers also laid out a proper 440 yard oval track.

Soon after this second festival, Mount Vernon was sold, so for the third festival in July 1864, now boldly titled the Grand Olympic Festival, the Zoological Gardens on Derby Road were hired.

The *Daily Post* was again on hand to report. 'Between half-past two and three o'clock London-road, Brunswick-road and West Derby-road were literally thronged with cabs, carriages and pedestrians moving towards the scene of the festival; and every omnibus running in the same direction was overloaded with passengers. Outside the gardens the state of affairs was remarkably lively. All the ingenuity of the police, and the good temper of coachmen, cab-drivers and conductors, was required to convey each vehicle, as it arrived, safely to the gates and back again into a clearer portion of the road. Flags flaunting from the walls invited all who were outside to venture nearer the centre of interest; and an insatiable crowd indulged with the utmost gusto in sarcastic observation on the dress and personnel of the favoured holders of tickets.'

Unsurprisingly this clamour did not go down well with Liverpool's elite. For them, the Zoological Gardens were tainted by their general reputation for drinking, gambling and prostitution. There were also reports that the Festival had been tainted by the 'nefarious craft' of the bookmakers.

Perhaps because of this, the fourth Olympic Festival of 1865 did not take place in Liverpool at all. Instead, it was staged in the emerging Welsh seaside resort of Llandudno. (Hulley himself was a keen advocate of sea-bathing.) »

▲ Representatives from Liverpool, Manchester, Blackheath and Richmond, gather at the Liverpool Cricket Club, Aigburth, for a match to celebrate the centenary of the **Liverpool Football Club**, in December 1957. But this was not the famous Liverpool FC of Anfield (which controversially usurped the name, despite protests, in 1892). Rather, this was a rugby club, and not only that, the first 'open' rugby club in the world.

In rugby's early days, when there was still no distinction between the football codes of rugby and soccer, the only clubs to play the handling game were attached to schools, universities or hospitals. Then in 1857, two former pupils of Rugby School (where the first rules had been formulated in 1846), Frank Mather of Bootle and Richard Sykes of Manchester, decided to invite other former public schoolboys to a scratch game at Edge Hill, then the ground of the Liverpool Cricket Club. In total, some 50 players turned up, on 19 December 1857, and thus was born the first rugby club to accept members on an open basis.

Manchester's contingent took a while longer to form their own club, in 1860. London's first club, Blackheath, followed in 1861.

A measure of the Liverpool club's prominence at this time was that it provided four of the England team to play Scotland in the first ever international match in 1871.

During the club's early years, various pitches were rented, at Edge Hill, Princes Park, Smithdown Road (behind the old Brooke House Hotel), and at Fairfield (near the Police Athletics Ground), until in 1884 Liverpool Cricket Club allowed the rugby club to play in front of their own recently completed pavilion at Aigburth (*see page 114*).

Then in 1889 extra land was acquired closer to the Mersey, where the club played until 1963.

At that point another pitch was found in St Michael's Hamlet, two miles along Riversdale Drive.

Nowadays the club plays at Moss Lane, St Helens, having merged with the local club to form Liverpool St Helens in 1986.

The club's 150th anniversary falls in December 2007.

No action images of the Liverpool Olympics survive. But from the *Illustrated London News* of May 1869 we can gain some sense of the atmosphere inside the Liverpool Gymnasium. This was an event organised by the Liverpool Velocipede Club, which had formed two years earlier, using the latest Pickering and Davies machines, imported from America. The etching shows cyclists tilting at rings, as in a medieval quintain, with the winner being the one to lance the most rings in ten attempts. Other trials included fencing, throwing the javelin, and 'fancy riding'. Alexander Alexander, later to be director of the Gymnasium, was one of the club's most enthusiastic members.

» A rather more significant development occurred shortly after the Llandudno festival. On 6 November 1865 Hulley and Melly opened their newest venture, the Liverpool Gymnasium on Myrtle Street, reputed to be the best of its kind in Europe (*see Chapter Fifteen*).

It was in this building that, also in November 1865, Hulley and Melly, together with William Penny Brookes from Much Wenlock, Ernst Georg Ravenstein of the German Gymnastic Society in London (whose gym still stands, next to King's Cross station) and a representative from Manchester, held the inaugural meeting of the National Olympian Association. Its motto: 'Civium vires civitatis vis' – the power of the state lies in the strength of its citizens.

The NOA's ethos was, of course, resolutely amateur. Professionals were forbidden from joining. The NOA also hoped to become the parent association for a variety of Olympian sports, including athletics, gymnastics, boxing, swimming and even cricket.

It should be noted at this point that the Liverpool Olympics were still in advance of other athletics meetings. Only in 1864 did Oxford and Cambridge hold their first Varsity meeting, while London's leading athletics club, alarmed at the growing influence of provincial clubs, organised their first championships in March 1866. Far from uniting the nation's Olympians, it would seem Hulley and Melly's efforts had only galvanised their rivals.

Hulley would organise only two further Olympic Festivals, at Llandudno again in June 1866, and back in Liverpool in 1867. At the latter, staged at the Liverpool Gymnasium and Shiel Park, with swimming in Wallasey Pool, athletes from Paris and Marseilles were among 300 athletes entered in 28 disciplines.

But instead of building from this, the 1867 Festival proved to be the last (at least until the idea was revived in 1892). The most commonly cited reason for this was the worsening finances of the Gymnasium. Hulley allegedly went bankrupt in 1871, then started travelling abroad to ease a chest complaint. However, another source claims that Hulley became *persona non grata* after he eloped with the daughter of a shipping magnate. He died in Liverpool in 1875, at the age of 42.

Another reason for Liverpool's Olympic efforts being curtailed was that the National Olympian Association had staged their own first set of games in London in 1866, followed by Birmingham the year after.

But this was not the end of Liverpool's Olympic aspirations.

Instead, a former apprentice of Hulley's, Alexander Alexander, now came to the fore. Most notably, in 1867 he founded the National Physical Recreation Society, with the aim of promoting fitness amongst the working classes. Under Alexander's directorship, from 1882, the Liverpool Gymnasium's influence also started to revive, and even achieve international status of sorts when it hosted two further 'Grecian Games', in February 1892 and November 1894.

If the link between the modern Olympics and those in Liverpool of the 1860s may be less direct, the 1892 Games anticipated the 1896

Athens games in various ways. Not least the French and Greek consuls in Liverpool attended. The latter, a Mr ED Barff, told the assembled crowd at the Gymnasium that the ancient games had consisted of just five events, whereas Liverpool's festival featured seven, including the javelin and the disc (which may have been based on the local game of quoits, as it had never been part of the ancient games). There was even a simulated chariot race.

For added authenticity each competitor was also kitted out with a toga, generously provided by Liverpool's Greek community. Winners received wreaths tinted in gold, silver and bronze.

Certainly Mr Barff seemed content. The 'games had been done correctly,' he declared. He also presented to Alexander Alexander a rare coin minted, appropriately enough, at the time of Alexander the Great.

Also of interest was that the 1892 festival was presided over by Herbert Gladstone, son of the former Prime Minister and president of Alexander's National Physical Recreation Society. Two years later Gladstone would be an adviser to Pierre de Coubertin at the birth of the International Olympic Committee.

Looking back, a lack of surviving documentation makes it hard to judge the extent to which Liverpool's Olympic festivals helped to shape the modern Olympic games. Certainly William Penny Brookes and his Much Wenlock games are cited as being of greater influence. But it seems inconceivable that the efforts of Hulley, Melly and Alexander had no influence at all, and therefore some recognition of Liverpool's contribution is surely due.

Late 19th Century sport

Olympian ideals, gymnastics, cricket and archery were all very well for the middle classes. But as a plaintive letter in the Liverpool Mercury of July 1853 records, not every sporting man had the time.

'Here have I been in an office for six years,' wrote the correspondent, 'and never had but three days holiday, with the exception of Sundays.'

Compared with such cities as Sheffield and Birmingham, where manufacturing patterns allowed certain workers free time on weekday afternoons – hence, for example, the formation of the Sheffield Wednesday cricket and football club – Liverpool's workforce had to lobby long and hard for a half-day holiday.

First to win this concession were stonemasons, who in 1857 negotiated the right to finish work at 1pm on Saturdays. By 1859 they were joined by coach builders and staff at the Central Money Order Office. But for many more skilled workers a shorter working week would not come about until 1872, and only then owing to the robust efforts of the Nine Hours Movement, which had emerged in Sunderland the previous year.

Skilled workers made up only a minority of Liverpool's workforce, however. Dockworkers, in contrast, owing to the casual nature of their employment, had much less bargaining power and would only gain their Saturday afternoons off from 1890.

Still, as each group of workers attained more hours of leisure, so their involvement in sport – as both participants and spectators – increased exponentially.

But of course this, combined with the virtual doubling of the city's population in the second half of the century, only added to the pressure on what little open space was available.

In May 1864 another Liverpool Mercury reader complained, 'I am a clerk... I take a stroll into Princes Park and there feast my eyes on that in which it is impossible I can participate – I mean the manly and health-giving game of cricket. The club there is composed principally of merchant's sons (I am only a tradesman's)... I have spoken to several of my friends of raising a club but the cry is "where will you get the ground?"'

Wavertree Park was already oversubscribed, while yet another letter in the Liverpool Mercury in 1865 suggested that sport had colonised Shiel Park too.

It read, 'I deeply regret that the footballs, which have been introduced into Shiel Park for general enjoyment of hundreds of young men that frequent it, should have caused any annoyance to any person.' (This, it should be noted, was at a time when the term football probably referred to a game more akin to rugby. Association football would catch on much later, in the late 1870s).

But a solution was in hand.

As proposed in the Liverpool Improvement Act of 1865, Liverpool Corporation, with Charles Melly to the fore, launched a scheme to create a belt of three new public parks: Newsham Park in the east (opened 1868), Stanley Park in the north (1870) and Sefton Park in the south (1872). Moreover, this new generation of parks was designed with specific areas allocated to sport.

As related in Chapters Five and Six, all three parks proved immediately popular, leading to a surge in cricket and rugby. But by the 1880s, soccer was ›

▲ Liverpool's large immigrant community played an active role in the city's sporting life, none more so than the Irishman **'Honest John' McKenna**, commemorated by this plaque at **Anfield**. McKenna arrived in the city in 1854 at the age of 17 and became a vaccination officer and a sergeant major in a volunteer regiment. A keen rugby player, he later came to the fore when Liverpool FC formed as an offshoot of Everton in 1892.

Meanwhile a Liverpool branch of the **Gaelic Athletics Association** was established in 1884, staging hurling matches in local parks.

Much earlier, members of the Caledonian Association formed the **Liverpool and Everton Curling Club** in 1839, which in turn led to the formation of the **Liverpool Skating Club** in 1855. Its members included Charles Melly and other individuals from the Gladstone and Hornby families.

In 1859 a **Highland Games** was also staged, in a private park in West Derby.

▶ Seen here in leisurely action at the turn of the 20th century, the **Childwall Quoiting Club** has two important claims to distinction.

Firstly it is the oldest club in Liverpool to have played the same sport since its foundation. The Mersey Bowmen may have formed earlier, in 1781, but that was for for archery, whereas now they play only tennis (*see page 76*).

Secondly, the club has been playing quoits at the same venue, the **Childwall Abbey Hotel**, on the corner of Childwall Abbey Road and Score Lane, since at least 1811.

Evidence for this is a trophy donated to the club in 1911 to celebrate the 100th anniversary of the championships being staged there. (In fact the club may predate 1811, as references to a Childwall club also appear in 1795).

Quoits itself is an ancient game, in which players throw heavy metal rings at a pin, or hob, driven into a bed of soft clay. One theory has it that quoits was played at the early Olympic games, and was a precursor of the modern discus. But it may equally have evolved from the throwing of horseshoes.

The earliest reference to quoits in Britain comes in 1361, when it was listed as one of three games prohibited to servants, apprentices and labourers, so as to concentrate their minds on archery practice. It was later revived during the 19th

century, particularly in the mining areas of Lancashire, the north east and Scotland, and is still played at several pubs around the country. There is also evidence of it being played in Birkenhead Park.

The Childwall club is steeped in tradition. Entry is limited to twelve members (men only), with a Lady Patroness appointed for ceremonial duties. Its minutes are still written in copperplate handwriting, while fines – for such transgressions as speaking out of turn or incorrectly addressing a fellow member – are levied in units of half a bottle of port, the cash equivalent of which is paid at the end of each season.

A rule requiring members to seek permission before getting married, is, however, no longer applied.

The club meets just six times a year, on consecutive Mondays either side of Midsummer's Day, and follows a time-honoured routine. Dinner is served at 5.30, always salmon, rib of beef and a shoulder of baked ham, followed by Black Cap pudding (which members liken to burnt Yorkshire pudding soaked in brown sugar and sherry). Play then starts on the hotel lawn at 7pm, ending at 10.30pm in time for supper.

One game a year is also played against members of the Liverpool Cricket Club, a tradition started in 1902 when one of the members, Danso Cunningham, donated a distinctive Royal Doulton challenge trophy (*shown left*). The venue for this alternates between Childwall

and the cricket club's headquarters at Aigburth (*see page 114*).

But even if players from other quoits clubs were to visit, they would encounter a quite different version of the game at Childwall. Known as 'the long game' the key difference is that Childwall throw a distance of 21 yards, compared with 18 in East Anglia and 11 elsewhere. The quoits vary too, being heavier, at 6–14lbs, and larger than those elsewhere. Childwall also score differently, with the quoit nearest the pin scoring a single point, as in bowls.

That Childwall have been playing to these rules, and on the same patch of lawn, for nearly 200 years, represents extraordinary continuity, by any standards.

» already starting to dominate. In 1882 the newly formed Liverpool County Football Association had just 12 member clubs. By 1886 over 150 teams were active. Thereafter, once the majority of the workforce gained Saturday afternoons off, the numbers grew further, so that by 1900 there were 13 football leagues in the city, most of them based in public parks.

As a result, the parks also became places of public assembly. In Stanley Park an emerging football team called St Domingo, later renamed Everton, attracted regular four–figure crowds from 1878–83, at which point it became imperative for the club to find a private ground where they could collect gate money. In March 1889, an exhibition game played by a visiting team of American baseball players drew 9,000 curious onlookers to Shiel Park. Soon after, the National Rounders Association was formed in the city. Rounders, a simple game, and arguably the forerunner of baseball, proved ideal for those players unable to afford cricket equipment. Even better, it could be played on almost any flat stretch of turf, without the need for a specially prepared wicket.

But rival sports were emerging also. The Royal Mersey Yacht Club had formed in 1844, to be joined by the Mersey Rowing Club a decade later. Before football took hold, athletics also proved extremely popular. Although Hulley's Liverpool Athletics Club folded in 1885, the example it had set was soon followed. Liverpool Harriers formed in 1876, followed by the Liverpool Gymnasium Harriers, the Newsham Cross Country Club, St. Cleopatra's Harriers, the Liverpool Police Athletic Club, Wavertree Harriers,

All Saints Harriers and Golden Eagle Harriers, all of which were formed between 1882–86.

In 1869 the Scottish game of golf was also put on an organised footing with the formation of the Liverpool Golf Club at Hoylake. This was followed in 1873 by the West Lancashire Golf Club at Blundellsands. Five more courses would open over the next 40 years.

In consequence, Merseyside today may claim to be the golfing capital of England. As Chapter Fourteen will relate, this has occurred not by chance but because the very landscape lends itself so perfectly to the sport.

Developed in the early 1870s, the new game of lawn tennis also found willing exponents in Liverpool's expanding suburbs, particularly amongst those more established residents who already had croquet lawns.

The Waterloo Croquet Club, for example, took up tennis in 1877, the same year that the All England Croquet Club at Wimbledon staged its first tennis championships. The aforementioned Mersey Bowmen were also converted, as was the Blundellsands Archery Club, which in 1880 borrowed £150 from Joseph Gardner, a Liverpool timber merchant, to lay four grass courts in Key Park.

Like croquet and archery before them, tennis had the great advantage of being suitable for both men and women, at a time when women were just starting to make an impact in sport.

One in particular was Lottie Dod, the daughter of a successful Liverpool cotton merchant. Born in 1871 across the Mersey, in Bebington, Dod is probably the greatest all round sportswoman this country has ever produced. »

▲ One of Liverpool's best known institutions is the **Liverpool Racquet Club**, founded by two members of the Childwall Quoits Club, Danso Cunningham and HB Parr, in 1874. Its first home was an adapted Georgian terraced house in Upper Parliament Street (*below right*), opened in 1877.

The club offered two courts for racquets (a game that had evolved, oddly enough, amongst inmates in London's Fleet Prison the previous century), 12 bedrooms, a billiard room and what was described as an 'American bowling alley'.

In 1894 this alley was replaced by two courts for the public school game of fives, while by 1936 racquets had been superceded by the newly popular game of squash.

For years the club formed a popular haunt until, in 1981, it was so badly damaged during the Toxteth riots that its members had to set up afresh in the Hargreaves Buildings, Chapel Street.

Since 2003 the Racquet Club has been run as a private hotel and restaurant business, although it retains two squash courts on its upper floor.

▲ Nowadays over 800 marathons per year are staged in cities across the globe, each measured at 26 miles and 385 yards, a distance established at the 1908 London Olympics so that the race would end in front of the royal box in the White City Stadium.

Liverpool, one of the first British cities other than London to stage such a race, in September 1927, arranged for their inaugural **City Marathon** to finish in front of the crowds at Anfield football ground.

Organised as part of Liverpool's Civic Week, 47 runners gathered in the Pudsey Street boxing stadium (*see page 156*) for a briefing, before setting off from outside St George's Hall (*above*), at a time fixed so that the lead runners would enter Anfield for one final lap of the pitch during the half-time interval of Liverpool's match v. Blackburn.

To great applause the winner was Sam Ferris, a northern Irish member of the Herne Hill Harriers, who had finished fifth in the 1924 Olympics, but had won the previous three British marathons, in Windsor in 1925 and 1926, and in Manchester the year after.

There were 102 entrants for the next Liverpool marathon in 1928, and this time Liverpool's FA Cup tie v. Southport had to be delayed so that once again the race would end at half-time. The crowd, many of them sheltering under the Kop's new roof, were also kept informed of the race's progress throughout the first half. Once again Ferris was the winner, with a time just three seconds short of the winning time recorded at the Amsterdam Olympics, weeks earlier.

For the fourth marathon in 1930 the end point was moved to the Stanley Recreation Ground, and there was then a gap until the race was revived in 1948, with Anfield once again hosting the finish, during the interval of a Reds v. Whites pre-season practice match.

During the following two decades the race became part of the annual Liverpool Show, with the last one in the sequence starting and ending at the Wavertree Playground in 1968.

Liverpool marathons since then have been rather larger events.

When the race was revived in 1982, between Speke and Bootle, over 5,000 runners took part.

Further marathons were run up to 1994, when it was decided to stage half-marathons instead. The 2006 race, which began at Sefton Park and finished at the Pierhead, attracted over 6,000 entrants.

However it is hoped that the full marathon will return in time for the Capital of Culture celebrations. But where might future marathons finish? On a point of tradition, Liverpool fans would argue that their new stadium in Stanley Park offers the perfect backdrop.

» She won the women's title at Wimbledon five times, only to give up tennis at the age of 21 and become the English women's golf champion in 1904. She then won a silver medal for archery at the 1908 Olympics, while also playing twice for the England hockey team. Dod proved similarly adept as an ice skater, showjumper, rower and yachtswoman.

Two other areas of sporting activity attracted women (as well as men). By 1889, as detailed in Chapter Eighteen, there were nine public swimming baths in Liverpool, the largest of which, on Westminster Road (opened 1877) had a 100 foot long gala pool.

Cycling also offered women much new found freedom, although in competition circles the sport was still male dominated.

In 1880, a gathering of recently formed cycle clubs from across the region – known as the 'Monstre Meet' – saw 300 cyclists from 35 clubs race from Sefton Park to the Town Hall, tailed by a further 400 unaffiliated riders. Among the clubs participating was the Anfield Bicycle Club, formed in 1879 and still pedalling to this day. One of its earliest presidents was the brewer and local councillor, John Houlding, known more widely since as the main backer of Everton football club.

Sport, as Houlding and many a publican in Liverpool increasingly realised, was not only good for the body. It was also wonderful for trade. Houlding owned the Sandon Hotel next to Anfield, which became Everton's headquarters in 1884.

So when a faction of Everton supporters fell out with their sponsor in 1892 and decamped to Goodison Park, instead of selling Anfield for housing, Houlding »

◀ A few miles north of Liverpool on The Withins fields near **Altcar**, two greyhounds, Perambulate and Rotten Row, are kept on a tight leash by the official 'slipper' as they prepare for the final of the 1937 **Waterloo Cup**, a hare coursing event so popular that at its height in the 19th century the Houses of Parliament would go into recess and the Stock Exchange suspend trading. Crowds of up to 75,000 would converge upon the small station at Lydiate for this, the Blue Riband of coursing.

Coursing – in which a pair of greyhounds pursue their prey by sight rather than by scent, and are judged by their pace and agility rather than on whether they catch the hare – is an ancient sport, introduced to Britain, it is thought, as early as 500 BC. For centuries ownership of hounds was banned to all but the ruling classes, until in 1776 the first public coursing emerged at Swaffham in Norfolk.

First staged in 1836, the Waterloo Cup was the brainchild of William Lynn, proprietor of the Waterloo Hotel in Liverpool, where the Earl of Sefton and his sporting cronies ran a dining club. In the same year Lynn also initiated the steeplechase at Aintree that would eventually be called the Grand National (*see Chapter Three*). Both events were held on Sefton's land, and successive earls acted as presidents of the National Coursing Club (formed in 1858) until the early 1970s. But coursing was equally popular in northern pit villages and industrial towns. Modern greyhound racing was developed from coursing in the 1920s to bring it to a wider urban audience, resulting in no fewer than four dog tracks opening in Liverpool (*see Chapter Ten*).

One key feature of the Waterloo Cup that has shaped many a cup competition since – football's FA Cup and the Wimbledon tennis championships, for example – was its organisation on a knock-out basis. Eight greyhounds competed for the first cup. By 1850 the total was fixed at 64 entries. Not only that but the draw was made from a jug, a method also adopted by other sporting organisations.

Although defenders of coursing argue that the hare is the natural prey of a greyhound, and that on average only one out of seven or eight hares is actually killed, opposition to the sport mounted throughout the 20th century, as shown by this poster from Liverpool campaigners in 1949 (*left*).

Finally, in November 2004 the Hunting Bill made hunting with dogs illegal, a ban which came into force two days after the last ever Waterloo Cup was staged at Altcar, in February 2005 (*below*), watched by an estimated 10,000 crowd.

▼ Recently refurbished for use as a youth and community centre by Sefton Council, the **Orrell Mount Pavilion**, built on Orrell Road c.1923, is the former pavilion of the Silcocks animal feed company, one of several Liverpool firms to create sportsgrounds for employees, to encourage a fitter and more loyal workforce but also as a means of attracting new recruits.

One of the city's first works grounds was that of the Cunard shipping company, at Bellefield, West Derby, opened in 1919 and now the Everton training ground.

Other companies to provide grounds were Metal Box, the shipping company Alfred Holt, and Jacobs Bakery, whose ground on Long Lane, Aintree, is still in use, as is the former Nalgo ground on Alder Road, West Derby, now home to the Alder Cricket Club.

For more on works sport, see Chapter Twelve, on bowls.

》 simply set up a new club of his own, Liverpool (*see Chapter Five*).

20th Century sport
The first full football season of the 20th century set a tone that was to define the sporting character of Liverpool thereafter. John Houlding's new Liverpool FC won their first League Championship in 1901. They repeated the feat in 1906, the same year that Everton won the FA Cup for their first time. (Between them, to date, Liverpool and Everton have won the League no fewer than 25 times, and the FA Cup on 12 occasions.)

Football was now a mass spectator sport, with the two clubs regularly attracting aggregate gates of over 80,000. By 1914 attendances for athletics, rugby, rounders, and even for cricket, had tumbled in the great stampede of converts heading to watch the mighty Reds and Blues. Both clubs' grounds were substantially redeveloped from 1906 onwards. Anfield's Kop became the largest covered terrace in football. Goodison Park became the first ground to have double-decker stands on all four sides.

In 1966, the year that Goodison Park also hosted matches in the World Cup, as in 1906, Everton won the Cup, while Liverpool won the League. As a result, that August the players of both teams were able to parade around Goodison Park holding not only the Charity Shield, the Football League trophy and the FA Cup trophy, but also the World Cup itself. (Ray Wilson of Everton and Roger Hunt of Liverpool had both played in the Wembley final).

At no other British ground has such an array of gold and silverware ever been witnessed.

In the present day, the Anfield museum also has on display the European Cup, held permanently by Liverpool following their fifth triumph in the tournament in 2005 (a record beaten only by Real Madrid and AC Milan).

Indeed such is football's pre-eminence in the city that, as detailed in Chapter Five, in 2006 the Council sanctioned the construction of a new stadium for Liverpool within the boundaries of one of the city's public parks, Stanley Park. It is hard to imagine a similar concession being granted in any other British city.

Football's popularity saw off a number of challengers during the 20th century.

Greyhound racing, an American import, made its debut in August 1927, at the purpose-built Stanley Stadium, on Prescot Road. Three more dog tracks would be built over the next six years (*see Chapter Ten*), with speedway, a sport developed in Australia, introduced at the Stanley Stadium in 1928.

Yet despite their early promise, the last of the city's greyhound and speedway stadiums closed in 1973.

Liverpool's dalliance with American baseball was even briefer. In 1933, building on the city's penchant for rounders (which had transmuted into English baseball during the 1890s), John Moores, founder of the Littlewoods Pools empire, helped set up in Liverpool a National Baseball Association.

One match at Wavertree attracted a 6,000 crowd in 1938. But, as related in Chapter Thirteen, the momentum was lost when war broke out the following year, and now only two local clubs remain.

Similarly fleeting was Aintree Racecourse's brave attempt to establish motor racing during the 1950s. Five Grand Prix events were staged at Aintree, until Silverstone won back its monopoly in 1963.

Rather more resilient was boxing.

As mentioned earlier, pugilism had enjoyed a long tradition on Merseyside. In the late 19th century dozens of small gymnasiums had opened up in the city's poorer districts, with large crowds turning out to see local heroes square up at the Adelphi Theatre, known to all as the Delly.

Then in 1911 local promoters combined to take over a roller skating rink in Pudsey Street (*see Chapter Seventeen*). Revamped with 4,000 seats, and grandly retitled the Liverpool Stadium, Pudsey Street was deemed to be Britain's finest boxing venue outside London. Its replacement, opened in St Paul's Square in 1932, also called the Liverpool Stadium, was even grander, with a fine Art Deco façade. Yet even this proved too small for some championship bouts, which were staged at Anfield instead. One such fight, in 1938, drew over 40,000 spectators.

As with greyhound racing, however, the Liverpool Stadium could never quite pay its way in the post war period, and was finally demolished in 1987.

A similar fate befell the city's only ice rink.

In fact the area's first ice rink, and only the fourth in Britain, had been built on Lord Street, Southport, in 1879, only to close ten years later when its primitive refrigeration system broke down. This was followed by a craze for roller skating. Liverpool had at least five rinks in the early 20th century. In addition to the Pudsey Street rink mentioned earlier there was roller skating at the Ritz, on the corner of Mulberry and Myrtle Streets, at Renshaw Hall, and at Heald Street, Garston.

By the late 1920s 'rincomania' had given way to a new fad for dancehalls. Dances were also held in several of the city's swimming baths during wintertime (*see page 178*). But this phase also proved shortlived, and in 1931 Liverpool's largest Palais de Dance, which had opened only three years earlier on Prescot Road, was converted into the city's first and only major ice rink. Named the Palace Ice Rink, it was one of more than 20 opened around Britain during the 1930s, and in common with most of its counterparts, it eventually had its own ice hockey team, the Liverpool Leopards. Formed in 1948, they disbanded when Mecca bought the rink and renamed it the Silver Blades in 1960 – a time when ice rinks and tenpin bowling alleys were, along with bingo halls, deemed to be the latest vogue in entertainment. (The Embassy Cinema in Formby was similarly converted into an ice rink during this period).

But as in most other cities, fashions moved on and the Liverpool Ice Rink, as it was later known, was demolished in 2001.

Not all sporting provision in 20th century Liverpool was commercially oriented.

Crown green bowls became established in the city during the 1890s, at a number of private members' clubs, many of which still operate today (*see Chaper Twelve*). Bowls was also among several sports which, from 1900–39, benefited from considerable investment by local authorities on both sides of the Mersey.

Indeed second only to the great behemoth football, the one defining aspect of sporting development in 20th century Liverpool was the growth of publicly-funded facilities.

Public bowling greens were laid out in almost every public park from around 1905 onwards. Municipal golf courses were created at Bowring Park, in 1913, at Allerton in 1922, and at Kirkby in 1929. All three remain in use today.

The construction of swimming baths and wash-houses, begun in 1828, also continued, resulting in six more indoor, and five outdoor pools opening between 1895 and 1936. Further baths opened in the neighbouring boroughs of Bootle, Crosby, Birkenhead and Wallasey.

Even so, there was no let up in demand. At the start of the century Liverpool's population stood at 711,000 (an almost ninefold increase since 1801). Partly owing to boundary changes – the absorption of Allerton, Childwall, Garston and Woolton in 1913 – but also owing to a continued influx of workers to the docks and other emerging industries, this total increased to an all time peak of over 846,000 by 1931.

But although the extent of public open space had also grown during this period – from around 1,000 acres in 1913, to 2,150 acres

by 1933 (according to a *Social Survey of Merseyside*, conducted by the University of Liverpool) – the total was still some way below the recommended standard.

This standard, formulated in 1934 by the National Playing Fields Association (established 1925), considered that for every 1,000 people there should be six acres of open space available for public recreation. If the University's 1933 survey was accurate, Liverpool's ratio was only 2.5 acres per 1,000. In densely populated Bootle, to the north, the deficit was even greater, at just 1.45 acres per 1,000.

Nevertheless, statistics show that major improvements were being made. By 1930 there were in the public realm 168 football pitches, 392 tennis courts, 70 cricket pitches, 54 bowling greens, 57 grounds for rounders and 12 for baseball, 25 hockey pitches and five boating lakes.

Combined, this was no small enterprise, particularly as, apart from occasional grants from the National Playing Fields Association and from charitable »

Designed by Denys Lasdun & Partners and opened in 1966, the University Sports Centre on Oxford Road is the only sports-related building in Liverpool to have caught the eye of Nikolaus Pevsner in his *Buildings of England* series, although he thought its set back angularity was 'a calculated insult' to the neighbouring Georgian terraces of Abercromby Square. Ironically Abercromby Square was itself built on the site of Mosslake Fields, where Liverpool Cricket Club formed in 1811. Another striking post-war building belonging to the University is the Geoffrey Hughes Pavilion, on Mather Avenue (*see page 110*).

» institutions, all had to be funded by the ratepayers.

Figures for useage were equally impressive. In 1931 alone the Corporation sold 236,400 tickets for bowling greens, 100,200 for tennis courts, 127,000 for municipal golf courses and 2.2 million for the city's swimming baths. The University's 1933 survey estimated that there were also 15–20,000 individuals playing football regularly, a figure that excluded schools and colleges.

As mentioned earlier, several of the area's larger companies also established sports grounds for the benefit of their employees.

But in Liverpool, as in every other major British city, this apparent golden era was to end by the 1970s. The dramatic decline of the docks, on both sides of the Mersey (caused by the introduction of containerisation in the late 1960s), allied to a downturn in the region's industrial fortunes in the 1980s, led inexorably to a reduction in the ability of local authorities to maintain their sports facilities and public parks.

Recent decades have also seen a marked increase in the number of sports facilities, and particularly isolated club pavilions, destroyed by arson attacks. In several cases this has resulted in priceless club records and memorabilia being lost forever, a terrible blow to the city's collective heritage.

Meanwhile, a steady decline in the population from the 1940s onwards has also had the rather more positive effect of reducing pressure on the city's open spaces.

Thus while the total extent of public open space in Liverpool has risen since 1945 to its current level of 2,500 acres, a corresponding drop in the population to 440,000 by 2001 – the lowest level since

the 1860s – has meant that the city now falls only fractionally below the six acres per 1,000 standard.

There are many reasons to feel optimistic about sporting life in Liverpool in the 21st century.

Considerable funds are being poured into the restitution of the city's historic parks, from the Heritage Lottery Fund, Liverpool City Council and numerous other public agencies. Funding worth £165 million from the European Community, English Partnerships, Liverpool City Council, the Northwest Development Agency and the private sector has also facilitated the construction of the 10,000 capacity King's Dock Arena, the most sophisticated sporting and entertainment facility yet constructed in the city.

This, combined with Liverpool's Stanley Park Stadium, and any future stadium development undertaken by Everton, heralds a turnaround in the city's sporting profile that could hardly have been imagined in the 1990s.

Allied to these commercial schemes, six centres of excellence have been identified for grassroots sport: Wavertree Athletics Centre, the Liverpool Tennis Centre (also at Wavertree), the Walton Soccer Centre, Lambeth Road Gymnasium (for boxing), and for swimming, a new £15 million 50m pool at Picton (*see page 183*).

So it is that as the city prepares to showcase its renewed vitality as European Capital of Culture – and celebrate its 800th anniversary – Liverpool's sporting heritage provides a timely subject for this *Played in Britain* study. For while modernisation is mostly to be welcomed, there is much worth celebrating – and conserving – from the past, as the march of progress take its inevitable toll.

1. **Formby Hall Golf Club** Southport Old Road (*134*)
2. **Formby Golf Club** Golf Road (*138*)
3. **West Lancashire Golf Club** Hall Road West (*141*)
4. **Waterloo Rugby Club** St Anthony's Road (*108*)
5. **The Northern Club** Moor Park, Elm Avenue (*118*)
6. **Crosby Leisure Centre** Mariners Road (*182*)
7. **Marine FC, Arriva Stadium** College Road (*105*)
8. **Merchant Taylors' School** Liverpool Road (*117*)
9. **Orrell Mount** Pavilion (*20*)
10. former **Vernons Pools** building, Ormskirk Road (*88*)
11. **Aintree** Ormskirk Road (*Chapter Three*)
12. **Kirkby Sports Centre** Valley Road (*102*)
13. **Olympic Bowling Club** Park Vale Road (*122*)
14. **Bootle Baths** Balliol Road (*172*)
15. **Bootle Cricket Club** Wadham Road (*116*)
16. **Gordon Institute** Stanley Road (*148*)
17. **Everton FC, Goodison Park** football ground (*Chapter Five*)
18. **Stanley Park** (*Chapter Five*)
19. **Liverpool FC, Anfield** football ground (*Chapter Five*)
20. **Billiard Hotel** Scotland Road (*78*)
21. former **Shrewsbury House Boys Club** Langrove Street (*153*)
22. **Newsham Park** (*50*)
23. former **Lister Drive Baths** (*174*)
24. **Fairfield Athletics Ground** (*126*)
25. **West Derby Bowls Club** Haymans Green (*125*)
26. **Huyton Cricket Club** Huyton Lane (*117*)
27. **Childwall Golf Club** Naylor's Road (*140*)
28. **Childwall Abbey Hotel** Childwall Abbey Road (*16*)
29. **Liverpool Bowling Club** Church Road (*124*)
30. **Wavertree Athletics Centre** (*103*)
31. former **Picton Baths** Wavertree (*175*)
32. former **Littlewoods Pools** building, Edge Lane (*93*)
33. **King's Dock Arena** (*163*)
34. **Merseyside Watersports Centre** Queens Dock (*32*)
35. **Florence Institute** Mill Street (*151*)
36. **Steble Street Gymnasium** (former baths) (*146/171*)
37. **Sefton Park** (*Chapter Six*)
38. **Geoffrey Hughes Memorial Ground** Mather Avenue (*110*)
39. **Liverpool Cricket Club** Aigburth Road (*114*)
40. **Woolton Baths** Quarry Street (*173*)
41. **Woolton Village Club** Allerton Road (*125*)
42. **Oval Sports Centre** Old Chester Road (*101*)
43. **Royal Mersey Yacht Club** Bedford Road East (*27*)
44. **Byrne Avenue Baths** Birkenhead (*177*)
45. **Tranmere Rovers, Prenton Park** football ground (*104*)
46. **Birkenhead Park** (*Chapter Four*)
47. **Wirral Rowing Centre** Poulton Bridge Road (*29*)
48. **Guinea Gap Baths** Seacombe (*177*)
49. **Wallasey Yacht Club** Hope Street (*30*)
50. **Wallasey Golf Club** Bayswater Road (*135*)
51. **Royal Liverpool Golf Club** Meols Drive (*132*)

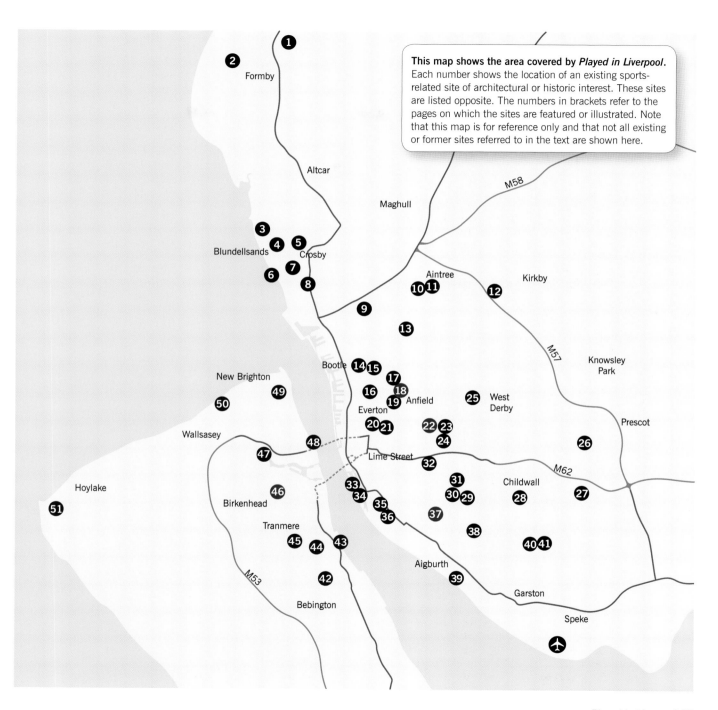

This map shows the area covered by *Played in Liverpool*.
Each number shows the location of an existing sports-related site of architectural or historic interest. These sites are listed opposite. The numbers in brackets refer to the pages on which the sites are featured or illustrated. Note that this map is for reference only and that not all existing or former sites referred to in the text are shown here.

Chapter Two

River Mersey

The Royal Mersey Yacht Club's Commodore, on board the *Moonraker*, signals for the start of a race at the 2006 Mersey Regatta, one of several annual regattas run by the region's long established sailing and rowing clubs. After decades of pollution from industry and shipping, the newly cleansed Mersey waters are once again awash with sporting activity, and marine life.

The Liverpool Victoria Rowing Club formed in 1884 (despite its name, on the Wallasey side of the river), and built its first boathouse – shown here in 1895 shortly after its completion – at Wallasey Pool. By this stage the club had secured its first boats with sliding seats, a great innovation at the time. The club is now based at the Wirral Rowing Centre (*see page 29*).

When the American novelist Herman Melville arrived in Liverpool as a ship's 'boy' in 1839, he was awestruck by the Mersey. In *Redburn*, his fictionalised tale of that journey, he compared the dock walls to the Great Wall of China, the enclosed docks reminded him of the Great Lakes, while the whole dock system was, to him, the equal of the Pyramids. Melville recognised that here was a great hub of the world, a wonder of the modern age.

At their peak the docks on the Liverpool side of the Mersey extended 14 miles, from Garston in the south to Seaforth in the north. Transport of all descriptions, horse, rail and canal barge, supplied the docks with manufactured goods for export. Thousands of dock workers filled hundreds of warehouses with goods from around the world. And yet remarkably, amidst all these comings and goings, the River Mersey was also a place for sport and leisure.

We have already noted how, throughout the 18th century, the port of Liverpool produced great

wealth. As the individual fortunes of merchants grew, increasingly they looked to exclusive forms of leisure to complement their lifestyles. Horseracing and blood sports had long been popular. Now they turned their attention to building private boats for such sports as yachting and rowing.

From various sources it would appear that the earliest recorded regatta on the Mersey took place in 1760 (compared with the earliest known at Chester, in 1733). There was definitely a Mersey boat race in 1783, as contemporary reports note a significant loss of life during the event. It is also known that professional watermen on the Mersey regularly raced each other during the 18th century, as did their London counterparts on the River Thames (where the Doggett's Coat and Badge Race,

still running, started in 1715). By 1828, however, evidence confirms that yachting and rowing regattas on the Mersey had become an annual fixture in Liverpool life.

Britain's earliest rowing clubs, all strictly amateur and based in the south, formed from around 1818 onwards. In Liverpool they started to appear from around 1840. For example the 1840 Chester Regatta featured three crews from Liverpool.

In July 1844, the city's first sailing club was formed, the Mersey Yacht Club, which just two months later was granted a royal warrant. The Mersey Rowing Club (*see opposite*) followed in 1854.

The emergence of the RMYC (*see pages 26–27*) would prove pivotal in the establishment of more regularised regattas, but its remit, at a time when the Battle

of Trafalgar was still within living memory, extended beyond social and sporting aims. As with other royal yacht clubs formed at this time, the RMYC in effect provided naval training, while acting as back-up for the Channel Fleet.

The earliest evidence of competitive swimming in the Mersey is a report in the *Liverpool Sporting Register* of two men racing in July 1825 between the Queen's Dock and Runcorn, a distance of 18 miles. For 3 hours 35 minutes they were swept along by the onrushing tides, being sustained along the way by tots of brandy and wine administered from bottles tied to a stick.

A cross Mersey swim also formed part of the Liverpool Olympic Festivals of the 1860s.

By the late 19th century however, the impact of dock activity, the accumulation of effluent from mills upstream as far as Stockport, plus the dumping of sewage, had turned the Mersey into reportedly the most polluted river in Europe and one hardly conducive to sport or recreation. An RMYC pamphlet of 1907 described the river water as a 'dirty fluid,' while the merchant Sir William Forwood complained that yachting and canoeing on the Mersey was increasingly limited by steamship movements.

Yet as this chapter relates, a number of clubs did continue to operate on the river throughout the century, and even swimming continued for long periods, albeit on the New Brighton side, where there was sufficient tidal outflow to create tolerable conditions.

Today, happily, the Mersey is in the process of being rejuvenated

Since 2002 oxygen levels in the river have risen sufficiently to sustain such fish as salmon. A cleaner river has even brought

back swimming to the Liverpool side of the Mersey, while modern water sports such as windsurfing and power boating are attracting greater numbers to the river.

Nor should it be forgotten that the annual Mersey Regatta offers an unbroken link with the pre-industrial era, before even Herman Melville had set eyes on the mighty river.

▲ The **Mersey Rowing Club** gather in 1885 at their floating boathouse, built in 1866 and moored during the winter at Birkenhead. Dressing rooms were on the upper level.

Formed in 1854 after the merger of seven other clubs – the earliest dating from 1840 – the Mersey RC became one of the most successful in the region, entering the Henley Regatta from at least 1861.

Alas the floating boathouse succumbed to a fierce gale at New Ferry in 1913, when 24 boats were also destroyed. But the club revived at a new boathouse at Wallasey Pool, where they shared the water with the Liverpool Victoria Rowing Club, until disbanding in 1959. Reformed in 1986, Mersey RC are now based at the Merseyside Watersports Centre (*see page 32*).

▶ Originally derived from fast sailing boats used by the Dutch Navy to pursue pirates, and subsequently introduced to Britain when Charles II returned to these shores in 1660, yachts were for many years the sole preserve of the rich. But as racing became more popular in the 19th century, so grew the demand for an affordable, one-design class yacht.

Seen here at the 2006 Regatta is a prime example of this trend, the **Mermaid**, one of five **Mylne Class** boats designed for the **Royal Mersey Yacht Club** by Alfred Mylne of Munro's boatyard on the River Clyde, and first raced on the Mersey in July 1935. Of those five, costing £185 apiece, each with oak hulls and mahogany decking and each with a name starting with MER, four remain in regular use, over 70 years later.

The RMYC owns several other Mylnes, including seven originally built in Bangor during the late 1930s for the Trearddur Bay Sailing Club, and five modern versions, built – in response to escalating timber repair and maintenance costs – with fibre-glass hulls from a mould made in 1980 and owned exclusively by the RMYC.

Both in looks and in its handling, the Mylne remains a classic, and to its admirers, no less emblematic of the Mersey skyline than the city's more familiar landmarks.

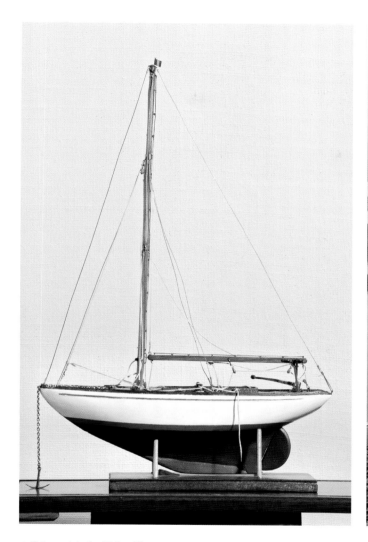

▲ This model of a **Mylne Class** yacht, together with the half-hull models on display at the clubhouse of the **Royal Mersey Yacht Club** (*above right*), represent a valuable historical record of yacht design over the last century (although they were originally crafted to showcase the work of competing boatyards).

After forming at the Mersey Hotel, Old Church Yard, in 1844, the RMYC first set up headquarters at the Union Gallery, Duke Street, until in 1852 the site was taken over by Liverpool's first public library. Boating activities were meanwhile based across the river at hotels in Birkenhead, then Rock Ferry. In 1876 they then moved to the former slipway and sheds of the Birkenhead Ferry on Mersey Street, until the expansion of the Cammell Laird shipyards persuaded members to purchase a pair of late Victorian semi-detached houses on Bedford Road, Rock Ferry (*see right*), from where the club has operated since May 1901.

It has proved an ideal location. Access to the river is only 200 yards away at the Rock Ferry Pier, while there is also a large yard for boat storage and maintenance.

▲ In stark contrast to the received image we have of rowing at the likes of Oxford or Henley, this view of an inter-war regatta, staged on the **West Float, Wallasey Pool**, by the **Liverpool Victoria Rowing Club**, illustrates just how incongruous were conditions for rowing on the Mersey for much of the 20th century. Indeed the very survival of the 'Vics' amid the docks, shipyards, flour mills and polluted waterways is a testament to the members' dedication.

In its original state Wallasey Pool was a two mile inlet from the Mersey, dissecting the townships of Wallasey and Birkenhead. Pleasure boating had long been popular there, and remained so even after the first dock developments of the 1840s created a new central section known as the Great Float (later divided into East and West Floats). But of several rowing clubs formed in the Pool in the late 19th century, only the LVRC, formed in 1884, would survive.

Although the scene is much altered today, the club still races on the stretch of West Float seen here, between Poulton, or 'Penny' Bridge and Duke Street Bridge.

▶ In 1930 the **Liverpool Victoria Rowing Club** was forced to vacate its original boathouse when the last remaining part of Wallasey Pool was redeveloped as Bidston Dock. Fortunately the Dock Board found the Vics a new site, on the Birkenhead side of the West Float (on what is now called Canada Creek), where they built this substantial timber boathouse in the shadows of the neighbouring mills and warehouses. It was here that the club – strengthened by an affiliation with Wallasey Grammar School begun in 1922 – clocked up numerous victories, including a record for any provincial club during their Jubilee year of 1934.

But West Float was hardly ideal. Unregulated discharge of waste oil and bilge water by visiting ships made for unpleasant conditions, forcing at least one regatta to be cancelled. Yet ironically, as dock activity decreased from the 1980s onwards, and more of the surrounding buildings were demolished, although water quality improved, the Vics' boathouse found itself increasingly vulnerable to vandalism and theft, a perennial problem for all rowing clubs in isolated, urban locations.

Finally, the boathouse was completely destroyed by an arson attack in August 1990.

For the next decade or so the Vics had to soldier on in the shell of a new, but spartan boathouse, built across the West Float by Poulton Bridge, until in 2002 they successfully applied for Lottery funding to modernise the boathouse and expand their remit to involvement with local schools.

As the region's oldest rowing club in continuous operation, the Vics' membership stood at some 220 members in the run up to its 125th anniversary.

Opened by Sir Steven Redgrave in April 2004 after a £1.5 million refit funded by the Lottery, Sport England, Wirral Borough Council and various other agencies, the Wirral Rowing Centre (*left*) – the new home of the Liverpool Victoria Rowing Club – may not possess the vernacular charm of its predecessor, but is secure, heated and well equipped. A 30m floating pontoon has also eliminated the problems associated with accessing the water at high and low tides.

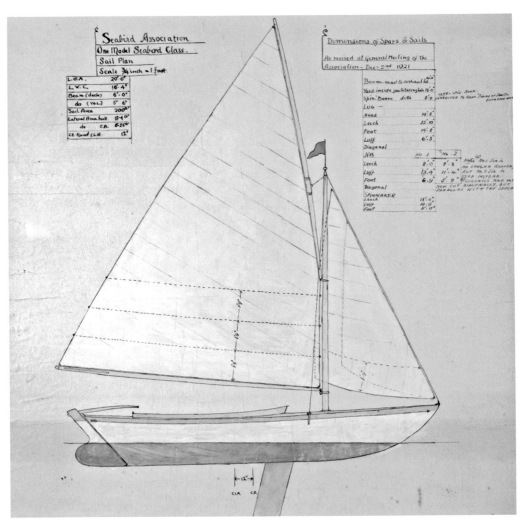

Ensconced since 1910 amid the terraced houses of Hope Street, 300 yards from the New Brighton waterfront, the Wallasey Yacht Club formed in 1903 after local would-be sailors decided that the existing clubs in the area were too exclusive (a common complaint at a time when sailing was still seen as the preserve of the rich). The club they formed was originally called the Magazines Sailing Club – named after the New Brighton district in which early meetings were held – until the current name was adopted in 1921 when Wallasey gained borough status.

▲ Just as the Royal Mersey Yacht Club adopted the Mylne Class in 1935, the boat most closely associated with the **Wallasey Yacht Club** is the **Seabird Half Rater**.

First built at a cost of £35 each for the West Lancashire Yacht Club and raced from the Southport Pierhead in 1899, the Seabird is thought to be the oldest one-design class boat still racing in Britain.

When the boat's centenary regatta was staged in the Menai Strait in 1999, an unprecedented total of 47 Seabirds, old and new, gathered, each of them named by tradition after sea birds. Apart from Wallasey Yacht Club, which has 25 of the boats, two other clubs were represented, South Caernarvonshire Yacht Club and Trearddur Bay Sailing Club.

This sail plan, on display at the WYC's clubhouse, shows various dimensions agreed after a meeting of the Seabird Association in December 1921.

A new 20 foot Seabird, built using the traditional method of carvel planking – in which longitudinal planks are fastened to the frame (making repairs easier) – would cost over £20,000.

▲ A stirring scene from the **Mersey Regatta** of 2006, showing a line of RMYC Mylne Class yachts embarking on the outward leg of the Henglers Cup race, while routine life on the Mersey carries on regardless. Although difficult to identify each boat, the roster of RMYC Mylnes follows a consistent pattern, with names such as Mercantile, Mercator, Merganser, Meridian, Merk, Merlin, Mermaid, Mermerus and, of course, Mersey.

As stated earlier, the Mersey Regatta may go back as early as 1760, making it by far the oldest sporting event in the region (predating even the Grand National). For many years it was also one of the most prestigious. The Grand Liverpool Regatta of 1840, for example, which included entries from London, offered silver plate to the value of £75 for the winners of the yacht races, and £100 for rowing. There was a further rowing prize of £10 contested by the Mersey boatmen who prepared the yachts. The regatta began at Monk's Ferry, Birkenhead and, according to the *Liverpool Mercury,* was watched by 500 ladies and gentlemen from the 'first families of Liverpool'. Following the regatta a firework display and dinner were enjoyed at the Monk's Hotel.

Modern Mersey regattas usually consist of nine races, each for a different class of yacht, and each starting at three minute intervals from close to the RMYC's base at Rock Ferry, on the Birkenhead side of the river. From there the boats follow one of six courses (depending on conditions), marked out by buoys, heading towards Dingle on the Liverpool side and reaching the furthest turning point – approximately three miles south from Rock Ferry – at Bromborough.

In all the RMYC runs 40-60 races a year on the Mersey between April and October. But they and the Wallasey Yacht Club are only two of several long established sailing clubs in the region, each with their own annual regatta.

These include **Hoylake Sailing Club**, formed in 1887 and based on the Promenade at Hoylake; the **Blundellsands Sailing Club**, first mentioned in 1891 and based on the mouth of the River Alt at Hightown; the **West Cheshire Sailing Club**, formed in 1892 and based on Coastal Drive, Wallasey, and **West Kirby Sailing Club**, formed in 1901 and based on Sandy Lane, adjoining the West Kirby Marine Lake (on the River Dee estuary).

To this list must be added the most recently established, and most centrally located **Liverpool Yacht Club**, formed in 1988 and based at the Coburg Dock Marina in Brunswick Dock (by Sefton Street), and the **Crosby Sailing Club**, based at the Crosby Marina, which opened in 1989.

In short, while the commercial shipping lanes might be quieter, for recreational sailors, the Mersey has never been busier.

▲ Sport has played a key role in a number of urban regeneration schemes around Britain, one fine example of which is the £1.2m **Merseyside Watersports Centre**, funded by the Merseyside Development Corporation in 1994 and located within Queen's Dock (itself nearly 200 years old). In an area of sport that has traditionally been the preserve of private members' clubs, its remit is to offer affordable opportunities to a wider sector of the community, thus helping to reconnect local people with the river. In addition to sailing, windsurfing and canoeing, it is also the home of the **Mersey Rowing Club**, which reformed in 1986 but, as seen on page 25, had a two-storey floating boathouse of its own during the period 1866–1913.

Although it appears to float, the club's new base is rather more permanent, being built on piles. It is, furthermore, one of the few modern sports-related buildings in Liverpool to have genuine architectural merit. Designed by David Marks and Julia Barfield (best known for the London Eye), among its numerous plaudits was a regional award from RIBA in 1995.

LIVERPOOL AND DISTRICT
SWIMMING & WATER POLO ASSOCIATION

52ND ANNUAL

Mersey Mile Championship
(Under A.S.A. Laws)

SATURDAY, 7TH AUG., 1937

Steamer "SKIRMISHER" will accompany the race.
Steamer leaves Liverpool Landing Stage at 6.30 p.m. prompt.

Adults 1/6 Each.

▲ From 1876 until 1939 one of the highlights of Liverpool's sporting calendar was the annual **Mersey Mile** swimming race, from New Brighton Pier to the north dock wall. This rare 1937 ticket is for a spectator to follow the event on board the steamer *Skirmisher*, from whose deck entrants dived to start the race (*as on the cover*).

Before it became a regular event, the earliest recorded Mersey Mile took place during the Liverpool Olympics of June 1863 when, watched by large crowds on both sides of the river, nine swimmers set forth. Of those, seven promptly gave up, unable to counter the estuary's notorious currents, while the remaining pair, Aitkin and M'Cullin, were swept downstream towards Albert Dock. At this point only M'Cullin was able to continue to the flagboat, moored off Prince's Landing Stage. Overall, he had swum between five and six miles to win the race, and was in the water for one hour and 40 minutes.

The decision to stage the event annually in 1876 appears to have been inspired by the exploits of Captain Matthew Webb, who the previous year became the

first person to swim the English Channel. (Webb was known in Liverpool, having previously begun his maritime career on the *Conway*, a Mersey-based training ship.)

Initially organised by the Liverpool Swimming Club, and subsequently by the Liverpool & District Swimming and Water Polo Association, the Mersey Mile soon grew in popularity, attracting entrants from all over Britain (each of whom received an ornate certificate for their efforts).

As the quality of entrants also improved, so too were new records set. For example in 1884, IWH Briton from Salford covered the mile long course in 23 minutes.

But in 1937 a St Helen's swimmer called Eric Gilvray won with a time of just under 17 minutes. Indeed Gilvray became the Mersey Mile's most successful entrant ever, winning three successive races from 1936–38.

Owing to growing concerns about water pollution the cross river race appears not to have revived after the war, although the Wallasey police force organised a swim on the Seacombe side of the river until the late 1980s.

▼ Directly mirroring the resurgence of watersports on the Mersey is the revival of swimming, due entirely to improvements in the water quality achieved since the 1980s. (New Brighton's beaches, for example, now regularly meet EU bathing water standards.)

One event started in 1990 and now popular with swimmers from all over Britain is the **Ivan Percival Open Water Championships**, a series of two and four mile races staged every May by the **City of Liverpool Swimming Club's Open Water Section** in the Albert Dock. Hardier souls then return to the dock for the annual Boxing Day dip.

In 1994 club members Robin Baynes, Bob Jones and Jimmy Tinsley (a cross-Channel swimmer), launched a further event, the successor to the pre-war Mersey Mile. Known in its modern guise as the **Across Mersey Swim**, this takes place every August, conditions willing, starting at Woodside Ferry, Birkenhead – from where this view of entrants to the 2003 race was taken – and ending across the river at Albert Dock, a distance of

1.25 miles. For absolute safety, a canoeist paddles alongside each swimmer, and the race is timed to coincide with slack water.

Interestingly, each of the first three events was won by a female swimmer, Rachel Godburn from Rotherham (another Channel swimmer). Since then the men, including Liverpudlian Dave Parry (brother of Olympic medallist Steve) have dominated. However no modern swimmer has yet approached Eric Gilvray's record of 1937, which suggests that he was racing with the tide, or on a shorter course. On the other hand, many of today's swimmers participate not to break records but in order to raise money for charity.

There is one slight sting in this otherwise welcome tale of the river.

Whereas in the past oil slicks, sewage and passing ships were the main threats to swimmers, now the Mersey teems with life, including such recent arrivals as lion's mane jellyfish, or worse, weever fish. But then open water swimmers have always understood that they can never quite rule the waves.

Chapter Three

Aintree

One of Liverpool's most celebrated pieces of public art is this fine bronze at Aintree. Red Rum won the Grand National a record three times in the 1970s, and was twice runner-up. After his death at the age of 30 in 1995 he was buried by the winning post. Intriguingly, the sculptor Philip Blacker was himself a Grand National jockey during the Red Rum era, achieving three top four placings in this epic test of man and beast.

Horse racing, the so-called Sport of Kings, is associated predominantly with rural settings; the likes of Newmarket, Ascot, Goodwood and Epsom Downs. Yet here at Aintree, on the outskirts of Liverpool, stands a racecourse of international renown, bordered by a canal, two railway lines, housing estates and a string of industrial units and retail outlets.

Manchester, Birmingham and London each lost their last remaining urban racecourses to development during the early 1960s, after the legalisation of off-course betting in 1960 had crippled their viability. And yet Aintree has survived, not only the economic pressures of the late 20th century, but the rapid urban spread of Liverpool in the second half of the 19th century.

The reason for this remarkable survival is simple. The racecourse is home to probably the world's most illustrious steeplechase, the Grand National, an event whose entire character is shaped by the topography and traditions of the course itself. The event, and the place, are virtually synonymous.

Aintree was not Liverpool's first course. The earliest recorded race was run along a four and a half mile stretch of sands between Crosby and Bankhall in 1576. William Blundell's diaries of 1654, and his list of rules, drawn up in 1682, confirm that racing continued there. These rules stated 'That a piece of silver plate... shall be exposed upon the stoop, commonly called the chair, where the horse course at Crosby doth usually begin and end.' In fact this same chair appears on John Eyes' 1765 *Plan of Liverpool*, located on the shore at Mile End. The Chair at Aintree (*see page 41*) is, of course, a more recent sporting landmark.

Crosby meetings were clearly popular. In 1705 the Liverpool Common Council donated ten guineas to sponsor a race, while a report in 1774 recounts: 'For seven miles... a stream of carriages. The sea was covered with sails, sloops, ferries and boats loaded with passengers discharged at the foot of the race ground...'

After Crosby, where the last meeting took place in 1786, from 1807–15 racing continued at Ormskirk, then reappeared in 1822 at Maghull, where, four years later, John Formby acquired an eleven year lease for the 'purpose of forming a race course'.

It was at Maghull that we find early references to the man who is generally regarded as the founder of Aintree and the Grand National. William Lynn, who donated the top prize at Maghull, the Waterloo Gold Cup, was the proprietor of the Waterloo Hotel, in Ranelagh Street, where several of the area's leading 'sportsmen' would dine as members of Lord Sefton's exclusive Altcar Club.

As one of several entrepreneurs around Britain who, at the outset of the railway age, was alert to the commercial potential of racing, Lynn then helped set up a syndicate to promote its own races, not at Maghull but on land owned by Lord Sefton at Aintree. Also part of Sefton's syndicate were the Earls of Derby, Eglington and Wilton, the lords Bentinck, Stanley and Grosvenor. Liverpool Corporation joined in with a donation of 150 guineas for the first races, held on 7 July 1829.

There are many famous courses in the width of English ground
Where the steeplechasing horses and the rainbow silks go round;
But it's Aintree, Aintree, Aintree where the champion chasers run
Where there's courage to be tested and there's glory to be won.

Will H Ogilvie (1869–1963)

Initially, as was then the norm in British racing, Aintree staged only flat racing (that is, with no obstacles). But in 1836 Lynn and Lord Sefton branched out. At Altcar they organised a sweepstake for coursing – an event that would become known as the Waterloo Cup (*see page 19*) – while at Aintree Lynn introduced a newly popular, but also highly controversial form of racing, the steeplechase.

In its early form, steeplechasing – literally a race between church steeples – was run cross country, with riders having to surmount whichever barriers, natural or otherwise, lay in their path. Thought to have originated in Ireland in the 1750s, then taken up by cavalry officers during the Napoleonic Wars, England's first formalised steeplechase began at St Albans in 1830.

Derided by the establishment as a 'tumbledown' affair, the St Albans Chase seemed a world away from the elitist ethos of thoroughbred racing. But that is what made it so attractive to Lynn.

So it was that on 29 February 1836, Aintree staged its first Grand Liverpool steeplechase, in front of a crowd reportedly 'composed principally of the middle class'.

Perhaps with the critics of steeplechasing in mind, Lynn had specified in his advertisement that only 'gentlemen riders' would be eligible. In fact the winning jockey, riding a horse called The Duke, was a professional called Captain Martin Becher, a farmer's son from Norfolk who gained his rank in the yeomanry. He was also a veteran of the St Albans Chase.

Racing historians are divided as to whether this 1836 race should be considered as the first Grand National. Aintree's own honours board (*see page 42*) and official

histories list the 1839 race as the first, and claim the 1837 and 1838 races took place at Maghull. However recent studies (*see Links*) clearly show that Aintree was the venue in both those years, and that, moreover, the course used was almost identical to the course used today. Yet it is the fourth Aintree steeplechase, run on 26 February 1839, that is continually billed as the first Grand National.

Various factors may explain this.

Firstly, 1839 was the year that Aintree became accessible by rail, thereby drawing entries from a wider catchment – 17 starters compared with only three the previous year – and larger crowds. One report estimated 40,000.

Secondly, reporters from London were in attendance for the first time. It was one of these, from *Bell's Life*, who described the race as The Liverpool Grand National. Not that this impressed everyone. In his popular novel *Mr Sponge's Sporting Tour*, RS Surtees, a critic of steeplechases, noted, 'The more snobbish a thing is the more certain they are to call it aristocratic. When it is too bad for anything they called it a "Grand"'.

But whichever race is deemed to be the first Grand National, for sure the 1839 race was a classic, not least for providing the first of what would turn out to be a rich store of anecdotes and legends when Captain Becher ⟫

Viewed from the north east, with New Brighton in the distance, Aintree Racecourse covers nearly 300 acres of well drained former farmland. In the foreground, between the racecourse and the Aintree housing estate, runs the Leeds & Liverpool Canal, opened 1774. Other than racing, Aintree is known for such companies as English Electric, Hartley's Jam and Vernons Pools (*see page 88*), but also for the Aintree Iron Company, known for its distinctive iron urinals in the docks area. Could this explain the reference to 'Aintree Iron' in the Scaffold's 1967 song *Thankyou Very Much*? Or did that refer instead to the iron-shape of the racecourse?

Since the very beginnings of organised racing in Britain in the 16th century, racecourses have been characterised by their odd mix of temporary grandstands, tents and booths. But surely none have been as quirky as the stands erected on barges seen regularly lining the Leeds and Liverpool Canal until the 1950s. This was one of them, in the process of being made ready for the 1938 Grand National, overlooking Valentine's Brook. At the 1931 National a reporter from *Time* magazine spotted what we may assume was a rather more luxurious barge in which 'the Duke of Westminster and his friends quaffed scotch and soda'.

» (winner of the 1836 race) was unceremoniously tossed into the first of two brooks that traversed the course, at a fence that has since become probably the most famous hedge in Britain, if not the world.

That 1839 race was the last organised by William Lynn. Worn down physically and financially, the founder of the Grand National retired, to be replaced by a new syndicate with fresh finance.

But they too struggled, until in the early 1840s a Yorkshire breeder, Edward William Topham, took over the lease from Lord Sefton, built stables and put the whole enterprise onto a firmer footing. It was Topham, for example, who took the decision to turn the Grand National into a handicap, in 1843, thereby creating a more balanced race.

As it transpired, Topham's family would continue to oversee Aintree until 1973. During this 130 year period, apart from a few lean spells, the Grand National's popularity as a spectacle and as an excuse for an annual frenzy of betting, in Britain and worldwide, held up remarkably well. In the

post-war period attendances peaked, according to some reports at 300,000 (which seems unlikely but reflects the trend in other sports at the time).

Also, in 1949 the Tophams purchased Aintree's freehold from Lord Sefton for £275,000.

This paved the way for a series of upgrades, including the addition of a motor racing circuit, opened in 1954 (*see page 44*).

However, as mentioned earlier, the advent of off-course betting shops in 1960, combined with changing social patterns, made life for racecourse owners increasingly tough in the 1960s, and Aintree, despite holding four race meetings a year at the time, was no different.

Escalating costs and, not least, growing unease with the rigours of the National and with Aintree's facilities, all paid their toll.

Also, in 1958 Ronald Topham died, leaving his wife Mirabel – albeit the real power behind the throne since they married in the 1930s – to face the future alone.

Eventually, in 1965 Mrs Topham put the course up for sale, and for the next eight years it seemed as if each Grand National would be the last. There was even talk of the race switching to either Doncaster or Haydock Park.

Finally, Aintree was sold in 1973 for £3 million to a property developer, Bill Davies, who in 1975 tripled admission charges, resulting in the lowest attendance – less than 30,000 – in living memory. Yet the reputation of the National itself was then at a high, thanks to a series of victories by the immensely popular Red Rum.

At this point the bookmakers Ladbrokes took over management of the race, but only when Davies eventually sold up in 1983 was the course finally safe. This time the

buyers were Racecourse Holdings Trust, an organisation set up by the Jockey Club in 1964 to assist ailing courses. (It had first rescued Cheltenham and would go on to buy twelve others.) Davies had originally demanded £7 million, and although a public appeal raised a considerable sum towards this, in the end £4 million proved enough to secure the deal.

But RHT still needed to raise further finance to modernise the now parlous facilities, particularly after a fire in 1984 destroyed half the County Stand. (A measure of how poor conditions were at this time was that, as one horrified visitor noticed, even the toilet in the royal box had only half a seat.)

Since then, stage by stage, Aintree has been almost totally revamped, largely thanks to an eight year sponsorship by the Canadian distiller Seagram, followed from 1992–2004 by Martell, and now the brewers John Smith. As described later, apart from the restoration and extension of the County Stand, two new stands were added in 1992 and 1998. In the interim a seven acre car park on Ormskirk Road was sold for a retail and hotel development, while a nine hole golf course was laid out within the Grand National course.

A further £34 million revamp started in 2005, resulting in the addition of two further stands.

Aintree today has never been so busy. It now holds seven days a year of racing, but just as importantly is in daily use for corporate hospitality, exhibitions and events.

But make no mistake.

Without its annual steeplechase, Aintree would not have survived. The place, and the event, remain inextricably linked.

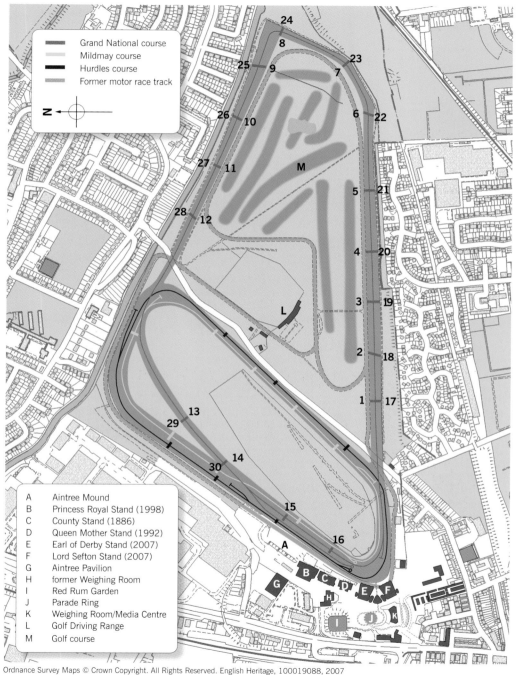

Legend:

- Grand National course
- Mildmay course
- Hurdles course
- Former motor race track

N

A — Aintree Mound
B — Princess Royal Stand (1998)
C — County Stand (1886)
D — Queen Mother Stand (1992)
E — Earl of Derby Stand (2007)
F — Lord Sefton Stand (2007)
G — Aintree Pavilion
H — former Weighing Room
I — Red Rum Garden
J — Parade Ring
K — Weighing Room/Media Centre
L — Golf Driving Range
M — Golf course

Ordnance Survey Maps © Crown Copyright. All Rights Reserved. English Heritage, 100019088, 2007

◀ Unlike a classical hippodrome, with its uniform track and symmetrical circuit, a National Hunt or steeplechase racecourse is moulded by the terrain.

Aintree consists of two unequal sections. The western third lies between the range of stands in the south west corner and Melling Road, which dissects the site from roughly north to south.

The upper, or eastern two thirds is that part of the course that before 1836 was open countryside. Even today when horses advance towards fence 1 (fence 17 on the second circuit), they are said to be 'heading into the country'. Indeed, until the course was fully turfed in 1885 much of the Grand National circuit was laid out on ploughed fields. (There are still farm cottages on the west side of Melling Road.)

The placement of the fences beyond Melling Road reflects this also. With minor amendments, each one marks the field boundaries as they were in 1836.

Since then the most significant alterations have been the addition of the Mildmay course in 1953 (named after the amateur jockey Lord Mildmay) and the tarmac motor racing track completed the year after. A nine hole golf course (M) and golf driving range (L) were also added, in 1994.

The present Grand National course starts opposite stand F, covering one circuit of 16 fences and a second of 14 (with fences 15 and 16 jumped only once). Its length is four miles, 856 yards.

The Mildmay course is just over three miles long and uses regulation steeplechase fences, while the Hurdles course has hurdles only (lower and flimsier than fences), and is also used for flat races (known as 'bumpers'), for potential steeplechase horses.

The oldest surviving structure at Aintree today is the much altered County Stand, which bears this discreet datestone for June 12 1885 on its south west corner. Unfortunately the identity of WRG, presumably the builder, remains unknown. The stand opened for the following year's Grand National in March 1886, the first in which the entire length of the course was both railed and turfed.

▲ Among dozens of paintings celebrating Aintree and the Grand National, this rendition of the 1843 race by **William Tasker** offers us the clearest view of the racecourse's principal architectural features during its early years.

The 1843 race was significant in that it was first to be run under the handicap system, introduced by Aintree's new manager, William 'The Wizard' Topham (who had previously worked at Chester, where Tasker painted two similar race tableaux, also in the early 1840s).

It was also the year in which the infamous stone wall reappeared – presumably to add extra excitement – having previously been erected for the 1840 race, resulting in several casualties. In truth the wall was not as evenly constructed as Tasker portrayed it, being a rather more informal pile of stones with a turf topping. But it did result, as shown, in the fall of both Tinderbox and Teetotum, with Lottery (the 1839

winner), ridden by Jem Mason, proving able to avoid the melee by leaping clear into the lead.

Tasker clearly used some artistic licence to portray both the action and the jockeys' colours. But his depiction of the stands appears to be more accurate. Most prominent among them was the **Grand Stand**, better known for obvious reasons as the Wedding Cake Stand. A typical racecourse construction of its era, with first floor balconies for the elite and two upper roof terraces for the more daring, its foundation stone was laid by Lord Sefton on 7 February 1829, five months before Aintree's inaugural meeting.

The architect was the Liverpool Corporation Surveyor, John Foster Junior, who at the time was also working at the Pierhead on Britain's first public baths (see page 168).

To the right, closer inspection of the open-topped stand shows it to be labelled Towers No 1 Stand, with dining rooms at the rear and

the names Peter Taylor and Wilson, possibly both bookmakers, above numbered doorways.

Also worth noting is the presence of spectators on both sides of the rail, a practice long since banned, and the presence in the lower right of onlookers on horseback. Apparently it was not uncommon at this time for individuals to ride freely around the course, following the action rather as television crews now do in vans alongside the rails.

Finally, the 1843 National was the first to have racecards issued. Could one of these be the white paper being held by the boy on the rails in the lower left foreground?

Few records survive to tell us more about other stand developments at Aintree, if any, until the completion of the **County Stand** (see left and opposite), in 1886. This was located immediately to the right of Foster's Stand, which was destroyed by a fire in September 1892.

▲ This view, taken at the start of Grand National in 2006, illustrates the mix-and-match architectural styling that is so characteristic of British racecourses, and sporting venues in general.

In the centre is the 1886 **County Stand**, whose central projecting balcony (*see left*) became the royal box after the Grand Stand burnt down in 1892. Note its ornate iron columns. Much of the stand had to be rebuilt after another fire in 1984, so that its original form is now largely obscured.

To the left is the **Queen Mother Stand**, opened at a cost of £3.25 million in 1992. This somewhat curious mix of gables, pitched roofs and clocktower marked the beginnings of Aintree's new life as an all-year round corporate entertainment facility.

To the right, replacing an earlier 20th century extension to the County Stand, is the rather more dashing **Princess Royal Stand.**

Built at a cost of £6 million and opened in 1998 as part of a more comprehensive remodelling of the general circulation areas, it was built by Birse Construction and designed by Lobb Sports Architects, the team that also worked on Bolton's Reebok Stadium. (Lobb had earlier worked at Cheltenham Racecourse and later became part of HOK Sport, architects at Ascot, Wembley, Wimbledon and Arsenal.)

As can be seen, in an attempt to provide a visual (and access) link between these three very different stands a continuous balcony has been added at mid-level.

In 2005 there began a further, even more radical phase of redevelopment (*see page 45*), culminating in the opening of two additional, and identical stands to the left of the Queen Mother Stand in April 2007.

It may come as no surprise that their style differs completely from their neighbours.

Becher's Brook 1839

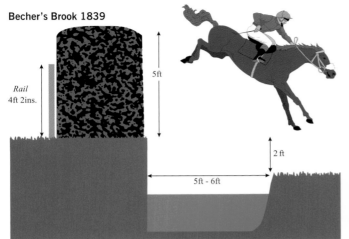

Becher's Brook 2007

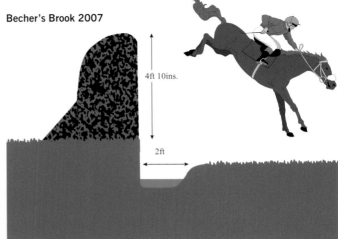

◄ Of all the fences at Aintree, none inspires greater awe or terror than fence Number 6 (22 on the second circuit), **Becher's Brook**, seen here on Jump Sunday, March 1952.

Held from 1906 to 1962, **Jump Sunday** was an Aintree institution, a chance for members of the public to walk the entire Grand National course on the Sunday before the race. This was the Topham family's way of thanking local residents for having to contend with the annual invasion of Aintree by 100,000 or more visitors every year.

Entry was free and it was not unknown for over 50,000 to turn up, along with an informal army of souvenir vendors, entertainers and three-card tricksters, thereby creating an event in itself.

Alas, after damage was caused to fences in 1961 and 1962 the Jump Sunday tradition came to an abrupt end. During Bill Davies' period of ownership it was revived in 1974. But with a charge of £5 per person and £2 for car parking, the experiment was not a success. Nor, sadly, in today's more security conscious climate is it one likely to be revived.

The diagram (*above left*) shows how Becher's Brook (known originally as 'the first brook') might have looked in 1839, with both a rail and hedge, and a drop in level of two feet onto the steeply sloping ditch side. (However one artist's impression depicts only a rail, and no hedge in front of the brook.)

Legend has it that when Captain Becher was thrown into the brook, during the 1839 National – the incident that gave the fence its name – he quipped, 'How dreadful water tastes without the benefit of whisky.' And in those days the brook was indeed wider and deeper. In 1928 spectators had to haul one horse out with ropes to save it from drowning.

Today's Becher's Brook is less steep on its landing side, having been partially levelled after two horses died attempting to clear it in 1989. The outer running rail was also splayed out to allow more room for horses landing wide.

Yet it remains a formidable obstacle, and one made tougher by the gathering of TV cameras and curious crowds at what is probably the best known fence in racing.

The Chair 2007

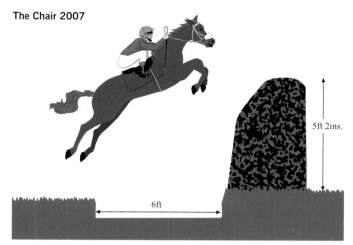

5ft 2ins.

6ft

The Water Jump 2007

2ft 9ins.

12ft

▲ Fence number 15, known as **The Chair**, is the tallest and widest fence at Aintree and although jumped only once during the Grand National circuit, its position directly in front of the stands offers spectators spectacular side-on views of jumping at its finest.

Note how the fence slopes at the top, or apron, of the take-off side. This design was adopted at several fences in 1961 to make them appear more inviting and easier to jump, and also to reduce injuries.

The fence itself takes its name from the raised chair on which, before the introduction of modern technology, the Distance Judge sat, 240 yards from the winning post. His job was to assess the distance between the first four – or 'placed' – horses. A horse that did not pass the Chair before the winner passed the post was said to be 'distanced'.

The chair in situ today is a plastic replica of the original, which for safety reasons was moved in 1994 to its current location near the parade ring (*below left*).

Two others fences at Aintree bear the names of horses. Fence 7 (23) (*right*) is known as **Foinavon**. In profile, it is typical of the majority of fences, yet at 4' 6" is the smallest obstacle on the course, apart from the Water Jump. Ironically, given its height, it was here in 1967 that a loose horse brought almost the entire field to a chaotic halt, allowing the trailing Foinavon to avoid the pile-up and romp home to a shock victory.

Fence 9 (25) is known as **Valentine's Brook** after a horse called Valentine jumped it in a curious corkscrew manner from an almost standing position in the 1840 race.

▲ Fence 16, the final fence on the first circuit of the Grand National, is the **Water Jump**. This replaced the fearsome wall (*shown on page 38*) in 1841, and like The Chair is positioned directly opposite the stands and jumped only once.

At only 2 feet and 9 inches tall it is the smallest of the Aintree fences, and even with its wide ditch on the landing side, offers a relatively easy obstacle for riders and horses. The water itself is barely 6 inches deep.

One other characteristic of the Water Jump is that it is the only current Grand National fence that is still a naturally growing hedge. All the others are built from scratch, by hand, using a thorn base, dressed with a form of spruce known as Sitka, supplied to Aintree from plantations in the Lake District.

For safety reasons no wires can be used in tying the bundles of spruce together, and the spruce has to be in place no earlier than two weeks before the National, otherwise it will start to turn brown.

Each Grand National fence costs around £10,000 a year to maintain.

Foinavon Fence

4ft 6ins.

▲ Volunteers from the Injured Jockeys Fund set up their stall by Aintree's enormous **Honours Board**. Every year the charity pays around £1.25 million in grants (compared with an estimated £63 million raised for the welfare of horses). In human terms Aintree is arguably no worse than many other courses. Only one jockey has been killed in a Grand National,

in 1862. But between 1997 and 2006 32 horses have died in action at Aintree, a figure exceeded in National Hunt racing only by Cheltenham. Aintree's management has therefore had to make a series of changes to the fences over the years in consultation with vets and owners, while at the same time facing considerable opposition from animal rights campaigners.

Meanwhile, according to recent research, the Honours Board is itself in need of revision. Historians argue that, contrary to the record shown on the board, both the 1837 and 1838 races were run at Aintree, not Maghull, while Captain Becher's victory in the very first race in 1836 is not listed at all. In this respect he too may be considered an injured party.

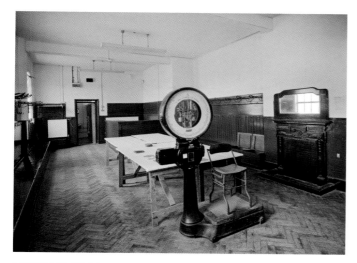

▲ Racing silks were first made compulsory at Newmarket in 1765 to make it easier to differentiate between riders. On display at Aintree are these two sets of colours. On the left are the silks of Manifesto's owner-breeder, Mr Harry Dyas, worn by jockey Terry Kavanagh when riding to victory in the 1897 Grand National. This was one of eight National appearances by Manifesto, an all-time record. Until recently, Manifesto's skeleton was on display at the University of Liverpool's Victoria Building on Brownlow Hill.

On the right are the woollen colours of Noel Le Mare, owner of Red Rum, carried in the horse's National victories of 1973 and 1974, ridden by Brian Fletcher, and 1977, ridden by Tommy Stack.

Also on display is an intricately decorated cigar box made by engraver Charles Hunt, to celebrate Lottery's victory in 1839.

▲ Until 2006, prior to each race every jockey had to be weighed on the Avery scales of the **Weighing Room** (*top*) next to the unsaddling enclosure (which, uniquely, was covered). Conditions may have been sparse, with simple benches for the jockeys to change and racks on which to hang their saddles. But the room was seen as part of Aintree's rather workaday charm.

Now, since a replacement was built on the far side of the former parade ring, the revamped **Old Weighing Room** (*above*) doubles as a bar area and as part of the racecourse's **Grand National Museum**. Note that the original parquet flooring, the decorative fireplace and some of the saddle racks have been retained amid the display of original artefacts.

Barely noticed by racegoers hurrying along Ormskirk Road is this humble entrance to Paddock Lodge, home to the Topham family from the late 19th century. The house itself, overlooking the old parade ring (now Red Rum Garden), is hardly noteworthy. But one of its inhabitants will never be forgotten. Mirabel Topham, a former Gaiety Girl, married into the family and became an Aintree director in 1935. It was under her doughty control that the freehold was secured, the Mildmay course laid out and motor racing introduced. Despite selling Aintree in 1973, Topham stayed on at Paddock Lodge until her death in 1980, aged 88.

▶ Just as William Lynn was persuaded that the thrills and spills of steeplechasing would be good for business in 1836, so did Mirabel Topham decide that the increasingly popular spectacle of motor racing might put Aintree onto a firmer footing in the early 1950s. After all, it had proved a great success for the Duke of Richmond at his estate in Goodwood, West Sussex, where a race track was laid in 1948, and also at the former wartime airfield at Silverstone in Northamptonshire, where 100,000 had converged to see the British Grand Prix in 1950.

Not everyone shared Topham's enthusiasm however, and it took two years of negotiations and the re-routing of a public footpath before the first race in May 1954.

Having spent £275,000 on buying Aintree's freehold in 1949, a further £100,000 was spent on laying a three mile, 35 feet wide tarmac track alongside the Grand National course, plus the building of a tunnel linking the track with a pit area, created in the infield.

These were exciting times in British motor racing. Engineers who had fine tuned Spitfires joined forces with a new generation of daredevil drivers such as Stirling Moss, Reg Parnell and Mike Hawthorn, to challenge the Ferrari team from Turin and the likes of the dashing Argentinian, Juan Fangio.

In total, from May 1954 until July 1962, Aintree hosted five Grand Prix races, including the 1957 race in which Stirling Moss became the first British winner of a Grand Prix since 1924. Later winners were Jack Brabham in 1959 and Jim Clark in 1962.

After that year the faster track at Silverstone won back its Grand Prix monopoly. But motor racing continued at Aintree under the

auspices of the **Aintree Circuit Club** until 1984, and was then revived in 2004 with a three day non-competitive Festival of Motorsport, featuring hundreds of historic racing cars (one driven by 75 year old Stirling Moss). The club's hope was that the festival would become an annual fixture, complementing two similar heritage racing festivals at Goodwood. Instead, members were

aghast to discover that Aintree's management had plans to build two new stands (see *opposite*), whose footprint would encroach upon the track, thereby ending any hope of further events.

A subsequent request to have the track listed failed, and the new stands are now in situ – a rare case, it would seem, of the horse having been put before the car.

▲ It is not so long ago that few punters would have bet on Aintree surviving as a racecourse into the 21st century. Yet not only does racing continue, it positively thrives. In addition to the Grand National there are now three other meetings, in May, October and November, together with a daily roster of conferences and events within the new stands' hospitality areas.

▲ Although the course itself has changed little since the 1950s, facilities for horses, jockeys and racegoers at Aintree have been transformed since 2005, thanks to a £35 million redevelopment drawn up by the Building Design Partnership (who masterminded a similarly radical revamp at Wimbledon during the 1990s).

Unsurprisingly, as at Wimbledon, BDP's plans raised fears that the scheme would detract from Aintree's historic character (not least by encroaching on the motor racing track). Yet nor could it be denied that decades of under investment had left Aintree ill-equipped to deal with today's more stringent demands.

This new **Parade Ring** and **Winner's Enclosure** was just one element of the two-year scheme.

Crowds of up to 4,000 can gather in this mini-arena, whose curving terrace leads up to a glass-fronted weighing room overlooking the new unsaddling enclosure. One sign of the times is that the jockeys' changing rooms cater for up to ten female riders. Also within this block is a restaurant and media centre, behind which is a pre-parade ring and 26 new saddling boxes.

But the most startling element of the scheme is a pair of matching stands (*below*). Named the **Earl of Derby Stand** and the **Lord Sefton Stand**, and opened for the 2007 Grand National, each has terracing for 1,400 spectators, plus three upper levels of 790 seats and hospitality suites for a further 1,000 guests under the shade of a distinctive cantilevered canopy.

Whatever one's view of gambling or of steeplechasing, Aintree's impact on Liverpool cannot be lightly dismissed. Estimates of between 400-700 million viewers worldwide follow the race on television – a figure rivalled by only one other British sporting event, the FA Cup Final – while in 2006 over 148,000 people visited Aintree during the three days of the Grand National meeting (including 12,000 travelling from Ireland), generating an estimated £17.5 million for the economy of the region. This figure was expected to rise in 2007.

The value of sporting heritage is often hard to calculate or express in real terms. But in this case there can be no doubt – 170 years of steeplechasing have made Aintree an out-and-out clear favourite.

Chapter Four

Birkenhead Park

Birkenhead Park Rugby Club, in whose possession is this tasselled cap from the club's early years, is one of three private sports clubs to rent a portion of what is otherwise a public facility. No doubt such an arrangement was far from designer Joseph Paxton's mind when he wrote to his wife in 1843, 'It is not a very good situation for a park as the land is generally poor but, of course, it will rebound more (to my) credit and honour to make something handsome and good out of bad materials.' Handsome and good Birkenhead Park turned out to be, a model copied both across the nation and overseas. But one of the lessons Paxton's successors learnt from it was that sport, in its right place, should be an integral part of any public park's design.

Our third cluster lies across the Mersey, but is included at this point because it offers a useful bridge in our understanding of how active team sport (as opposed to passive recreation) emerged as an integral element of Victorian park design.

Birkenhead Park is, of course, widely considered to have been the first municipal park in Britain.

This claim is based upon the fact that, in 1842, Birkenhead became the first local authority to apply to Parliament – through legislation called the Third Improvement Act (Birkenhead) – for the right to allocate public funds towards a park development. (However it should be noted that nine years earlier Preston's Moor Park had also been publicly funded, and without recourse to Parliament.)

Birkenhead's population at that time was relatively small compared with Liverpool's, but was increasing rapidly, from just a few hundred in 1801 to over 8,000 by 1841. The park therefore seemed an ideal way to implement the conclusions of an 1833 Select Committee on Public Walks that

open spaces for the 'comfort, health and content' of the growing urban masses were now a necessity, rather than a privilege.

Birkenhead's Improvement Commissioners nevertheless still expected the rich to subsidise the creation of the park. Of the 185 acres of apparently unpromising fields and marshland purchased, 60 were marked out around the perimeter for sale to house developers. (This was a model first used for London's Regent's Park two decades earlier, and one being employed in Liverpool at the time for the development of the privately financed Princes Park.)

Leading Birkenhead's design team was Joseph Paxton (later to design the Crystal Palace), who was then also working on Princes Park. He was joined by Edward Kemp, with whom Paxton had worked at Chatsworth House, and a Liverpool architect, Lewis Hornblower.

Paxton's brief was to create an idealised version of the English countryside (a countryside that, ironically, so many of Birkenhead's population had left behind in search of work).

The first set of plans appeared in November 1843, and made no specific provision for any organised sporting activity.

Yet no sooner had they been made public than Kemp was approached by a group of local cricketers wishing to play in the park under the title of Birkenhead Park Cricket Club. That Hornblower was himself a cricketer no doubt helped, and terms of £10 a year were soon agreed. Kemp even allowed the new club to enclose their pitch with railings, designed very probably by Hornblower.

And so it was that from the very outset, a portion of Britain's first municipal park was set aside for use by a private members' club.

Birkenhead Park Rugby Club's half-timbered pavilion was built in 1892 but carries the club's original initials, this being from before the days when any distinction was made between the rugby and football codes. The lion on the club's emblem is taken from the crest of the former County Borough of Birkenhead.

No cricket was played on the park's official opening day in April 1847 however. (The ceremony had been delayed to coincide with the opening of the new Birkenhead Docks.) Instead, a crowd of 10,000 people were entertained by bands, bellringers and such 'rural sports' as sack races, porridge-eating contests and a competition to catch a pig whose tail had been shaved and lathered with soap.

Birkenhead Park's significance cannot be overstated. When an American landscape designer, Frederick Law Olmstead, visited in 1850, he was so impressed that he based his plans for New York's Central Park on what he saw. As did a whole generation of park designers in Victorian Britain.

In recognition of this, in 1986 English Heritage awarded Birkenhead Park a rare Grade 1 listing on its register of Parks and Gardens. Moreover, in 2005 the Heritage Lottery Fund, English Heritage, Wirral Council and various other funding agencies allocated a combined £11.5 million for the park's renovation. This included £1.2 million for a new visitor centre, opened in 2006.

Sport, meanwhile, has turned out to have a major presence in the park, albeit almost by default.

That is because several of the areas originally allocated for housing failed to sell as the years went by (*see right*), leaving plenty of space for sport to colonise. Rugby arrived in the early 1870s, followed by a second cricket club in 1878. Bowls and tennis would follow over the next few decades, by which time sport had become an accepted element of park design.

Thus this, the first municipal park was indeed a model, but not quite as the Improvement Commissioners had envisaged.

▲ Looking east towards Liverpool, **Birkenhead Park** appears, as Paxton planned, as a veritable *rus in urbe*. Yet had circumstances been different, the park would have been rather smaller than this.

For example, both the pitches of **Birkenhead Park Rugby Club** (*centre left*) occupy an area that in 1850 was put up for sale, unsuccessfully, for housing.

Just above these are **tennis courts**, and beyond these, just above the new visitor centre (the semi-circular white building) are six **bowling greens**. Again, both these areas were intended for sale, as were the **playing fields** at the far end, bordering Park Road East.

Two areas for sport that were always planned as open areas are the ground of **Birkenhead Park**

Cricket Club (*centre right*) and that of **Birkenhead St Mary's Cricket Club**, in the dead centre.

Hardly visible amongst the trees are two lakes, both used for fishing, though no longer for **curling**, as was popular in the 19th century.

More recently the park has seen up to 5,000 female runners take part in an annual 5km **Race For Life** charity run.

▶ Joseph Paxton may not have planned it this way, but the rural idyll he helped to create could hardly have been more suited to cricket. Shown here is the pitch used by **Birkenhead St Mary's Cricket Club**, who formed in 1878. Alas, despite their enviable setting, the club suffered a devastating blow in 2003 when an attack on their pavilion resulted in most of their records and memorabilia being destroyed.

In contrast, their neighbours at Birkenhead Park Cricket Club occupy a building that is a piece of history in itself (*below right*).

For their first three years at the park the club used a tent, until in 1849 they gained permission to erect a permanent pavilion (but only on condition that they repaired the damage caused to the turf by the tent). The result was the Grade II listed clubhouse we see today.

A charming single-storey brick structure with slate roofs and three gables forming a verandah, it is thought to be the work of Lewis Hornblower, an early playing member of the club and designer also of the park's Grade II* listed Grand Entrance Gateway (of which Paxton apparently disapproved).

If the pavilion's date can be verified, it is almost certainly the oldest sports-related structure still in use on Merseyside today, and one of the oldest in Britain too.

Hornblower also designed the railings which enclosed the ground, but regrettably these were removed during the Second World War.

Adjoining the pavilion, the white tented-roof structure is an indoor cricket school, opened in 1993.

Birkenhead Park CC were founder members of the Liverpool Competition (*see Chapter Eleven*), but today play their cricket in the Cheshire County Cricket League.

From 1887 until the 1920s, Gold Medal cards produced by John Baines of Manningham (Bradford) sold in their tens of millions to eager schoolboys. This card features Percy Dale Kendall, one of Birkenhead Park's finest. 'Toggie', as he was known, captained 'Park' for five seasons, scoring 76 tries in 196 games. He also won three England caps between 1901–03. Within hours of war being declared in August 1914 Kendall had signed up for the 10th Battalion of the King's Liverpool Regiment and offered Birkenhead's ground for military training. 'Toggie' added just one more honour to his name, that of the Military Cross, before being killed in action at Ypres in January 1915. A memorial board at Twickenham commemorates his sacrifice for king and country.

▲ On the northern edge of the park lies **Upper Park**, the home of **Birkenhead Park Rugby Club**.

The 'Park' are one of Britain's oldest rugby clubs, having been established in 1871 (the same year that the Rugby Football Union formed), after two clubs, Claughton and Birkenhead Wanderers combined with several members of the Liverpool Rugby Club who lived in Birkenhead. They were later joined by players from the disbanded Rock Ferry club.

During those early years the club played in the Lower Park section of the park, but then switched to a ground called St Anne's, on the north side of Park Road North, before moving to their present location in the Upper Park in 1886.

In order to secure this new site, club members formed a limited company, which in turn raised the capital to build the timber framed pavilion seen above, in 1892.

Since then, although the ground appears basic by modern standards, Upper Park has hosted a number of international matches, the first of which was England v. Wales in 1894. The New Zealand All-Blacks have been regular visitors since 1905, while North of England representative games have also been played against Romania, Tonga and the West Indies.

During the 1970s it appeared that the 'Park' might not survive much beyond their centenary, as the club entered a long period of decline, exacerbated by mass levels of unemployment in the region. Nor were 'Park' able to adapt easily

to rugby's controversial embrace of professionalism in 1995, a move which left many clubs like Birkenhead struggling in its wake.

But survive they did, and started a steady climb up the regional divisions, to reach the Powergen North Division One by 2002. The club now runs eight teams, from under-10s to seniors, has two squash courts, and plays an active role in community sport.

'Park' have also begun a major phase of redevelopment at Upper Park, funded by a £773,000 Lottery grant. This includes new floodlighting, improved pitches, a new changing room block and the modernisation of their historic pavilion which, happily, will be retained and adapted for community use.

Chapter Five

Stanley Park

Since it opened in 1870, sporting activity at Stanley Park has been dominated by football. This plaque records the first game played by Everton after the club's name had been changed from St Domingo, in 1879. Their opponents were another church-based team, St Peter's (whose modern premises in Langrove Street incorporates the youth club where the plaque is displayed). Coincidentally, the match was played on the corner of Stanley Park where rivals Liverpool are now building a new stadium. The stadium will adjoin the pitches (*below right*) where many a young player has honed his skills since the Victorian era.

The eminence of Aintree notwithstanding, our next cluster may with some justification be described as the epicentre of Liverpool's sporting renown.

As is common knowledge within football circles, astride Stanley Park may be found two of the most historic grounds in the world, Anfield and Goodison Park. What is less well appreciated is that this unique juxtaposition is no historical quirk. Rather, it reflects Stanley Park's role as a cradle for the development of working class team sport in the city as a whole. From the very outset, Stanley Park was indeed 'the People's Park'.

As the mayor of Liverpool, Joseph Hubback, declared to an estimated 25–30,000 gathering on its opening day on 14 May 1870, 'Although the Corporation of Liverpool have several parks, such as the Shiel Park, the Wavertree Park and the Newsham Park, there is no park that has yet been opened to the public which deserves the name of "the People's Park" more than Stanley Park.'

He continued, 'When I consider what large masses of people live within the space which stretches from the outskirts of this park down to the Mersey, and the confined habitations in which they dwell, and when I look at the grand scene around me today, I cannot but believe that the park will be the greatest benefit... to all classes of the community... both morally and physically.'

This was no mere rhetoric. In 1868 a Parliamentary report had noted that Liverpool's population of 500,860 was concentrated at a density of 100 inhabitants per acre. By comparison, Manchester and Salford's density was 46 per acre.

With so little open space, this meant that there were few outlets for outdoor recreation other than for a privileged few, for whom cricket, at such private clubs as Liverpool, Dingle and Bootle (*see Chapter Eleven*), was the dominant sport prior to 1860. The private Princes Park, opened in the 1840s, was also still largely out of bounds.

To an extent this situation was eased by the creation of the parks referred to in the mayor's speech; Wavertree Park, opened in 1856, followed by Sheil Park in 1862.

But with both those parks oversubscribed by local clubs and the city's population continuing to rise, the pressure on space grew so acute that in 1865 the Corporation launched its boldest scheme yet, the creation of a belt of three new public parks.

Newsham Park, in the east, was the first to be ready, in 1868. Stanley Park, in the north, was the second. Sefton Park would follow in the south two years later, as detailed in the following chapter.

Named after the Stanley family of Knowsley Hall – Edward Stanley, the 14th Earl of Derby and three times Prime Minister, had died in 1868 – Stanley Park was laid out on what had partly been Mere Farm, and partly land belonging to Councillor Robert Vining. In total these acquisitions cost the Corporation £115,000, plus a further £40,000 for landscaping.

The park's design was drawn up by Edward Kemp, who by then had clocked up 20 years experience as superintendent at Birkenhead Park (*see Chapter Four*). Kemp had also designed Anfield Cemetery,

opposite the park, in 1863, and Newsham Park, five years later.

At 100 acres Stanley Park was smaller than Newsham. But in concept it was similar; that is, there was to be a 40 acre core of formal gardens and lakes, dotted artfully with lodges, pavilions and bridges (designed by ER Robson). East of this were 50–60 acres of open turfed areas, suited to sport. (An indication of how social trends had changed in the two decades since Birkenhead Park's opening was that specific provision for sport was made in the design of all three of the new parks.)

At the same time, based on the Birkenhead Park model, plots of land surrounding the parks were to be sold for housing.

As it transpired, Newsham Park would never quite attain the elegance of Stanley Park, and in both cases the type of housing to emerge was on a more modest scale than was planned for Sefton Park. By way of illustration, the 'Rotten Row' Kemp had laid out for horse riding in Stanley Park did not attract many takers, and was restyled as a cycle track c.1907.

But its open expanses were immediately popular. Prior to the park's opening, it is estimated that there were were at least 40 teams playing cricket on assorted parcels of private land in the neighbouring areas of Everton and Walton, most of which would soon be swallowed up by housing. Thus within two months of the park's opening, a Mr A Monteith and 236 other signatories wrote to the Corporation requesting that they be allowed to play cricket and rounders on the park. A cricket league was soon established.

However, it would be a few years before Stanley Park played host to the newly codified game

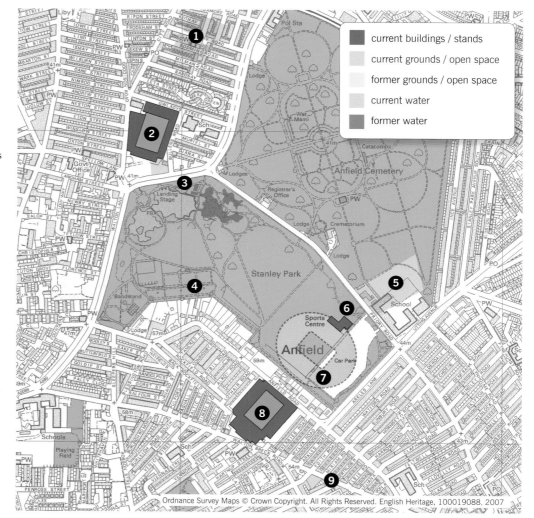

Ordnance Survey Maps © Crown Copyright. All Rights Reserved. English Heritage, 100019088, 2007

of Association football. This was largely because, as explained in Chapter One, the majority of Liverpool's unskilled men – that is, those most likely to take up the new game – had yet to win shorter working hours. By comparison, some 800 teams are recorded in Birmingham by 1880, whereas in Liverpool organised games only started around 1878. »

Stanley Park and Anfield Cemetery occupy an area that once formed common land known as Hongfield, attached to the medieval manor of Everton. The main sites of sporting interest, past and present, are:
1. Walton Stiles, home of Liverpool Association FC (1880s)
2. Goodison Park (1892–)
3. Stanley Park Open Air Swimming Pool (1923–60)
4. Bowling greens (c.1906–)
5. Cruitt's Field, home of Everton (1883–84)
6. Vernon Sangster Sports Centre (1970)
7. Everton pitch 1879–83 / site of new Liverpool Stadium (in pink)
8. Anfield, home of Everton (1884–92) / Liverpool (1892–)
9. Sandon Hotel and former bowling green

This unusual tiled panel, some 2m tall, was uncovered in 1986 during renovations to the Sandon Hotel – Everton's base when they moved to Anfield in 1884. Although neither the artist nor the player's identity are known, the salmon coloured shirt and dark blue shorts suggest a date of c.1892. The panel is now on display at Goodison Park.

» Of the handful of early teams playing in Stanley Park, the most successful was that of St Domingo, a recently opened Methodist church a few hundred yards south, on the corner of St Domingo Vale and Breckfield Road. Within a year the team had renamed itself after the district, Everton, and played its first game under this title in December 1879 (see page 50).

For the next four years Everton gained in stature, attracting ever larger crowds to their regular pitch on the park's south eastern corner. But being a public park they could not collect gate money, so in 1883 Everton rented a field on Priory Road, adjacent to the cemetery. However their landlord, William Cruitt, a cattle merchant, ended the agreement after only one season – Everton's growing crowds were too noisy for his liking – and so Everton moved to their second private ground, this time opposite their original pitch, on a field between Anfield Road and Walton Breck Road.

This was the ground that would be known thereafter as Anfield.

Jointly owned by two brewers, John and Joseph Orrell, the cost of laying out Anfield was borne by a man known locally as the 'King of Everton', a local councillor and landlord of the nearby Sandon Hotel, John Houlding, who now became Everton's chief backer.

Anfield staged its first game on 28 September 1884, and although according to *Athletic News* its pitch 'could only sport about three blades of grass,' Everton's annual receipts leapt from £45 to £200. To further cement their dominance of the local scene (in which Bootle were the main rivals), in 1888 they became founder members of the Football League, and won their first Championship in 1891.

Meanwhile more men, (including dock workers freed from Saturday afternoon shifts following an agreement in 1890), were not only watching football but playing it, so that the number of teams in the city, which had risen from 151 in 1886 to 293 by 1890, now grew to fill 13 leagues by 1898, each with several divisions.

Football now dominated the open spaces of Stanley Park.

The story of what happened next is a familiar one to football fans.

Briefly, arguments over whether Everton should become a limited liability company and buy Anfield (which now could hold up to 20,000 fans), led Houlding to increase Everton's rent. Bitter wrangling ensued, culminating in the split that would forever define the footballing map of Stanley Park, and of Liverpool.

In 1892 an Everton faction broke free and bought a former nursery (described as 'a howling desert') 800 yards north of Anfield, while Houlding, left with a ground but no team, instead of selling up to developers responded by forming his own club.

And so, on 1 September 1892, a new chapter began. At Anfield, the newly created Liverpool FC, a team composed entirely of Scots, made their debut v. Rotherham in front of barely 200 onlookers, while across the park, Everton played their first game at Goodison, v. Bolton, watched by 10,000.

But Houlding – soon to become Lord Mayor – and his right hand man and fellow freemason John McKenna (see page 15), were not to be outdone. In 1901 Liverpool clocked up their first League championship, by which time their gates had also caught up with Everton's. And the rest, as they say, is history.

One of football's greatest and, it might also be said, friendliest of all rivalries, came to dominate the city's sporting agenda until, in the late 1990s, it came to dominate the political agenda too.

The reason? The very future, not only of both Anfield and Goodison Park, but of Stanley Park too.

In 1999 Liverpool City Council secured an 'in principle' pledge for £967,000 worth of Heritage Lottery funding to revamp Stanley Park, which had fallen into sad disrepair but had also been listed Grade II on English Heritage's Register of Parks and Gardens.

But before the grant could be finally approved, in 2001 Liverpool FC submitted plans to build a new 60,000 seat stadium on the very part of Stanley Park where Everton had first played in 1879. Most of this area, it was argued, had been covered by tarmac since the 1960s and used on match days as a car park. Others contended that the area was still part of the park, and therefore should not be built upon.

After four years of debate, permission for the stadium was granted in 2006, as part of a much wider regeneration scheme for the Anfield area as whole.

Meanwhile in 2003 Everton failed in an attempt to build a new stadium at King's Dock. An indoor arena has been constructed on the site instead (see page 163). Having then been rebuffed in their request to share Liverpool's new stadium, in 2006 Everton decided that their future might well lie in Kirkby.

This is, of course, to simplify matters greatly.

And yet underlying this complex web there is a simple irony. Stanley Park, 'the People's Park', was once a cradle of local football. Now, it is football that will shape the fate of the park.

Boat House, Stanley Park, Liverpool

◀ The **boating lake** was a popular feature of Victorian parks, often with ornate boathouses attached. But as park keepers discovered, the lakes proved equally attractive to small boys hoping to cool off during the summer. This resulted in many a lake having a corner sectioned off specifically for swimming.

Stanley Park's **open air pool** (*centre*) was built in a corner of the lake by Walter Spencer of Aintree at a cost of £6,515. Opened in July 1923, it measured 75 x 35 feet, with a paddling pool attached. In common with the Corporation's other open air pools (*see page 180*) its water was also heated.

The pool was the city's last open air facility to close, in August 1960, and no traces now remain.

Other sports provided for in Stanley Park have been tennis, netball and, on the upper terrace, bowling greens, laid out c.1906 and served by a charming iron and glass **pavilion** (*below left*). Now derelict, this is one of 16 listed park structures, most designed by ER Robson in 1870. The others include the so-called monkeyhouse (a small pavilion), a bandstand, five bridges, a lodge, and three stone pavilions facing the bowling greens.

All will be restored as part of a £12 million refurbishment planned as part of the new stadium development, together with the park's grandest structure, the Gladstone Conservatory, built in 1899. However it is possible that the bowls pavilion and monkey house will be relocated within the park and the bowling green area restored to Kemp's original designs.

The park's least attractive, but most well-used building, the 1970s Vernon Sangster Sports Centre (*not shown*), will also be demolished and its facilities incorporated within the new stadium.

▶ These rare postcards tell us much about football ground design at the turn of the 20th century.

Anfield, viewed c.1903-06, from what is now the Kop end, was a typical late Victorian ground, with irregular timber crush barriers on unterraced slopes and basic iron and timber stand roofs and bench seating. In the top right, behind the terrace cover on Anfield Road (completed in 1903), can be seen the chimneys of **Stanley House** (still extant), the home of John Houlding. On the left is the Main Stand, completed in 1894 and presumably, like the ground's earlier fixtures and fittings, partly funded by Houlding (whose pub, the Sandon Hotel, on what is now **Houlding Street**, off Walton Breck Road, served as Everton's early headquarters).

The image of **Goodison Park** (*right*) was probably taken in 1895, when the Bullens Road Stand on the far side of the pitch was in the process of being completed. This stand alone cost £3,407 to build, to add to the £8,090 Everton had spent on buying the site in 1892, plus a further £3,000 on its layout and on the terrace cover, at the Gwladys Street end (on the left).

When opened in 1892 Goodison was regarded as the finest ground in England, in recognition of which it became the first and only club venue to host an FA Cup Final, in 1894. By 1905 its capacity was 55,000, double that of Anfield.

Note that the small boy in the foreground appears to be shoeless.

Liverpool *Football Ground*

The Wrench Series No. 4489

A Football Match at Goodison Park, Liverpool.

◀ Sixty or more years on, and both Anfield and Goodison Park have changed beyond recognition. But although the two stands shown here in the 1960s appear quite different, they are by the same designer, the Scottish engineer and leading ground designer of the early 20th century, Archibald Leitch.

Leitch's first commission in the city was Anfield's **Main Stand** (*left*), in 1906. Although its distinctive roof gable exudes tradition, the stand was actually the first reinforced concrete grandstand ever built in Britain. Indeed its subframe remained in situ when the stand was expanded and re-roofed in the early 1970s, and will remain intact until Liverpool depart for their new stadium in the park.

Clearly impressed by his work, Everton hired Leitch to design their own new main stand in 1908 (*seen here during the 1966 World Cup*). Seating 3,500 on its upper tier, with room for 21,000 on its vast lower terrace, the stand featured two trademark Leitch details; the pedimented roof gable and criss-cross steelwork balcony.

Measuring 80 feet tall, the stand was compared by one impressed reporter to the *Mauretania*, the world's largest ship.

For his part, Leitch clearly took to Liverpool, because in 1909 he left his native Glasgow and bought a family home in Blundellsands.

▲ This 1922 view of **Anfield** shows the ground as it was remodelled by Archibald Leitch in 1906, and before the **Spion Kop** was roofed in 1928. This huge terrace was given its name by the sports editor of the *Liverpool Echo*, Ernest Edwards, within weeks of its completion, as a reminder of the South African hill on which 322 British soldiers, many from Liverpool, died during an infamous Boer War battle, six years earlier (although the first terrace named Spion Kop was at Woolwich Arsenal, in 1904).

Only one 19th century structure survived by this time; the frame of the Kemlyn Road Stand (in the foreground), originally built as the Main Stand in 1894 and moved across the pitch when Leitch built the new Main Stand in 1906.

Behind the Kemlyn Road Stand is a row of terraced houses that, after years of trying, Liverpool bought up and demolished to make way for the much larger Centenary Stand in 1992. This apart, and despite the rebuilding of all three other sides between 1970 and 1998, Anfield's footprint in 2007 remains essentially the same as shown here.

▲ Pictured in the 1950s, **Goodison Park** is equally hemmed in by its surrounds, although Everton pre-empted Liverpool by demolishing one row of houses to make room for the expanded Gwladys Street Stand (*left*) in 1938. This was the third stand designed by Leitch's company, to complement the colossal 1909 Main Stand (in the foreground), and the opposite Bullens Road Stand, completed in 1926. The only surviving pre-Leitch stand was at the Park End, designed by Liverpool architect Henry Hartley in 1907. Goodison was in fact the first British ground to have double decker stands on all four sides – one reason why it, rather than the smaller Anfield, was selected as a venue for matches in the 1966 World Cup.

A unique quirk of Goodison is the presence, in the nearside corner of the site, of a church, St Luke's, and church hall, built in 1901 and 1908 respectively. Until screened off in recent years, the church roof provided a popular vantage point on more crowded match days.

Also visible is the Stanley Park lake and open air pool, with Anfield Cemetery in the top left.

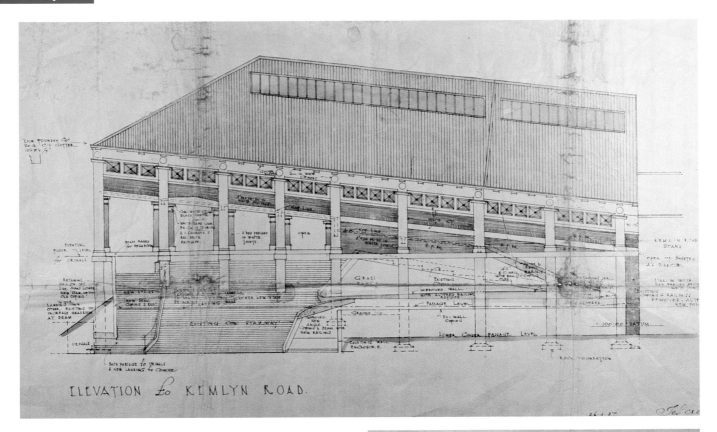

ELEVATION to KEMLYN ROAD.

▲ These hitherto unpublished plans show Joseph Watson Cabré's 1928 designs for the roof over Leitch's original Anfield **Kop**.

Based in Crosby, Watson was a surprise choice, given that he worked mostly on private houses, church restorations and memorials.

Opened on 25 August 1928 by Liverpool's John McKenna, who was then President of the League, it measured 425 feet wide and 80 feet high and, with a covered capacity of 28,000, was the largest of its type in Britain at the time. Watson also drew up plans for a double-decker stand at the Anfield Road end. But by then, Liverpool felt that they had spent enough.

In truth, despite its instantly recognisable metal framed windows and deep overhanging roof trusses, the Kop was never a well designed terrace. Injuries were routine. Circulation routes were so limited that it was common for fans to have to urinate on the spot where they stood. In 1987 a section of its terracing subsided when a sewer shaft collapsed. As a result, successive safety measures reduced its capacity to 16,480 by the time of its demolition in 1994.

And yet its demise represented a genuine watershed in British football history. Though not the best, it was certainly the most famous terrace in the world.

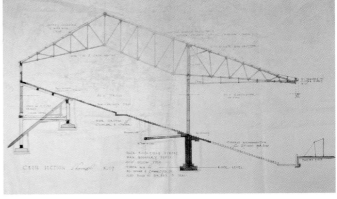

CROSS SECTION Liverpool KOP

Not just any old piece of concrete but a lump of the Kop, now on display at the Anfield museum. The back-fill upon which the terracing was originally built in 1906 came from Priory Road, which was being dug up at the time to lay tracks for Liverpool's tramway system. The concrete was then relaid in 1928 and on several occasions subsequently, until as recently as 1990. But such was the terrace's potent symbolism that when it was cleared in 1994 to make way for a new 12,000 capacity all-seater stand, sales of Kop rubble raised £200,000 for charity. Some of it was turned into key rings, crystal pyramids and even bird baths, but much of it has been simply displayed on sideboards or mantlepieces as tokens of a passing era. When the readers of *France Football* magazine voted Anfield as having the best atmosphere of any ground in the world, in 1991, there was no doubt as to why. When the Kop was in full song, the earth really did seem to move.

▲ For its regulars, standing on the Kop was a ritual affair. Pre-match routines such as wearing one's scarf in a certain way were adopted to bring luck. Koppites would each have their own 'spec' on the terrace, from where they would sway, side to side, scarf aloft, singing the latest Merseybeat track or the famous Kop anthem *You'll Never Walk Alone*, as recorded by another Koppite, Gerry Marsden.

Here was a place where comradeship was converted into lifelong friendships. To be a Koppite was to wear a badge of honour.

During the match a mazy dribble down the wing or a corner kick at the Kop end would send cascades of fans hurtling down the steps as they strained to gain a better view. The banter, the pushing, the sweat, the singing, the affinity with players plus the adulation shown towards the Kop's spiritual leader, Bill Shankly (manager from 1959–74), all contributed towards the Kop's iconic status. Small wonder that reporters and documentary makers were drawn to its swaying masses time and again throughout the 1960s and 1970s. When it closed in 1994 memories of the Kop filled an entire book (*see Links*). Even visiting fans, including Evertonians, would brave standing there, just to be able to say that they had sampled the Kop experience.

Most memorably of all, in 1989, after 96 Liverpool fans died at Hillsborough, the Kop became a shrine, as thousands of scarves and floral wreaths covered the entire terrace in a tribute to the dead.

▲ One manifestation of football's growing, if belated appreciation of its heritage is the number of statues now appearing at grounds.

This one, sculpted by Tom Murphy and unveiled in May 2001, is of Birkenhead-born **Bill 'Dixie' Dean**, Tranmere and Everton centre forward during the inter-war period and one of the most profilic goal scorers in the game's history.

Appropriately the statue is at the Park End of Goodison Park where, in 1928, Dean scored his record-breaking 60th league goal of the season, a tally that will surely never be surpassed. Railings surrounding the statue contain 60 circles to commemorate his feat. Dean once lived in a terraced club house close to this spot, and died at Goodison during a Merseyside derby in 1980.

▲ Also by Tom Murphy is this statue outside the Kop, based on images of **Bill Shankly** receiving the adulation of fans after Liverpool's eighth League title in 1973. Before his arrival in 1959, Liverpool had been struggling in Division Two.

But more than just rack up honours, Shankly, who had been raised in a Scottish mining village, engendered the fierce collective spirit that provided the foundations for Liverpool's current international status. 'Shanks' was a genuine man of the people, a teetotaller who lived humbly and preferred to operate out of Anfield's famed 'bootroom' under the stand.

Awarded an OBE in 1974, his death in 1981 was marked by a minute's silence at the annual Labour Party conference.

▶ One of the great curiosities of Anfield is this flagpole, standing by the Kemlyn Road entrance to the Kop Stand.

Standing 18m tall, with a further 2m below ground, and made from pitch pine sections dovetailed together, the flagpole was originally one of six masts belonging to Isambard Kingdom Brunel's third, and last iron ship, the **Great Eastern**, launched from the Millwall Docks in London in 1858. (Although powered by steam, masts and sails were fitted as a back up). Unfortunately for its backers the *Great Eastern* – then the largest vessel the world had ever known – had only a short life on the ocean waves, ending its days at a breakers' yard in Rock Ferry, Birkenhead, in 1888, where most of its fittings were auctioned.

But the topmast must have remained unclaimed, because 18 years later someone had the bright idea to transport it to Anfield to stand alongside the newly completed Spion Kop, where it has stood ever since.

To transport it to the ground the mast was floated across the Mersey to the Pierhead, from where it was then hauled up to Anfield by a team of four horses.

Such is the pole's unique status, not to mention its historic provenance, that when Liverpool move to the new stadium in Stanley Park, the pole will go with them.

From boats to trains, and another great treasure, the Everton railway nameplate (*right*), now on display at Goodison Park.

Sport and the railways have long enjoyed a symbiotic relationship, as seen in the location of golf courses between Liverpool and Southport (*see page 134*). Indeed the emergence of mass spectator sport in the late 19th century was partly

a consequence of the railway age, with companies laying on 'football specials' for thousands of travelling fans, plus teams and officials, on a weekly basis.

One such company keen to nurture this lucrative business was the **London & North Eastern Railway**, which in 1936 and 1937 named 25 of their B17 locomotives (designed by Sir Nigel Gresley) after leading football clubs. In practice it proved difficult to match up each engine with the appropriate football special, but the gesture was warmly appreciated by both fans and train spotters alike, and to this day the engine nameplates are richly coveted by collectors.

Everton's nameplate was attached to loco number 2863, built in 1937 at the Robert Stephenson railway works in Darlington and painted in LNER's standard apple green livery.

After the engine was finally taken out of service in the late 1950s it was presented to Everton in 1960.

Also in 1937, engine number 2864 was named after Liverpool, but alas this nameplate was sold by the club in the 1990s and its present whereabouts are unknown, although it is known to have been sold at an auction in Sheffield in 1992 for £40,000.

Intriguingly, also somewhere in private hands, there is another nameplate called Spion Kop, once attached to LNER loco number 2752, built in Doncaster in 1929. However this was named not after the famous Anfield terrace but after a racehorse called Spion Kop, which won the Derby in 1920.

Needless to add, it would be wonderful if the Liverpool nameplate were restored to the club in time for it to be displayed at their new stadium, along with the *Great Eastern* flagpole.

▲ At no other British ground are there as many memorials as at Anfield. Most poignant of all is the **Hillsborough Memorial**, on Anfield Road, where the names of the 96 Liverpool fans who died as a result of the April 1989 disaster are listed. Despite the intense rivalries that exist between clubs, on every match day visiting fans pay their respects at this sombre memorial.

When Liverpool's new stadium is complete the memorial will form part of a garden on the Anfield site.

Another reminder of the hurt still felt by survivors and bereaved families is the **Hillsborough Justice Campaign** office (*right*), facing the Kop on Walton Breck Road.

The **Shankly Gates** on Anfield Road (*top*), are a tribute to Bill Shankly, the Reds' charismatic manager from 1959–74. These were unveiled by his widow Nessie in 1982. Also commemorated by gates outside the Kop (*above*) is **Bob Paisley**, who managed Liverpool from 1974–83, the most successful era in the club's history.

Starting as a player, Paisley served 44 years at Anfield. The blue Hetton crest on the left denotes his roots in County Durham.

▲ Various analogies have been used to describe the cultural role that stadiums fulfil. Most often they have been likened to cathedrals, but also, in the darkest days of hooliganism, to prisons and battlegrounds. More recently stadiums have acquired the status of tourist attractions. Liverpool have their own museum, while both they and Everton run regular stadium tours. At some grounds couples can even get married on the pitch.

But perhaps the most telling of all analogies is that of the shrine.

Surrounding the perimeter at **Goodison Park** are dozens of discreet plaques, each recording the name of a fan whose ashes have been scattered on the pitch. This practice is surprisingly common, with some clubs conducting up to 20 such ceremonies a year. Increasingly, owing to the corrosive nature of the ashes and the sensibilities of players, groundsmen prefer ashes to be scattered only by the touchlines, or to be buried in urns.

But that is not the end of the mattter, for should Everton ever relocate, they will be obliged to provide some memorial to all those dearly departed left behind.

The top picture shows Liverpool footballer Cyril Done greeting boxing officials before what was probably the last boxing match at Anfield, in 1949. Above, the world featherweight champion Freddie Miller is seen on his way to a points victory over seaman Tommy Watson at Anfield in 1937. The windows of the Kop can just be seen in the background.

▲ Both Goodison Park and Anfield have hosted numerous sports other than football. Indeed Goodison's inaugural event on 24 August 1892 was an **athletics** meeting, followed by a concert and fireworks display. A week later when the first football match was staged, a reporter from *Out of Doors* was so impressed he reckoned Goodison 'rivals the greater **American baseball** pitches'.

He must have been prescient because in 1924 the Chicago White Sox and the New York Giants did indeed play there (*top right*), as did several local teams when baseball established itself in the city during the 1930s (*see Chapter Thirteen*). Goodison also hosted games featuring US servicemen during the war, before staging its last baseball match – a Lancashire Cup Final between Halton Trojans and Formby Cardinals – in 1948.

Anfield, meanwhile, became a regular venue for **boxing**, following the closure of the Pudsey Street Stadium in March 1931 (*see page 156*). With the ring set up on the pitch in front of the Kop, Anfield's first fight took place in October 1931, when local hero Nel Tarleton defeated Johnny Cuthbert for the British featherweight title.

So well received was this bout that although a new purpose-built indoor boxing stadium would open on Bixteth Street the following year (*see page 158*), promoter Johnny Best continued to hire the much larger Anfield for several subsequent world title contests.

Of these the most illustrious was a fifteen round world flyweight title fight between Warrington's Peter Kane and the Californian Jackie Jurich, in September 1938, won on points by Kane. Officially the attendance was given as 35,000, though many present thought it well over 40,000. In either case, it was the largest attendance ever at a boxing match staged in the city.

Boxing continued at Anfield throughout the war years before the last bout was held there in 1949.

Another sport staged at Anfield was **tennis**. This took place in June 1937 when Fred Perry, originally from Stockport, who had controversially turned professional earlier that year, played a series of games against other leading pros of the day, including Bill Tilden and Ellsworth Vines of America, watched by an estimated 11,000.

Also making just one appearance at Anfield was **basketball**, courtesy of an exhibition match staged in 1958 by the Harlem Globetrotters (in whom, coincidentally, George Gillett, Liverpool's new American co-owner, once had an interest).

More recently Anfield has been an occasional venue for **rugby**, for example, the 1989 Rugby League Charity Shield, and a game involving the All Blacks in 1993.

Finally, Anfield has served on several occasions as the end point for the **Liverpool City Marathon**.

As detailed earlier (*see page 18*), this began in 1927, with the race's finish being timed to coincide with half-time during a Liverpool home game. The practice was repeated in 1928 and 1929, and then resumed in 1948.

Anfield's last marathon finish came in the 1950s, after which the race became part of the Liverpool Show, with its climax transferred to the Wavertree Playground.

▲ Everton's motto *Nil Satis, Nisi Optimum* – only the best is good enough – goes back to their early days. But their **official crest** is a more recent invention, having been created by club secretary, Theo Kelly, to adorn a new club tie in 1938. It first featured on the club shirts in 1980.

In the crest's centre, flanked by olive wreaths (ancient Olympia's equivalent of a winner's medal) is a representation of the oldest building in the Everton area, a small sandstone structure with a conical roof that stands in public gardens on Shaw Street, in the heart of what was once the village of Everton. Built in 1787, the Grade II listed building was originally a lock-up, used to detain felons overnight (although it is also erroneously referred to as Prince Rupert's Tower – Rupert camped out on Everton Brow during his siege of Liverpool in 1644 – and also as the Everton beacon, which actually stood on a nearby site until 1803).

Another Everton characteristic is the club's nickname, the Toffees, which in turn has led Goodison Park to be occasionally given the rather grand title of 'Toffeeopolis'.

Before Everton was absorbed into Liverpool's boundaries in 1835 it was a pleasant, hilltop village, much favoured by the local gentry and well known for its toffee shops. Legend has it that **Everton toffee** was originally produced there in the mid 18th century by one Molly Bushell, in a cottage close to where the lock-up was later built.

Bushell's enterprise, it is said, led to other toffee shops being set up, one of which, on Village Street, was close to the Queen's Head, the football club's first headquarters. One version of this story, never proven, suggests that in the 1880s the newly developed Everton mint – toffee encased in mint – was given black and white stripes to mirror Everton's colours at the time.

True or not, in 1894 another firm called Noblett's took up toffee making, using on their packaging a caricatured image of Molly Bushell (renamed Mother Noblett), complete with bonnet, basket and umbrella. The story then goes that in order to stymie Noblett's, a

descendant of Molly Bushell sent her grand-daughter Jemima to hand out their own Everton mints to the crowds at Goodison, a pre-match tradition that continues to this day.

The mints, later manufactured by Liverpool confectioners Barker and Dobson, are now mainly made in York by a subsidiary of Cadbury Trebor Bassett.

During the 1950s the familar role of old Mother Bushell was carried out at Goodison Park by Mary Gorry (*above*), whereas today's toffee ladies are chosen on a match-per-match basis from the ranks of the club's junior season ticket holders. But whoever wears the costume, it is a fine tradition, and one quite unique in British football.

▲ When the citizens of ancient Rome packed into the Circus Maximus, loyalties were divided between four teams of charioteers, the Reds, Whites, Greens or Blues.

Modern day Liverpool is divided in much the same way, albeit not as many outsiders might imagine.

True, the question most often asked when Liverpudlians first meet is this: 'Are you a Red, or a Blue?'

Yet the reason why they answer one way or another is often down to pure chance. Unlike in Glasgow, the choice has nothing to do with religion (though some historians have tried to make that assertion), and both teams have an equally strong fanbase in Ireland (although because of its European success, Liverpool has developed a larger following from further afield).

Certainly the part of the city from which you come has no real bearing, and not even family traditions are necessarily decisive. Many a Merseyside family is split, the most famous of which was the Moores. John Moores, founder of the Littlewoods Pools empire in the 1920s (*see Chapter Nine*), owned shares in both clubs before finally becoming Everton's chairman in

1960. Yet his nephew David would later be chairman of Liverpool.

Even in the aftermath of the big split of 1892, when John Houlding formed Liverpool in retaliation for Everton's members breaking away, the two clubs often shared resources. For example they printed a joint matchday programme until 1930, and both employed the same architect, Archibald Leitch.

But what makes the city's divide even more random is the fact that for the first 24 years of their existence Everton wore a variety of colours; first white, then black and white, then blue and white, then black with a wide scarlet sash. In fact when Everton played their first League match at Anfield in 1888 they were actually dubbed 'the Reds'! Next, at Goodison in 1892,

they adopted salmon pink and dark blue, before switching to ruby shirts with blue trim and dark blue shorts. For the first ever local derby in the League in 1894 – watched by a record 40,000 fans – Everton wore blue while Liverpool played in blue and white squares. Only in 1896 did Liverpool opt for red, and it would be another five years before Everton finally settled on blue.

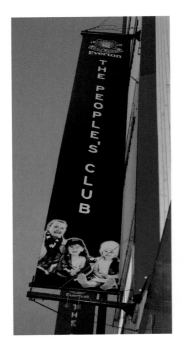

▲ When newly appointed manager David Moyes dubbed Everton as 'the People's Club' in 2002 he may not have realised that its first games in 1878 were played in what was then called 'the People's Park'. But his meaning was clear.

While Liverpool's status as five time winners of the European Cup had brought them international status and a squad full of imported stars, Everton sought strength, and perhaps even solace, in adopting a contrasting, rather homelier image.

This distinction – justified or not – was further accentuated when Liverpool were bought by two American businessmen in February 2007, and were thus able to proceed with their hotly disputed plans to build a new stadium in Stanley Park, while all Everton's plans to relocate had, until then, been scuppered by funding shortfalls and planning obstacles.

Yet the two clubs do share at least one common problem.

Since football grounds were converted to seating-only, following the 1989 Hillsborough disaster, Everton's capacity has fallen to 40,100, down from a peak of 78,299, recorded in 1948.

Moreover, Goodison's facilities and spectator accommodation are now quite outdated compared with other leading stadiums.

Thus the People's Club has concluded that its future may well lie elsewhere.

Even taking into account Leitch's two surviving stands – neither one a gem – there are no preservation issues at stake, should Goodison be demolished. But these two clubs have faced each other across the park since 1892. Their separation will end one of the greatest double acts in sporting history. In heritage terms that, surely, is the real loss.

▲ It was Bill Shankly's idea to place a sign above the player's tunnel, reminding visitors of the cauldron they were about to enter. But despite expenditure of over £25 million on three stands since 1992 – including the 12,000 seat Kop (*left*) and an upper tier added to the Anfield Road Stand (*below, at the far end*) – Anfield's capacity is still only 45,360, compared with 76,300 at Manchester United and 60,000 at Arsenal.

As at Goodison, Anfield's demise will result in no significant architectural loss. In place of the ground there will, furthermore, be an Anfield Plaza, leading to the new stadium in the park beyond. So this site will still be Anfield, of sorts, though no doubt with different signs and almost certainly causing less trepidation for visitors.

▲ Billy Liddell, the Liverpool player thought to be the subject of this sign at The Park pub – facing the rear of the Kop – retired in 1961. Yet he will never be forgotten. Players' kits will change in style, but the colours will remain the same, just as Everton will carry on playing Liverpool long after the fate of Goodison Park is settled, one way or another. At The Park, the Sandon, the Albert, the Arkles and the Winslow, and at every other pub in the vicinity, every fan is both an historian and a soothsayer, waiting for the next great hero to emerge, and for the next pint to be as good as the last. In short, the power of place is only one element in football's heritage. Wherever they are based, the story of the Reds and the Blues will wind on.

▲ Stanley Park and its adjoining grounds have been part of the Liverpool landscape for well over a century. Now, starting in 2007, a substantial portion of the park – the upper third as shown opposite, including the car park and the site of Everton's original pitch in 1878 – is to be built over with a new 60,000 seat stadium for Liverpool (*above*), designed by the club's longstanding architects, Atherden Fuller Leng (who of course have also worked for Everton in the past). Anfield, meanwhile, will be razed to the ground and an Anfield Plaza of hotels and shops put in its place. Over £12 million will be spent on the remaining parts of Stanley Park, plus a further £84 million on the regeneration of the Anfield area.

Still to be determined is the fate of Goodison (*top*). In February 2007 Everton submitted plans for a stadium at Kirkby. Should this proceed, or if Everton move elsewhere, Goodison will probably be redeveloped by housing – handy for any Reds fans wanting to be close to their new stadium, and with some delightful park views thrown in for good measure.

Chapter Six

Sefton Park

Sefton Park Bowling Club, formed in 1884, is one of three long established private sports clubs based in Sefton Park. The others are the Mersey Bowmen Tennis Club, originally an archery club when established in 1781 and one of the oldest tennis clubs in the world, and the Sefton Cricket Club, who formed in 1862 and moved to the park in 1876. Such a clustering of three historic clubs in a public park is rare, and yet to most visitors to the park – the largest in Liverpool – their presence is quite discreet.

Sefton Park, opened in 1872, two years after Stanley Park, is Liverpool's largest urban park, covering 266 acres (108 hectares).

It is also judged sufficiently important to be granted a Grade II* listing on English Heritage's Register of Parks and Gardens.

But although most widely celebrated for its elegant paths, floral displays and wooded areas, its Palm House (also Grade II*), its waterfalls and grottoes, and not least for its bronze statue of Peter Pan (unveiled in 1928), Sefton Park is also an important focal point for bowls, tennis and cricket – a sporting profile that reflects not so much its design but rather the social make-up of its surrounding residential areas.

As outlined in earlier chapters, Sefton Park was one of three parks proposed by Liverpool Corporation in 1865, and was by far the most expensive.

Laid out on former agricultural land that had, until the late 16th century, formed part of the Royal Park of Toxteth (reserved largely for the hunting of deer), the Corporation paid the Earl of Sefton

It is often said that fishing is still the most popular participation sport in Britain, with over three million anglers wielding a rod at one time or another every year. In Sefton Park's seven acre lake, fed by two streams, the most common catches are roach, bream and tench, with catches of both carp and pike, each over 25lbs in weight, being recently recorded.

and a Mr Livingstone a total of £250,000 for its purchase. Overall the site amounted to 387 acres – almost equal to London's Hyde Park – of which, as at Stanley and Newsham Parks, just under a third was allocated to housing to help defray the costs.

But whereas at the previous two parks the resulting residential developments were, with some exceptions, relatively modest, comprising mostly terraced houses, around the edges of Sefton Park a much grander set of detached villas would emerge, several being commissioned by some of the city's foremost merchants and public figures (Charles Melly, chairman of the Parks Committee, included).

From the very outset Sefton Park was envisaged as the jewel in the city's crown. Unlike the other parks, an international

competition was staged for its design, with a prize for the winner of 300 guineas.

Of 29 entries submitted, the one chosen was a joint scheme drawn up by the Liverpool architect, Lewis Hornblower, whom we encountered earlier in the chapter on Birkenhead Park, in collaboration with a 27 year old Frenchman, Eduoard André, the City of Paris's much admired Jardinier Principal.

As shown on page 74, their masterplan called for a complex network of curving pathways, dividing the park into numerous sections, each with their own character. Several of these sections, amounting to 190 acres – almost four times the extent allocated at Stanley Park – were set aside for sport and recreation, including 12 acres for a cricket field (perhaps at the insistence

of Hornblower, who had been an early member of the Birkenhead Park Cricket Club 20 years earlier).

Hornblower and André's plans turned out to be far costlier than anticipated, and even after being trimmed they still amounted to £147,000, nearly twice the original budget. Not built were botanical gardens and a selection of lodges and recreational buildings designed by Hornblower.

Selling off all the housing plots, on Aigburth Drive, Croxteth Drive, Ullet Road and Mossley Hill Drive, also took longer than anticipated, and even then some plots remained empty until the following century.

That said, the creation of this Parisian-style park represented a significant watershed in Liverpool's efforts to achieve respectability in mid-Victorian Britain, as was confirmed on 20 May 1872, when a mile long procession of 77 carriages accompanied Prince Arthur to the opening ceremony, watched by some 4–5,000 guests in a temporary grandstand.

The park would later benefit from the addition of the splendid Palm House in 1896 by the same Glasgow company, Mackenzie and Moncur, who three years later designed the Gladstone Conservatory at Stanley Park.

Like Stanley Park, a lack of funding in the late 20th century led to serious deterioration at Sefton Park. However, thanks to a £3 million refurbishment funded by various local and national bodies the Palm House was re-opened in 2001, while a grant of £4.7 million from the Heritage Lottery Fund, matched by £1.6 million from Liverpool City Council, has enabled restoration work to start on the rest of the park in 2007.

▲ Viewed from the east in 2005, **Sefton Park** and its smaller and older neighbour, **Princes Park**, stand out as noble bulwarks against the city's urban spread, with Princes Avenue cutting a leafy path through to the distant Anglican Cathedral, and the Three Graces and River Mersey beyond.

In the centre of Sefton Park stands the recently restored circular Palm House. To the left of this is the boating and fishing lake, while to its right is a tree-enclosed playing area that was originally intended as a deer park on André and Hornblower's plan. (This area had, after all been a hunting ground, until the 17th century.)

Also visible, just above the Palm House, are the terracotta and green hard courts used by the Mersey Bowmen Tennis Club (see page 76). The smaller enclosed area below this is the green of the Sefton Park Bowling Club (page 77). Not shown, in the north east corner of the park (beyond the right edge of the photo) is the ground of Sefton Park Cricket Club (see page 75).

Note that apart from an avenue of trees, there is hardly a straight line in the park's design.

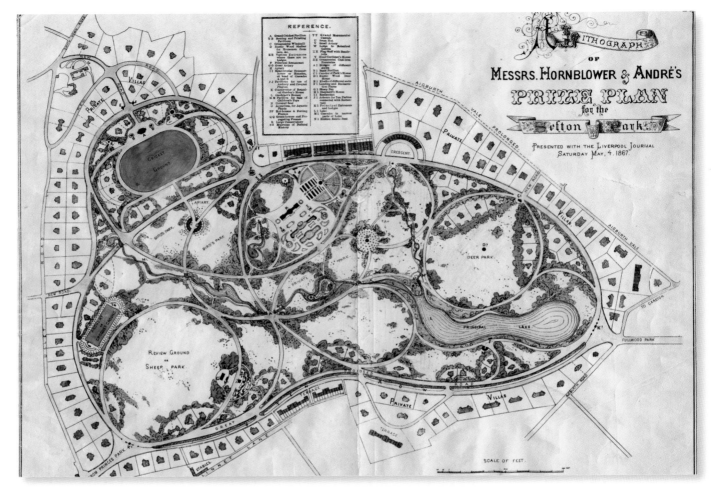

▲ This is Lewis Hornblower and Edouard André's prize winning scheme for **Sefton Park**, and although some elements were not implemented, its organic network of winding, interlocking paths had the effect of creating a series of circular and elliptical zones, each with their own character and function.

In this way, any sporting activity would not impinge upon neighbouring zones.

Edouard André had been closely involved in the implementation of Baron Hausmann's masterplan for the wholesale remodelling of Paris in the early 1860s. He had also been influenced by the work of a French park designer Adolphe Alphand, whose Parc de Buttes Chaumont opened in Paris to huge acclaim in 1867.

So we can only imagine what he thought of the eccentric English game of cricket that his colleague Lewis Hornblower was clearly so keen on, and which would now occupy a corner of his creation.

As to the other sports, Sefton Park's original bylaws made it clear that apart from cricket only more refined forms of recreation would be permitted; that is, archery and croquet, both very much the preserves of the middle classes. Bowls was a later addition.

The park also featured, as did Stanley Park, a 'Rotten Row' for horse riding – as in Hyde Park – although Sefton Park's version was apparently known as 'the jockey sands' instead.

▲ **Sefton Cricket Club** face Wallasey in a Liverpool Competition match at Sefton Park on 26 May 1934, in front of their largest crowd of the season.

Sefton CC originally formed in 1862 at a ground on Smithdown Road, but moved to Sefton Park in 1876 after receiving an invitation from the Corporation's Parks Committee. Clearly the park's cricket ground needed a reliable tenant for it to be properly maintained. Equally, the club's presence would bring more people to the park. And so it proved.

In their first match there in June 1876 Sefton beat Woodcroft, a team from Greenbank Park, by one run. A year later the legendary WG Grace made an appearance.

Obviously quite content with their new tenants, two years later the Corporation arranged for the pitch to be relaid and donated £6,000 towards the cost of a handsome pavilion (*left centre*).

In 1984 that same pavilion was all but destroyed in a fire, although fortunately its replacement follows the original design closely. The smaller ladies pavilion (*seen above to the right of the main pavilion*) also burnt down, the following decade, but has not been replaced.

Now known as **Sefton Park Cricket Club** (since 1998), the club has recently built a second pavilion which, thanks to a grant from Sport England, looks out over a new pitch, known as the Lower Ground and used by the club's Third XI.

▲ It may not possess an especially historic or impressive pavilion, but the **Mersey Bowmen Tennis Club** in Sefton Park is almost certainly the oldest surviving sports club in Liverpool, and also one of the oldest lawn tennis clubs in Britain, and therefore the world.

The fact that so few of its records have survived is therefore a matter of some regret.

What we do know is that the Mersey Bowmen are said to have formed in 1781, as the name suggests, as a gentlemen's archery club (at a time when the sport was enjoying a particular revival in high society). Their first headquarters were in a lodge on Cazneau Street, off the modern day Scotland Road.

Indeed the panels shown above, on display inside the current pavilion – featuring two crossed arrows flanked by a wreath, and in the centre panel by a hunting horn – were apparently replicated from emblems engraved on the walls of

that original Cazneau Street lodge.

A further indication of the social standing of club members was that next door to this lodge were tennis courts; that is, indoor courts for real, or royal tennis (a game that predates lawn tennis and was then largely the preserve of the elite).

By 1860 the club had relocated to the Lodge Lane area, from which

they moved again in 1867 to a farm meadow on Ullet Road. When the Earl of Sefton then sold this land to the Corporation for Sefton Park, the Mersey Bowman were offered a replacement home within the new park's boundaries.

Within a few years, and certainly by 1877, the club took up the newly popular game of lawn

tennis (which had been adopted at Wimbledon only in 1875), and this would eventually supercede archery, as it would at several other archery clubs around the country.

The club's present, rather modest pavilion, on the Aigburth Drive side of the park, dates from 1887, but has clearly been modified since.

Not all the Mersey Bowmen wore trousers. Here the lady members go for gold at a Merseyside Archery Shield event at Sefton Park in the inter-war period, when both archery and tennis were integral to the club's activities.

This stainless steel wall sculpture by Cheshire-based artist Stephen Broadbent depicts a basketball player in a wheelchair. Unveiled in 1999 by Princess Anne, it is to be found on the east side of Sefton Park, at the Greenbank Sports Academy, one of Britain's most advanced training centres for athletes with disabilities, to a Paralympic standard. Apart from basketball and table tennis the Academy offers boccia (a form of bowls played from a seated position, now contested at an international level), and uni-hoc (an indoor hockey game). The centre also hires out hand cycles for those who wish to do a few circuits of Sefton Park.

▲ A few yards south of the Mersey Bowmen's tennis courts lies the home of the park's third, and youngest private sports club, the **Sefton Park Bowling Club.**

Unlike cricket, archery and croquet, bowling did not feature on Edouard André's original plans. But then that was true of most public parks before the 1870s. (Stanley Park's greens were not laid out until the Edwardian period.)

Certainly when the Sefton Park Bowling Club formed in 1884 it was strictly a gentlemen's club, with an annual subscription of one guinea, plus an entrance fee of 10s 6d. Also, membership was limited to just 95 individuals.

Despite this, the club had only a modest pavilion; a half-timbered shelter costing £126. It can still be seen today, serving as a storeroom.

In 1919 the members took the momentous decision to allow ladies to bowl on the green. Then two years later they took over as their new pavilion an adjacent building known as the Island Tea House, one of several small refreshment rooms dotted around the park.

Seen above, it is now more widely called The Roundhouse.

Even so, ladies were not allowed inside the Roundhouse until 1968, and then only on weekend evenings for a trial period. They were finally granted full equality in 1975.

On the southern perimeter of Sefton Park is a second bowls club of historic interest. This is the **Aigburth People's Hall Bowling Club**, on Aigburth Vale.

The club itself traces its origins to a temperance club called the Aigburth Cocoa Rooms, set up in

Aigburth Vale in 1876. Its current headquarters and bowling green, opened in 1901, were gifted by a wealthy businessman and Sefton Park resident, John Temple.

As reported in the *Liverpool Weekly News*, 'It is desired that in the Hall the people of the district, shall at the close of their day's toil, find a congenial rendezvous where they may exploit their wit, discuss amongst themselves the topics of the day, play games – bowls, billiards, quoits, draughts, chess etc., smoke if they like, and in short, do everything which they would feel at liberty to do in... a public house, except partake of intoxicating liquors...'

A century later the People's Hall continues to provide just such a rendezvous but, with the added congeniality of a well stocked bar.

Chapter Seven

Billiards

British billiards champion from 1849–70, John Roberts played his first game, aged nine, at the Rotunda, Bold Street. After a spell working in Manchester he returned to run a billiard room at the George Hotel, Lime Street, where his son, also John, took up the cue and went on to become champion from 1870–85. This water colour of John Roberts Senior forms part of the Norman Clare Collection, one of the great treasures of Britain's sporting heritage.

Liverpool entrepreneurs and individuals have contributed greatly to sporting life in Britain, and beyond. In this section of the book we look at three such contributions, relating to the manufacture of billiards and snooker equipment, the invention of goal nets (*Chapter Eight*) and the development of the global football pools industry (*Chapter Nine*).

Billiards is an ancient game, originally played on the ground, and converted, it is thought by the French, to an indoor table-top game by the 15th century. Mary Queen of Scots was an avid player, until her very end, while that great chronicler of English games and pastimes, Joseph Strutt, wrote in 1801 that billiards was 'so generally known' as to need no further description.

Britain's first known maker of bespoke tables and equipment was a cabinet maker, John Thurston, who set up in London in 1799, and whose company developed the billiards table as we know it today – with pockets, a slate bed and vulcanised rubber cushions – during the 19th century.

As billiards reached its peak in popularity in the late 19th century, pubs, clubs and hotels all over Britain adapted or expanded their premises to house tables. Not many chose to name themselves after the game, however. This is the Billiards Hotel, now known as the Throstle's Nest, on the corner of Scotland Road and Chapel Gardens, Everton.

A host of companies followed Thurston's lead. In Lancashire between 1870–1914 there were at least 18 manufacturers, spread across Manchester, Burnley, Accrington and Liverpool.

The city's earliest recorded maker of equipment was William Bayliff of Paradise Street, set up in 1847. But the largest was James Ashcroft & Co. Established in 1869, in 1883 Ashcroft opened its own six storey showrooms and factory on Victoria Street, a resplendent building that still stands today (*see page 83*).

Ashcroft and its rivals sent out legions of salesmen to spread the gospel. For working men, the new breed of billiard halls and rooms in pubs offered a seductively lit refuge from the outside world. For tennis, golf and bowls clubs a billiards table offered winter solace and extra bar revenue, while establishments such as the Kursaal United Temperance Billiard Hall, on Overton Street,

Edge Hill, offered an alcohol free alternative. At the same time no royal residence, country house or gentlemen's club was without its expensively fitted billiards room.

But if billiards, with its green baize, ivory balls and soft light, was highly seductive, the game itself was slow, highly technical and difficult to watch. In contrast, the new game of snooker, invented by British Army officers in India in 1875 and using more balls, but otherwise the same tables and basic equipment as billiards, was fast, colourful and far more entertaining for non-purists.

By the late 1920s, snooker had won the battle of the baize. Partly this was owing to media coverage of emerging stars Joe and Fred Davis, who made several appearances in Liverpool, including the one featured on the inside cover of this book. But also crucial was the creation of more accessible, modern snooker halls, many of them built above high

street retail stores. One of the first of these was above Woolworth's in Church Street, rebuilt in 1923 on the site of Britain's first Woolies store (opened in 1909).

Montague Burton also adopted this model. Sensing that working class men were reluctant to visit tailors, from 1928–38 Burton built a chain of nearly 600 light and bright outfitters, many of which, designed by the company architect N Martin, featured snooker halls on their first floor.

In Liverpool only one former Burton's of this type survives, on the corner of County Road and Spellow Lane, where the snooker hall is now a gymnasium.

Otherwise, regrettably, no historic billiards halls or rooms survive in Liverpool. (See instead *Played in Manchester* and *Played in Birmingham* for examples.)

But if lacking in architectural examples, the city has much to celebrate in terms of billiards related manufacturing.

During the late 20th century the majority of British companies either merged, went out of business or started importing their wares from the Far East. But of the dozen or so companies still making equipment in Britain, two are based in Liverpool. Alliance Snooker Ltd are based on Edge Lane. The other is EA Clare Ltd on St Anne Street in the city centre.

EA Clare is an important company for two reasons.

Firstly, it is the largest surviving maker of billiards and snooker equipment in Europe. Secondly, it is home to the largest collection of billiards and snooker related equipment, documentation and memorabilia outside the USA.

Edward Arthur Clare, the company's founder, learnt his trade at J Ashcroft & Co and later

as a representative for Orme & Sons of Manchester, before setting up his own workshop on nearby Fraser Street in 1912. For decades Clare's was a comparatively small business. And yet as trade dwindled in the post war period, then revived with television coverage of snooker in the 1970s, the company hung on.

The first rival to fall into Clare's ambit was also the most venerable, when Norman Clare, son of the founder, became joint chairman of Thurston in 1963. Three years later he took on a similar role at Padmore's of Birmingham (established in 1830).

Clare then moved to its current premises in 1970, before buying up the cue-tip makers EL Fletcher & Son of Baldock, Herts, in 1972, and transferring their works to Webster Road, Edge Hill. Fletcher

were subsequently merged with Peradon (Britain's first cue making company, established in Willesden, London, in 1885).

Other companies to merge with, or sell up to Clare were Fitzpatrick & Longley of Sheffield (established 1843), Chas. Parker & Son of Barnsley (1879), Van Laere of Brussels (1896), MacMorran of Chalk Farm, London (1923) and Weildings of Acton, London (1924). Two Liverpool firms were also absorbed; the oldest, William Bayliff, and finally, the once mighty Ashcroft, in 1987.

As each company entered the fold, so Norman Clare took in their hordes of assorted artefacts and records, going all the way back to Thurston's foundation in 1799.

The result is a remarkable collection, unique to Liverpool, and of great credit to the company.

▲ A cornucopia of delights – the inner sanctum of the **Norman Clare Collection** has at its centre a rare Thurston 'Octangular', made in 1908 to fit a room with a bay window and said to 'enable ladies to meet their menfolk on more equal terms by reason of the great variety of possible strokes'.

When not in use for play the Octangular was easily convertible into a dining table.

As well as being an inveterate collector, Clare, who died in 1990, aged 76, was forever being offered obscure items, such as a late 19th century, London-made cast iron table that had been found in a house in Ireland, having also seen service in the Indian colonies.

Note the two miniature billiard tables, used by manufacturers as showroom samples and as children's novelties.

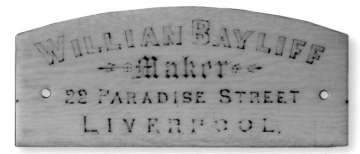

From the hundreds of engraved table nameplates that form part of the Norman Clare Collection we can draw up a fascinating list of manufacturers and suppliers active in Britain since the early 19th century. These from the Liverpool area include two companies later absorbed by Clare. Among others not shown are George Metcalf of Fonthill Road, Kirkdale, and GA Wright of Birkenhead.

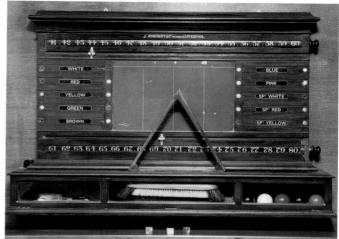

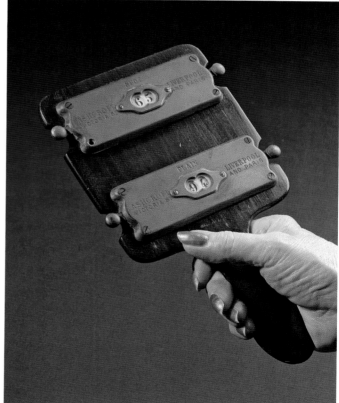

▲ Also part of the **Clare Collection** are hundreds of accessories, some more practical than others.

Standard fare was this cast iron table iron (*top left*), used to smooth down the baize before play. However, manufacturers showed much more ingenuity when it came to scoring devices. Thomas Ollis of Liverpool patented this thief-proof, coin-operated billiards marking board (*above*) in the late 19th century, while Ashcroft made hand-held boards (*right*) for spectators at billiards matches.

Separate from the collection is a classic Ashcroft marking board (*top right*) still in use at the **Wallasey Yacht Club** (*see page 30*). The side panels are for scoring the once popular game of Life Pool, in which up to 13 players could join in.

◄ Billiards and snooker cues are still crafted by hand. Marketed under the brand name **Peradon** (a firm originally set up in London in 1885), the cues made at EA Clare consist of a long shaft made from maple or ash, into which a shorter, four pointed hardwood butt, usually made of ebony, is spliced and glued. More expensive cues are then further enhanced by additional splices of veneer.

If the cue is to be sold as a two-piece, as favoured by afficionados, once its length – usually measuring 58 inches – is planed and sanded to the right shape, weight and balance, the shaft is then cut in two and a threaded brass joint fitted so that when screwed together the timber grains of both sections match up exactly. (If different timbers were used in each section the cue would be less strong and more prone to warping.)

Finally, after more sanding and varnishing the all important leather tip is added (an invention credited to a former French infantry officer, in 1807, who experimented with cuttings from a leather harness whilst serving a prison sentence).

Billiards manufacturers have always been keen to have their wares gain a celebrity endorsement. Peradon cues were, for example, endorsed by the greatest billiards player of all, Joe Davis.

A Joe Davis cue today can cost from £75 upwards, with top of the range models costing £100–200.

EA Clare also make tables, ranging from £4,000 for a basic full-sized model up to £17,000 for the top model with accessories. But because tables last so long – a century old table is not uncommon – the company's main business today is renovation, for which it employs a roster of six fitters to service clients all over the world.

▲ An 1890s Thurston set of ivory balls for billiards, life pool and pyramid (a precursor of snooker), held in the **Norman Clare Collection**. In 1890 alone, 762 tonnes of ivory passed through the Port of London, with one company proudly claiming that 1,140 female elephants had to be slaughtered just to supply one year's demand. From each tusk deemed suitable (some 6-8 per dozen), no more than five balls could be made.

But although a celluloid ball was invented in the United States in 1868 and marketed under the name of Bonzoline (or Crystalate in Britain), not until the 1920s would many of the top players admit that these new 'composite' balls were in fact more truly spherical and consistent in all temperatures.

Ashcroft's Billiard Works.

ONE OF THE LARGEST WORKS IN THE KINGDOM.

▲ Barely noticed amid the shop fronts and office blocks of Victoria Street, in central Liverpool, is the red Aberdeen granite doorway and the red brick and Cefn stone exterior of the **Ashcroft Buildings**, once the headquarters of Liverpool's most successful billiards manufacturer, J Ashcroft & Co.

Designed by Hoult and Wise architects, and completed in 1883 at a cost of £13,000, until 1987 the buildings housed the firm's showroom at street level (now occupied by a Chinese restaurant). The first and second floors were rented out as office space, with the third and fourth floors fitted out as Ashcroft's offices and workshops – this at a time when many a city centre façade hid a factory or warehouse at the rear. (In fact Victoria Street was then dominated by fruit and produce wholesalers).

The roof was flat, reinforced with concrete and coated with asphalt to serve as storage for up to 400 tons of timber and slate beds used in billiard table construction.

In order to lift the materials up to this roof, and back down to the workshop and then showroom when required, a large cage-hoist was fitted. To power the machinery and electric lights, there were two gas-powered, eight horse power 'Otto' engines, supplied by Crossley Bros of Manchester.

The uppermost corner turret housed the Ashcroft studio, in which all the latest lines were photographed for the annual catalogues, several of which are now held as part of the Clare Collection.

In an ideal world the old building would be restored for use as a permanent home for the collection.

Instead, the public must visit the Thurston shop at EA Clare in St Anne Street, where Peter Clare, Norman's son, hopes to create a public exhibition to coincide with the 2008 Capital of Culture year.

Chapter Eight

Goal Nets

JA Brodie was a remarkable man. Appointed as Liverpool City Engineer in 1898, he planned the city's first ring road, Queen's Drive, invented a system of prefabricated concrete panels for cheap housing construction, and a method for collecting refuse. He worked in New Delhi and Spain, became a leading town planner and advocate of both cars and trams. He is commemorated by Brodie Avenue, and by a plaque at his home, at 28 Ullet Road. But for all his achievements, Brodie is best remembered for perhaps his simplest invention...

Liverpool has numerous claims to fame in the world of football. But one of the city's most important contributions to the development of the modern game is the humble goal net.

For this the credit must go to John Alexander Brodie (1858–1934), the ingenious Liverpool City Engineer, who, in the tradition of all the best inventors, saw a problem and then sat down to solve it.

For make no mistake, football without goal nets was riven with problems. Here was a game that had evolved piecemeal throughout the 19th century, from a barely defined field game played to local rules, to a strictly codified national sport attracting thousands of paying spectators.

The key stages of this evolution occurred between 1863, when the newly formed Football Association drew up its first rules, and 1902, when the current pitch markings were adopted (apart from the penalty arc, added in 1937).

The rules agreed in December 1863 stated that a goal should consist of two upright poles, eight yards apart. For a goal to be scored the ball had either to pass between the posts, 'or over the space between the posts (at whatever height)'.

Clearly this was a recipe for discord, so in 1865 the rules were amended to require a tape to be extended between the goalposts at a height of eight feet. In 1875 it was agreed that these tapes could be replaced by a fixed cross bar, and crossbars were then made compulsory in 1882.

Thus it took nearly 20 years simply to settle on the form of goal that has been in use ever since.

But this still left the thorny issue of judging, in the heat of the action, whether a ball had passed inside the posts, for a goal, or outside, for a goal kick or corner.

It can easily be imagined how disputes of this nature led to virulent arguments, and even riots.

In Liverpool, the main needle match of the 1880s was between Everton and their local rivals Bootle. Such games drew high-spirited crowds far in excess of what the grounds were able to accommodate, which in turn resulted in spectators hugging the touchlines and frequently encroaching upon the pitch.

At a Liverpool Cup match in 1886, for example, 10,000 fans crammed into the Bootle Cricket Ground on Wadham Road, the highest number yet recorded in the city. At one point the Bootle goalkeeper dropped the ball after being hampered by a group of boys crowded behind the goalposts. Everton scored easily, and the goal was controversially allowed.

They scored again, this time a shot rebounding off a spectator standing on the goal line.

Bootle and their fans were furious, especially as the referee had disallowed an earlier goal of theirs, scored in similar circumstances, claiming that he had been unable to tell which side of the post the ball had passed.

The game ended prematurely with a pitch invasion, Everton being declared the winners.

The formation of the Football League in 1888 brought no resolution of the matter, despite the much higher financial stakes now at play, and as newspaper ›

This extract from John Brodie's 1889 patent application shows that he was also thinking of rugby, his first love, as well as football. Note his suggestion for bells or other alarms to be attached to the nets to confirm that a goal has been scored.

N° 19,112

A.D. 1889

Date of Application, 28th Nov., 1889
Complete Specification Left, 28th Aug., 1890—Accepted, 4th Oct., 1890

COMPLETE SPECIFICATION.

Improvements in or applicable to Goals used in Football, Lacrosse, or other like Games.

I, JOHN ALEXANDER BRODIE of 5 Kelvin Grove, Liverpool in the County of Lancaster, Engineer, do hereby declare the nature of this invention and in what manner the same is to be performed, to be particularly described and ascertained in and by the following statement :—

My invention relates to those games in which the object of the contending sides is to kick or otherwise propel a ball through the goal defended by their opponents.

It frequently happens in such games that it is extremely difficult to decide whether the ball has passed just within or just without the assigned limits, and the object of my invention is to overcome this difficulty.

According to my present invention I attach boarding, canvas, netting, or other suitable material to the limiting lines of the goal within which the ball is required to pass, the said material being carried back from the field of play and inclined outwards from the goal mouth. The material may be painted white so as to form a back ground by means of which the path of the ball in passing over the goal line can be more readily observed than is the case with the goals at present in use.

Where it can conveniently be done I prefer to enclose the space thus formed behind the goal so as to form a pocket in which the ball may lodge after passing through the goal.

In this case I prefer to use netting as it does not obstruct the view and not being rigid the ball is not so liable to rebound therefrom, the said netting being supported by suitable posts or rods behind the goal.

Where found desirable one or more bells or other suitable alarms may be connected with the netting or other material forming the pocket so as to indicate the impact of the ball.

In order that my invention may be readily understood, reference is made to the accompanying drawings in which Figs. I, II, and III show my improvements applied to a goal for Association football, Fig. I being a front view, Fig. II a side view and Fig. III a plan ; Figs. IV, V, and VI are analogous views showing my improvements applied to a goal for Rugby football ; Fig. VII is a plan of a modification. Throughout the drawings similar parts are indicated by the same reference figures.

Referring to Figs. I, II, and III, 1, 1 is the goal line 2, 2 are the goal posts and 3 is the cross-bar.

An enclosed space or pocket is formed behind the goal mouth by the side nettings 4, 4, the top netting 5 and the back netting 6 ; the nettings 4, 4 and 5 being attached as shown to the goal posts and cross-bar respectively, and all being further supported by the light framing 7. The nettings which extend to the ground are or may be pegged thereto.

Referring now to Figs. III, IV, and V :—In this case the ball is required to pass between the goal posts 2, 2 or their indefinite prolongations and over the cross-bar 3 ; the pocket is in this case accordingly open at the top and is formed by the side nettings 4, bottom netting 5 and back netting 6, the nettings 4, 4 and 5 being as before attached to the goal posts and cross-bar respectively and all being further supported by the framing 7. The back netting 6 stops short of the horizontal bar 7 so as to leave room for the ball to roll out at the back.

Whilst I have shown the pockets as formed by netting it is to be understood that any suitable material may be used and it may be supported by any convenient means.

Fig. VII shows in plan a modification which may be used when it is not desired to form a pocket behind the goal.

Dated this 27th day of August 1890.

SLOAN & LLOYD BARNES,
26, Castle Street, Liverpool, Agents for the Applicant.

London : Printed for Her Majesty's Stationery Office, by Darling & Son, Ltd.—1890.

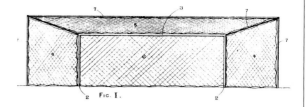

FIG. I.

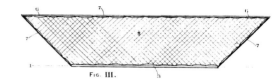

FIG. III.

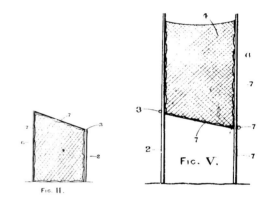

FIG. II.

FIG. V.

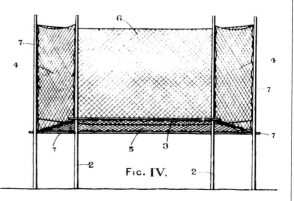

FIG. IV.

▼ This *Football Echo* sketch of a match at Anfield between Everton and Bolton on 17 October 1891 is one of the first known, accurate representations of **Brodie's Patented Goal Nets**.

According to the *Football Echo* Everton had been using the nets for some time, and were the first Football League club to adopt them in general play. The paper also noted that only 50 sets were known to be in use at that time. Two weeks later they became compulsory at all League matches.

There were some teething problems. Brodie and the League had to agree on a maximum price of £3 12s 6d for a set (a figure which would soon drop as more companies started to produce nets). It was also noted that some goalkeepers forgot the nets were in place and ran into them when trying to retrieve the ball.

» reports from around Britain during this period show, disputed goals were now a regular occurence; England's first goal against Wales in 1889 being just one example of where defenders insisted the shot had been wide.

As the *Athletic News Annual* of 1894 recalled, 'How often prior to the invention of goal-nets has a referee been hoodwinked by the gesticulations of an over-anxious forward, and allowed a goal for a shot a few inches over the bar?'

How exactly John Brodie became interested in this issue is not clear. Unsourced snippets from various football histories only muddy the waters.

One version states that goal nets were first tried in Birmingham in 1885, four years before Brodie's involvement. Another unsubstantiated tale has it that Brodie hailed from the fishing town of Bridport, in Dorset, and was therefore familiar with nets.

If, as often stated, Brodie actually witnessed a match in which a disputed goal was scored, we do not know which one. It could just be that as a keen rugby

player in his youth, Brodie had seen many footballers arguing on a neighbouring pitch.

Whatever, according to Brodie's own account, he sat down one afternoon in August 1889 to consider the problem, and within half an hour had come up with a solution that no football official had managed in the previous 25 years; that is, a simple 'pocket in which the ball may lodge after passing through the goal'.

The next stage was to test his design, apparently at a match staged in Stanley Park with the help of a group of players later described as Northern Old Etonians, but who may well have been members of the Liverpool Ramblers (who were formed by former Etonians).

The date of this trial is not recorded. However we know for sure that Brodie submitted a provisional application to patent his designs on 28 November 1889, and that his revised specifications, submitted in August 1890, were finally approved by the Patent Office on 27 November 1890.

It has been suggested in some sources that the first trial of Brodie's Patented Nets took place at Pikes Lane, Bolton, for a match between Bolton Wanderers and Nottingham Forest, on New Year's Day 1891. But no report of that match mentions the nets.

Instead, possibly thanks to the secretary of the Liverpool & District FA, Bob Lythgoe, acting as Brodie's intermediary, the first official trial was conducted at the Town Ground, Nottingham, on a cold and frosty Monday afternoon, on 12 January 1891.

As reported by the *Nottingham Evening Post*, 'Mr Brodie's net, which was used in the 12th annual North v. South Match, is likely

to become popular. It has been smartly styled "a trap to catch referees."'

Describing the net as 'a huge pocket' the report added that it was designed to assist referees 'in difficult cases of shooting at goal' and 'at the same time in no way interferes with the goalkeepers'.

In a later memoir, the editor of *Athletic News*, Jimmy Catton, recalled one of the FA officials, 'the late Dr Morley, of Blackburn, smoking the inevitable cigar and wearing the inevitable silk hat, walking out to inspect the novelty'.

Appropriately, the first player ever to 'net' an official goal was an Everton man, Fred Geary. The North added two more goals for a 3-0 victory, watched by an estimated crowd of 4,000. (One of the umpires, incidentally, was Sam Widdowson, whose own contribution to football was the introduction of shinpads).

Clearly impressed by what they saw, three weeks later the FA invited Brodie to a meeting, and concluded that 'the Council approve the use of Nets as under Mr. Brodie's patent, but cannot take any steps to amend the rule so as to make their use compulsory until some satisfactory arrangement can be made with the patentee as to the prices to be charged to Clubs'.

Brodie gained further encouragement when the FA also agreed to use nets at the forthcoming FA Cup Final, played on 21 March 1891 at the Oval.

Once more, however, football history becomes confused at this point.

A sketch of that Final, played between Blackburn Rovers and Notts County, clearly shows a net placed behind a goal. But it looks more like a screen than a

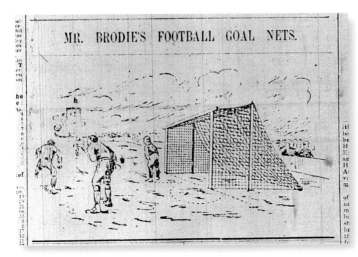

MR. BRODIE'S FOOTBALL GOAL NETS.

Brodie net, and is not attached to the posts. This may have been an oversight by the artist, for the *Nottingham Daily Guardian* certainly mentions the use of Brodie nets at the match. And yet all official FA histories consider the 1892 Final, also at the Oval, to have been the first at which nets were used.

In this instance it would seem that the official accounts may well need correcting. Moreover, two weeks after the 1891 Final, on 4 April, Brodie's nets were also reportedly used for the England v. Scotland international at Ewood Park, Blackburn.

What is for sure is that two further decisions confirmed that nets were here to stay. In September 1891 both the Football League and Lancashire League resolved that Brodie nets were to be compulsory for League matches from 1 November onwards. Brodie then received one final stamp of approval in 1894, when the FA recommended that nets also be used for all Cup ties.

Just four years had passed since Brodie's first experiments on Stanley Park.

Brodie himself would go on to have an even more profound influence on Liverpool and on town planning generally. But as he admitted himself, the invention of goal nets was the best idea he ever had.

Net profits – Liverpool sports retailer Frank Sugg Ltd advertises its latest goal net styles c.1906, with supporting poles positioned outside and behind the goal posts. This arrangement regained popularity in the late 20th century after numerous controversial incidents in which the ball entered the net but struck an inner goal stanchion, only to bounce out.

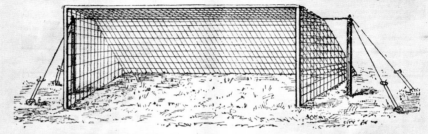

Chapter Nine

Football Pools

A clocktower on Ormskirk Road, Aintree, is all that remains of the headquarters of Vernons Pools, completed in 1934 and the first purpose-built offices constructed by any pools company in Britain. Their 1936–37 handbook started off 'A is for Aintree, where Vernons reside, Spacious the building, an object of pride. Lovely to look at both inside and out, One of the finest, of that there's no doubt.' Following Vernons' departure for nearby Park Lane in 1991 the building was used as a nightclub, until all but the clocktower was demolished in 2006.

Sport has always been associated with gambling. Indeed until the 20th century to engage in a bit of 'sport' was synonymous with having a bet, amongst both rich and poor, and in every conceivable arena of competition, be it bowls or cricket, horse racing or cockfighting. The emergence of mass spectator sport extended gambling's hold on the public even further.

But the football pools, a truly British invention, are a somewhat different phenomenon. True, they are a form of gambling. But whereas in traditional fixed odds betting, a punter – dealing directly with a bookmaker – knows in advance what he might win from his stake, in pools, or 'combination betting' (as it was often called), winners are in effect paid a dividend, or a share of a much larger pool of stake money. The amount of this dividend depends on the size of the combined weekly total, the accuracy of one's predictions across a range of fixtures, and how well one fares in relation to all other entrants.

The pools may therefore be deemed a more inclusive, collective experience, and as a result, one whose weekly grip on the nation was no less intense than that of its modern day successor, the National Lottery.

Throughout the pools' hey day, from approximately 1930 to 1994 (when the introduction of the Lottery effectively ended their dominance), opinions were sharply divided as to their social merit. For example, while Anglican officials told a 1949 Royal Commission that the pools were a 'menace to social and personal life,' the Roman Catholic Church felt they were 'relatively harmless' and even beneficial, 'since in many homes, happy evenings are spent by the family remaining together and filling up their coupons'.

But whatever their pros or cons, one fact is certain. While dozens of pools companies operated around Britain, Liverpool was the absolute powerhouse of the industry. When the politician AP Herbert wrote in 1951 of sending coupons 'to the great building in the north', every reader took this to mean Liverpool.

That this was so was initially down to one man, John Moores, the founder of Littlewoods, who ironically was a Mancunian. Moreover, the idea was born not in Liverpool but, according to various sources, either in Edinburgh or in Birmingham, in the early 1920s.

Betting on football was already hugely popular by then and had attracted regular opprobrium from officials within the game and from guardians of public morality. A 1907 survey carried out by the National Anti-Gambling League, for example, claimed improbably that 250,000 fixed-odds betting coupons were being circulated in Liverpool alone, every week.

William Murphy, a miner, and Thomas Strang, issued what may have been the earliest genuine pools coupons in 1918, in Edinburgh. Three years later, a Birmingham bookmaker, John Jervis Barnard, followed suit. He could not make it pay, but one of his coupons made its way to Manchester, where it was picked up by Moores, then working as a telegraphist. What happened next is part of Liverpool folklore. »

▲ Visitors to the vast 'poolrooms' of Liverpoool, it was said, were always amazed at the quiet, orderly fashion in which the coupons were checked by thousands of women in serried ranks. Voices seldom rose above a whisper, and it was rare to see even the tiniest scrap of paper on the floor. By 1954 it was estimated that seven per cent of Liverpool's female working population worked for the three main companies, Littlewoods, Vernons and Zetters.

This was Irlam Road, a former boat building factory, one of six Liverpool buildings occupied by Littlewoods in the 1950s. There was another immense poolroom at their Walton Hall Avenue premises, plus two others in Glasgow and Cardiff.

At the time this photograph was taken in 1949 a report found that one third of all British adults entered the pools weekly, and that Littlewoods processed half the national total. Vernons enjoyed the second largest share, at 25 per cent of the market, as a result of which they too had to find three extra buildings to supplement their main offices at Aintree.

▲ Training was a vital part of the pools operation. Here staff at **Littlewoods** are being trained as permutation clerks (*top*), a specialised task arising from the introduction of treble chance in 1946. Under this system points are awarded for home wins, away wins and draws, with 24 points being the target. Given the huge sums involved – Littlewoods paid out their first £75,000 jackpot in 1948 to a man in Aldershot – every step required meticulous attention. This extended to the coupon's layout (*above*), which had to be clear both for the checkers and the millions of punters for whom, at five o'clock each Saturday, as they tuned into the BBC's *Sports Report*, this would be the most important piece of paper in the world.

» Briefly, Moores and two work pals each invested £50 – a huge sum for such young men – in setting up their own pools business. To avoid alerting their bosses at the cable company they named this enterprise after one of the trio, Colin Askham (born Colin Littlewood). It may also have been to avoid detection that they set up offices in Liverpool, on Church Street, rather than in Manchester.

The business soon floundered. But Moores persisted, bought out his partners, and with the help of his brother Cecil and other relatives increased weekly receipts from £37 in 1925 to £2,000 a year later. By then, 2,000 coupons were being submitted per week.

Meanwhile, Vernon Sangster from Preston was making similar headway after setting up Vernons in 1926, while other firms emerged in London (Copes), Cardiff (Shermans) and even Belgium, where Zetters, later to move to London and Liverpool, set up.

The full story of how this industry developed and overcame a string of obstacles – put up by legislators and the football authorities – is well told elsewhere (*see Links*). But in the context of this study, the pools' impact on Liverpool, and on sport generally, is worthy of summary.

In social and economic terms, hardly a family in Liverpool was untouched by the pools. Between them Littlewoods and Vernons grew to employ over 20,000 people, mostly women. In the 1930s, when unemployment reached 30 per cent, this helped the city's economy greatly.

John Moores himself proved to be an astonishing entrepreneur and benefactor in his adopted city. In 1932 he set up the Littlewoods mail order company. In 1937

he opened the first Littlewoods department store, in Blackpool. Another major employer within the Moores empire was its printing business, set up initially to print coupons but soon developing into a business in its own right.

While brother Cecil ran the pools operation, John also became actively involved in sport. In the 1930s he set up a baseball league (*see Chapter Thirteen*), then became managing director of Liverpool's prime boxing venue (*see Chapter Seventeen*). In 1960 he became chairman of Everton, although the family also owned shares in Liverpool, where Cecil's son David would later become chairman.

Family funds would further be directed towards the local polytechnic (now John Moores University), the John Moores Foundation, and to such initiatives as the Liverpool Exhibition Trust.

After years of rebuffing the pools industry on moral grounds, football itself became a beneficiary in 1959, when the Football League started charging for the use of its fixtures. From 1975–2000, the Pools Promoters' Association also contributed nearly £200 million to the refurbishment of British football grounds. Each Liverpool club, for example, received £2 million to help implement the government's all-seater policy. This was in addition to the pools companies' profits being taxed at levels varying from 20 per cent in 1949 to 42.5 per cent by 1990.

Meanwhile other sports, including rugby and cricket, would benefit from the Foundation for Sports and Arts, set up in return for a reduction in pool betting duty to 37.5 per cent in 1991. The FSA, now funded solely by Littlewoods, has since given grants of £350 million. »

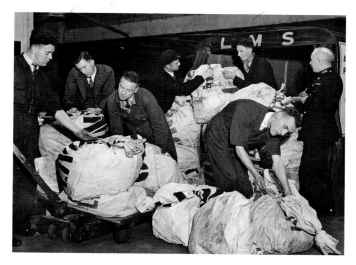

▲ Servicing the pools industry required considerable logistical planning at a national level, particularly on the part of railway companies and the Post Office (both of whom profited greatly in return). By the late 1930s it was estimated that pools coupons were being delivered to six out of every ten homes in Britain. To ease this burden, the Postmaster General had to persuade Littlewoods and their counterparts to send out two weeks worth of coupons at a time.

The Post Office was also at times severely stretched by the demand for postal orders (which were cheap to send and, unlike cheques, did not appear on bank statements).

In order to guarantee security and guard against fraud, incoming mail bags, each sealed with a timed lock, had to be logged at each stage of the journey.

Another feature of the business in the pre-computer age was that all coupons were sorted by postal address, rather than by name, so that the same clerk would deal with entries from a whole street or even an entire village, every week.

Validating each coupon was a vital part of the process. This was done first by a 'joey', a stamping machine that recorded the date and time of receipt. Then, as each coupon passed from one clerk to the next, a series of security marks and secretly coded impressions tracked its progress. For additional security, work rotas were regularly changed so that no pool clerk knew in advance which coupons she would be checking, and also that she did not mark those from her own postal region of clients.

Such rigour required discipline at every level. Chatting on the job was frowned upon, even if it could be heard above the clatter of stamping machines. Yet at the same time the pools companies generated tremendous loyalty. Staff were comparatively well paid. Not every day was intense, and both Vernons and Littlewoods offered high standards of staff welfare.

Most famously, the Vernon's all-girl choir went on to achieve national fame as the Vernon Girls, appearing on the televised music show *Oh Boy* from 1958 onwards.

Pools companies were at the forefront of adopting efficient work practices and modern technology, from adding machines at Vernons in 1955 (*above*) to optical scanners at Littlewoods in 1961. Now five coupons per second could be checked, requiring half the workforce and much less office space. In 1966 Littlewoods became one of the first British firms to install an IBM computer.

>> But the economic ripples have extended far beyond these shores. Since 1945 punters all over the world have either played the British pools or local versions. When a Nigerian won £75,000 from Littlewoods in the 1950s it sparked a national mania.

In countries such as Sweden and Hungary, income from pools financed massive expenditure on sport, prompting British critics to argue that our own industry should be put into public ownership. Instead, in 1994 the National Lottery was established.

Its effect on the last remaining pools companies was devastating.

In November 1994 Littlewoods paid out a record jackpot of £2.9 million. Yet within two years 2,500 Littlewoods workers lost their jobs, as pools entries fell to a new low of two million.

Yet there is hope. Some 12,000 door-to-door collectors still work for Littlewoods, who have diversified into other areas of gaming under new owners, SportTech (who also own Zetters). Vernons are now owned by Ladbrokes. Online pools may also provide a means for future growth.

But for now, the immense role the pools have played in British life should not be forgotten. For 60 years the pools ensured that millions of men and women, rich and poor, young and old, turned their attention not merely to football, but to the evocative names and places of their island home, and that for one magical moment, the result of Crewe Alexandra v. Accrington Stanley bore equal importance to that of Manchester United v. Arsenal.

Here was a unique cultural phenomenon, and one that would have been impossible without the British love of 'a bit of sport'.

▲ Littlewoods may have moved on to premises more appropriate to their current needs, but their former **Edge Lane** headquarters, opened in 1938 and resplendent on a rise overlooking Edge Hill and the distant Welsh horizon, survives as a dazzling monument to the ambition and vision of the Moores family.

Designed, it is thought, by local architect Gerald de Courcy Fraser (otherwise responsible for offices and department stores, such as Lewis's in Renshaw Street), it is both finely proportioned and defiantly functional. Littlewoods required extensive, roof-lit open plan spaces that would be adaptable to accommodate changing technologies. (They had noted how Vernons had soon outgrown their Aintree building within years of its completion.)

Part of the Edge Hill building, for example, housed an immense printing press, able to turn out millions of coupons, fliers, envelopes and letters every week. At the outbreak of the Second World War these same presses were commissioned to print 17 million National Registration forms in just three days. Later in the war the building was also used to assemble Halifax bombers. In fact Littlewoods as a company played a significant role in the war effort, partly owing to the Moores' patriotism, but also because their buildings and work practices were very much geared to modern production and fast turnaround.

After Littlewoods vacated Edge Hill in 2003 the building's future seemed uncertain, until in 2006 it became the latest in a line of landmark 20th century buildings – including Morecambe's Midland Hotel and Birmingham's Rotunda – to come under the wing of the property development company, Urban Splash. Their plans are to undertake an extensive £48m refurbishment, including the replacement of the run down east wing with a complex containing a hotel, bars, offices and an open public space. The classic bookend west wing, which overlooks the Botanic Gardens, will be converted into flats and apartments aimed at the first-time buyer. These renovations, it is hoped, will be complete by 2008.

Meanwhile, another former pools building, Zetters in Clerkenwell, London, has been converted into a boutique hotel.

Chapter Ten

Stadiums and Grounds

A rare example of decoration in an area of sporting architecture dominated by utilitarian structures. This is one of sixteen ornate iron capitals adorning the grandstand at the Oval, Bebington, built in 1902 as part of an agricultural showground and later taken over for use by workers at the nearby Lever Brothers' Port Sunlight factory village. Now owned by Wirral Borough Council, the structure is the oldest grandstand in Merseyside.

It has been noted before in the *Played in Britain* series that the stadium enjoys the highest public and political profile of all sports-related buildings. But as this chapter demonstrates, the term 'stadium' is laden with ambiguity.

Both Anfield and Goodison Park, Liverpool's largest spectator facilities (*see Chapter Five*), are increasingly described as stadiums because of their size and status (and also because the term has become fashionable). But traditionally they have always been referred to as 'grounds'.

From an architectural viewpoint there is an important distinction.

Strictly, a stadium is considered to be a sports venue that has been pre-designed as a single entity, and built, whether in one phase or more, according to a masterplan. Few historic British sports venues, Anfield and Goodison Park included, were ever planned in this fashion. Rather, they were developed piecemeal, over the years, as funds became available or as planning regulations changed, almost always with different architects overseeing each phase.

Equally, a stadium is generally held to be an open air venue. Yet the Liverpool Stadium, opened in 1932, was an indoor arena for boxing (*see page 158*), while the present day Bootle Stadium, on Stuart Road, is hardly more than a playing field, with not a stand or terrace remaining.

Semantics apart, in this chapter we turn to those venues – be they called stadiums or grounds – in which such track and field events as athletics, greyhound and speedway racing, football and rugby, are staged.

What links them all (apart from the final example, at the University of Liverpool's sports ground on Mather Avenue) is that they are laid out to fairly standard dimensions and are sufficiently enclosed for spectator access to be controlled.

In Liverpool, as in the rest of the country, this type of permanent venue started to appear in the 1880s, primarily for the newly professionalised sport of football (for which the collection of gate money was essential). Athletics and rugby followed, with two new track-based sports, greyhound racing and speedway, being introduced in the late 1920s.

As detailed here, Liverpool had no fewer than four of these new tracks, none of which survive.

Partly their demise was owing to changing trends. However, legislation arising from three major disasters also had a profound effect on the design, economics and management of all enclosed stadiums and grounds.

After the Ibrox disaster of 1971 senior football grounds were designated under the 1975 Safety of Sports Grounds Act, which required local authorities to issue annual safety certificates.

A homely turnstile block greets spectators arriving at the St Anthony's Road ground, Blundellsands, home of Waterloo rugby union club since 1921 (*see page 108*). Waterloo is the highest ranking rugby club on Merseyside.

In Liverpool this affected only Anfield and Goodison Park.

Then in May 1985 a fire in the wooden stand at Valley Parade, Bradford, led to the 1975 Act being extended to all lower division football grounds (such as Tranmere's Prenton Park) and all senior rugby league grounds, while more stringent fire regulations were extended to any other ground having a grandstand holding 500 or more spectators.

The impact was felt across Merseyside. Ground capacities were slashed. Dozens of timber structures were condemned.

Meanwhile, as the economy faltered, a number of Merseyside grounds fell into decline. Several clubs also suffered from arson attacks; in the case of South Liverpool, the city's third ranking football club, the damage was serious enough to force them to abandon their Holly Park ground in 1990, after which it died a slow death at the hands of vandals.

Even more sweeping were the effects of the 1989 Hillsborough disaster, in which 96 Liverpool supporters died on the terraces of Sheffield Wednesday's ground. Following the recommendations made by Lord Justice Taylor, all terracing at senior grounds was ordered to be closed by 1994. This resulted in Anfield, Goodison Park and Prenton Park becoming all-seater; an expensive measure which not only reduced capacities even further but also required major changes in the cultural patterns and behaviour of fans.

But smaller clubs were also affected. Several had to bring their terracing up to newly formulated national standards. All became subject to equally demanding minimum standards imposed by each league organisation.

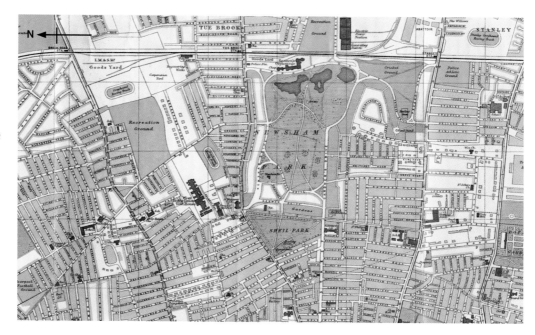

Those clubs who could not afford to upgrade, or whose grounds were, owing to planning restrictions, unable to meet the new standards, were then forced either to find a new home or to drop down to a lower league.

It would be false to assert that these changes resulted in the loss of any buildings of architectural merit. Before and since the 1990s, the main characteristic of most grounds, on Merseyside as in the rest of Britain, has been functionalism born out of pragmatism.

Nevertheless, the network of grounds is, in itself, part of the region's collective heritage, with each ground having its own distinctive character and history.

That the buildings seen on the following pages may not amount to much in design terms is, to their users, much less important than the very fact of their existence.

▲ The region's penchant for the sport of hare coursing – of which the Waterloo Cup at Altcar was the leading event (*see page 19*) – may explain why Liverpool had such a concentration of **greyhound tracks**. Not even in London, where there were 17 tracks altogether by 1939, were there three tracks so close together, as seen on this Bartholomew map of 1935.

The first to open, in 1927, was **Stanley Stadium** (*top right*). This was followed in 1928 by **Breck**

Park Stadium on Townsend Lane (*top left*). A third track, the **White City Stadium** (*centre*), just left, or north, of Newsham Park, opened in August 1931, followed, remarkably, by a fourth in **Seaforth** (*see next page*) in 1933.

Yet by 1973 none would remain, and today very few Liverpudlians even recall how closely they were bunched together.

Note also **Shiel Park** (now built over), the **Police Athletic Ground** (*top right*) and **Anfield** (*lower left*).

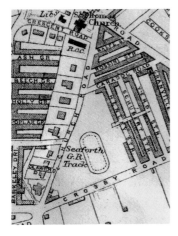

As if three dog tracks in the city were not enough, on 25 February 1933 a fourth one opened on Crosby Road South. But although the Seaforth Greyhound Stadium had a substantial, three storey brick grandstand, a second smaller stand opposite, plus terrace covers behind both curves – an unusual amount of cover overall – no images of the venue in operation have been traced. From 1948–53 the stadium was also home to the shortlived Bootle Athletic FC (not the original Bootle FC or the current one). Eventually the stadium was purchased by Crosby Corporation for housing. The final meeting took place on New Years Eve 1965, and Church Grove now occupies part of the site.

▲ Viewed from the north in 1930, the **Stanley Greyhound Stadium**, the first of its type in Liverpool, was opened on 17 August 1927 by the Electric Hare Greyhound Company. Prior to this the site had been occupied by the Stanley Athletic Ground, one of several privately owned sports grounds to have been laid out in the city during the late 1880s and 1890s.

Accessed from Prescot Road (*top right*), the new stadium was ideally located between Stanley and Edge Lane stations (*see map on previous page*), and became a regular haunt for workers at the Old Swan cattle market and at a new abbattoir (now the Stanley Meat Market) that opened across the road in 1929.

Note the tower in the centre of the dog track. It was from here that a controller regulated the speed of the electric hare as it sped around the track on a rail, making sure that it was neither slow enough to be caught by the dogs, but not so fast that they lost sight of it.

Across the railway line can be seen the **Police Athletic Ground**, Fairfield (still extant), also laid out in the 1880s and a popular venue for baseball, cricket and bowls.

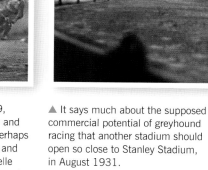

▲ Riders from Liverpool's Stanley speedway team, known as 'The Chads', take the first corner at a race in 1951. The **Stanley Stadium** was one of 37 British speedway tracks active that year – compared with 36 today – all but a few them based at greyhound tracks. (The cinder speedway track may be seen opposite, inside the 516 yard sand track used by the dogs.)

Originally called dirt track racing when first developed in Australia in 1923, speedway made its British debut in Essex in February 1928. Within months it had been trialled all over Britain, arriving at Stanley Stadium in September 1928.

Not only was speedway daring and spectacular – especially when staged at night under trackside lights – but it also helped bolster the uncertain finances of many a newly built greyhound stadium.

But it was costly to stage. The riders were professionals. Nor, unlike greyhound racing, was betting sanctioned. And so in Liverpool, as in several other cities, promoters and their teams came and went. The Chads disbanded

in 1937, resurfaced in 1949, and despite nurturing the up and coming star, Peter Craven (perhaps one of the riders seen above and soon to join Manchester's Belle Vue Aces), they dropped out again in 1953, to be replaced by a shortlived team called The Pirates.

Note that apart from the one grandstand, the only other cover at the stadium consisted of eight basic shelters formed by timber Belfast roofs (*see opposite*). Thrills aplenty, perhaps, but precious few frills.

LIVERPOOL SPEEDWAY

6D

Official Programme
May 27th, 1957.
No Betting Allowed

▲ It says much about the supposed commercial potential of greyhound racing that another stadium should open so close to Stanley Stadium, in August 1931.

Built at the comparatively lavish cost of £70,000 on the former sports ground of the St George's Roman Catholic Industrial School on Lower Breck Road, the **White City Stadium** was one of a chain operated by the Greyhound Racing Company, and was named after the former exhibition site in west London where the 1908 Olympic Stadium was built, and which staged its first greyhound racing in June 1927. Other White City stadiums were at Manchester,

Newcastle, Hull, Nottingham, Glasgow and Cardiff.

Few images of the stadium survive, although as this snapshot from the early 1970s shows, it was one of the few, if only, British venues whose track was covered by an extension of the stand roofs.

It was also the longest surviving track in Liverpool, managing to stay in business for over 40 years, before closing in October 1973. (Only two other White City tracks lasted longer. Manchester's closed in 1981, followed by the west London flagship three years later.)

The Liverpool site is now occupied by St Margaret's Church of England Junior School.

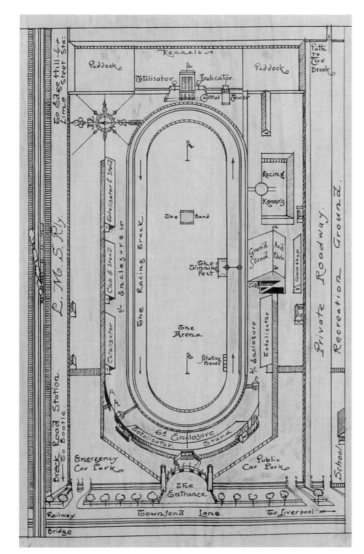

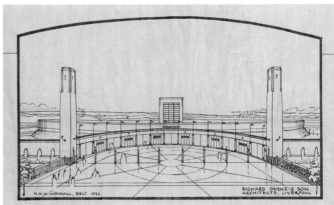

▲ Liverpool's best documented dog track was also, ironically, its least developed. Opened in 1928 (although some reports suggest that racing there may have started the year before), **Breck Park Stadium** was built by the Liverpool Greyhound Club Ltd, next to a goods yard on Townsend Lane.

These oddly contrasting drawings, drawn up in 1932 by the Liverpool architects Richard Owens & Sons, show the company's plans, only partially realised, to develop the stadium further, with a grand Art Deco entrance (*above*) and modern bars (*not shown*).

Note on the rather fancifully drawn main plan (*left*) that the proposal included the addition of a Totalisator Board. This was a mechanically operated display board that showed the state of Tote, or cumulative betting on individual greyhounds (a system invented in Australia in 1913 and first installed in Britain at London's Harringay Stadium in 1930).

Apart from greyhound racing's obvious appeal to gamblers, the use of track lighting, public address systems and Totalisator boards formed key elements of the sport's attraction. Traditional greyhound coursing had taken place on open fields, with the dogs chasing a live hare (as at the Waterloo Cup at Altcar). In addition to accusations of cruelty, coursing was difficult for spectators to follow.

It was in response to this that in 1912 an American, OP Smith, invented the mechanical hare. But more than that, he realised that for it to be seen by larger crowds, an oval circuit, as in athletics, would be ideal. Britain's first modern track opened at Belle Vue in Manchester in July 1926. Thirty more tracks would open within a year, attracting a total of 5.6 million spectators.

By 1928 this figure had more than doubled, to 13.7 million, making greyhound racing second in popularity only to football.

Breck Park was damaged during the war when a passing ammunition train en route to Kirkby was attacked by German bombs.

The stadium finally closed in February 1948 and was converted into a sports ground for the Merseyside Dock Workers Sports & Social Organisation, who have been there ever since. It was renamed Edinburgh Park after the Duke of Edinburgh, who opened the ground in April 1953.

◄ A grainy aerial view of **Breck Park Stadium** in May 1948 (*top*), shows how comparatively basic it remained, although the twin towers proposed in 1932, seen on the right, do appear to have been built.

Also completed was the ultra modern Totalisator Board (*centre*), shown here in July 1932 shortly before being switched on by the Lord Mayor. Note that the track was turfed. Sanded tracks only became standard in post war years.

The quality of kennels provided was another important factor, and Breck Park's, shown here in April 1928 (*lower left*) had just received the approval of the sport's recently created governing body, the National Greyhound Racing Club.

To the rear, backing onto a Corporation Yard (which still exists), can be seen a training area and a further range of kennels.

To recoup costs Breck Park tried to establish itself as a venue for boxing, with two fights staged in September 1928 (*see Chapter Seventeen*). But as this poster shows, by the 1930s there would be racing there six nights a week. With four tracks operating by then, clearly the local racing scene was highly competitive.

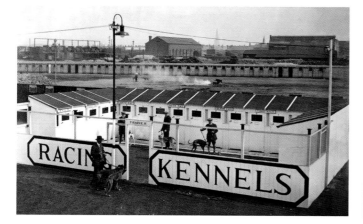

▲ In late Victorian Britain a stadium for the staging of sports and spectaculars was a prerequisite for any ambitious seaside resort. At **New Brighton** in 1896 they went a stage further by constructing their own version of the Eiffel Tower. At 544 feet, it was the tallest structure in the country.

Seen here in 1946 is the base of that tower (right), which alas had to be dismantled after the First World War. The sports ground itself, opened in 1897, became the home of **New Brighton Tower FC**, a club created by the tower's backers and elected to the Football League the year after. But despite the ground's scale and its seaside setting in the shadow of the illustrious Tower Ballroom, the venture lasted only three seasons.

Nor was a second attempt to establish League football there, by a new club called New Brighton, between 1946–51, much better.

The ground did however stage some memorable events; the World Cycling Championships in 1922, and in 1957, an FA Cup tie between New Brighton (then a non-League team) and Torquay, which attracted a record crowd estimated at 16,000. The club used the profits to buy the freehold, but eventually sold up to Wirral Borough Council in 1976. The site of the ballroom (demolished after a fire in 1969) is now open parkland. The site of the sports ground is now housing off Molyneux Drive.

Another lost treasure is New Brighton's 1930s **lido** (*see page 181*), seen on the distant shore.

▲ The Wirral's most historic sports ground is the **Bebington Oval,** Chester Road, originally laid out in 1902 as the showgrounds of the Birkenhead and Wirral Agricultural Society, whose patron at the time was William Lever, co-founder of the nearby Port Sunlight factory and model village.

In 1919 the Lever Brothers took over and renamed the site the Port Sunlight Recreation Ground, and for many years it staged a regular programme of company sports, including football, rugby and hockey. The former trotting track was converted to an athletics track for use by the **Wirral Athletic Club** (formed in 1911 and still active today). The track also staged motor cycle displays as part of Port Sunlight's annual Founders Day celebrations between the wars.

However the ground's main claim to fame is that the 1902 grandstand made an appearance in the 1981 film *Chariots of Fire*, when it doubled as the Stade de Colombes in Paris, venue for the 1924 Olympics.

Another noteable feature of the Oval, as it was renamed in 1966 when taken over by Wirral Borough Council, is its charming, timber-clad entrance lodge (*left*) designed by the architects Grayson & Ould, designers of several buildings at Port Sunlight and many more in Liverpool city centre.

▲ When City Architect Lancelot Keay planned for the village of Kirkby to become a dormitory town for Liverpool in the late 1940s, a 25,000 capacity stadium formed the centrepiece of his masterplan. It did not materialise. Instead, the **Kirkby Sports Centre** was opened by Huyton MP Harold Wilson, in June 1964, on the edge of Kirkby.

The stadium itself, latterly run by Knowsley Borough Council, had an 8,000 capacity, a 532 seat grandstand, a seven lane athletics track and a banked cycle track, which was soon in use by the newly formed **Kirkby Cycling Club**. A later sports hall – typical of late 20th century multi-purpose sports barns in its brutal functionalism – also became home to the **Kirkby Amateur Boxing Club**, of which the light heavyweight champion John Conteh was a member.

In late 2007 the sports centre is to replaced by an £11.3m facility featuring a 25m pool, sports hall, a six lane athletics track and two artificial pitches, on nearby Cherryfield Drive. And although the old centre will not be missed, it was an important part of the new town's formative years all the same.

In May 1895 the residents of Wavertree, a district newly absorbed within the boundaries of Liverpool, received some unexpected news. An anonymous benefactor had purchased the Grange Estate, plus other adjoining plots of land totalling 108 acres, and instead of building houses on it, had donated the site to the Corporation; not for a park, the donor made clear, but for active recreation. For a playground.

An estimated 60,000 people turned up for its inauguration the following September, when they were treated to displays of morris dancing, sports and fireworks.

Rumours abounded that the unnamed donor was the shipping magnate Philip Holt. But these were never confirmed, and ever since the **Wavertree Playground**, as it is officially titled, has been called 'The Mystery.'

As this view from 2005 shows, there need be no mystery as to the importance of the Playground to sports development in the area. **The Wavertree Athletics Centre** is now a hub of excellence for tennis, athletics and soon, for swimming, when the city's first 50m pool (*see page 183*) is completed in the top corner of the park, to the rear of the former Picton Baths (whose pool roofs are visible in the centre right). Whoever the donor was, he, or she, would surely approve.

Local authorities are no different from private stadium operators in that functionality usually takes precedence over aesthetics. But they must also design for robust, daily useage. This metal clad 475 seat grandstand at the **Wavertree Athletics Centre** on Wellington Road dates from 1992 and is used for a range of events, including meetings staged by one of the city's oldest clubs, the **Liverpool Harriers**. Since their formation in 1882, the Harriers have nurtured over 50 international athletes, of whom ten have performed in the Olympics.

▲ While Everton and Liverpool draw support from all parts of Mersyside, and beyond, the region's third highest ranking football club, **Tranmere Rovers**, carry the flag for the Wirral. Formed in 1884, Rovers moved to **Prenton Park** in 1912.

In common with most smaller clubs forced to compete with more powerful neighbours, life has often been precarious for Rovers. In 1939 the Lever Brothers offered to relocate them to the Oval (*see page 101*), but only if they changed their name to Port Sunlight. But with astute land sales, donations from supporters and from Wirral Borough Council when the club faced extinction in 1982, Rovers hung on to become a model club.

Seen here from the Cowshed Stand (which affectionately recalls a previous terrace cover on the site), the Main Stand (right) dates from 1968, while the three other stands were all built in 1994, in response to the Taylor Report, at a cut price £3.1 million. The tallest is the Kop Stand, at the far end (*also shown right*). This variation of height and depth at least helps to add some character to what is otherwise a functional, though tidy ground, holding 16,567.

◀ Tucked behind College Road and the semi-detached houses of Rossett Road, Crosby, is **Rossett Park**, now called the Arriva Stadium, home of Liverpool's most senior non-League football club, **Marine FC**, since 1903.

Marine have unusual origins. They were formed in 1894 at the Marine pub on South Road (still extant), by a group of professional middle class men, described in one source as being mainly connected with banking, accountancy, teaching and the civil service; professions normally associated with rugby union. Even as late as the 1950s, by which time they were playing in the semi-professional Lancashire Combination, Marine would draft in the occasional Oxbridge student enjoying his university vacation.

Despite once holding a record estimated crowd of 8,000, for an FA Cup tie in 1920, Rossett Park is so compact that on its northern side (seen left) there is room only for dug-outs, not for spectators. This constraint means that while the club now plays in the Unibond Northern Premier League, the ground would not conform with the standards required by the next level of non-League football.

Nevertheless its current capacity of 3,185 is more than enough to cope with Marine's average gates of 200-400.

So tight is the Rossett Park site that its main stand – the 400 seat Millennium Stand (*left*), built in 1999 to replace its 1922 predecessor (*above*) – is behind the goal. A narrow covered terrace lines the southern side, with a larger terrace at the opposite end.

The Moor Lane ground of Liverpool Ramblers, in Thornton – their home since 1934 – is no more than a pitch with a pavilion. But the club is very much part of the city's sporting heritage. Formed in 1882 after a match at Stanley Park involving locally-based Eton and Harrow schoolboys, the Ramblers adopted the orange and blue colours of one of the Eton College houses, and beat Everton 5-0 in their first season. Now, only they and Everton survive of the original members of the Liverpool County FA. Not only that but to this day the Ramblers maintain their amateur status, playing mostly against public schools such as Shrewsbury, Malvern and Repton.

▲ Taken in 1978, this rare colour view of **Holly Park**, Garston, home of **South Liverpool** from 1935–90, provides a glimpse of how tough the latter years of the 20th century were for non-League clubs.

And yet in their heyday, South Liverpool – successors to a club of the same name that played in Dingle until 1919 – attracted healthy crowds and made seven applications to join the League. Their stand and terrace cover were built by the Garston steelwork engineers, Francis Morton & Co, who also supplied several major grounds, Goodison Park included.

Most famously, inspired by a tour to the Continent after the war, South Liverpool became the first British football club, at any level, to install permanent, albeit rudimentary floodlights. Mounted on eight pylons (not those shown here), the lights were first used during a match against a visiting Nigerian XI (some of whose players

played in heavily bound feet, rather than boots), on 28 September 1949. This, it should be stressed, was two years before the Football Association had sanctioned any competitive games under lights.

Watched by a record gate of 13,007, this historic match was broadcast live to Nigeria on the BBC World Service, with Kenneth Wolstenholme commentating.

But South Liverpool would soon be struggling. An arson attack gutted the stand in 1955. Gates fell to below 200, and in 1990, after another major fire, the club finally departed. (They now play parks football.) For the next decade the rotting Holly Park attracted ghoulish interest from passing fans, until it was redeveloped as the South Parkway rail and bus interchange.

◄ Stricter ground standards and development pressure on land have forced a number of Merseyside's small football clubs to relocate over the last decade, thereby ending years of tradition and habit for spectators and players alike.

Formby FC, known as the Squirrels, were based from 1920–2002 at the slightly ramshackle but homely **Brows Lane** (*top left*), where the record gate was 2,500 for a Cup tie v. Oldham in 1973. They now play a short distance away at a pristine but exposed ground on Altcar Lane.

From 1977–99 **Bucks Park**, on Northern Perimeter Road, Netherton (*centre left*), was home to **Bootle FC**, who had formed in 1953 at Edinburgh Park, site of the former Breck Park Stadium (*see page 98*). In 2006, after seven years of groundsharing, including a spell at the Kirkby Sport Centre (*page 102*) the club opened the New Bucks Park, on Vestey Road.

Football has been played at **Kirklands**, on St Peter's Road, Rock Ferry (*lower left*), less than a mile north of the Bebington Oval, since 1922. **Cammell Laird FC**, the resident club, trace their origins to 1889 when a team from the giant Laird Brothers shipyard, later Cammell Laird, formed in Birkenhead Park (*see page 46*). Ties with the shipbuilders remained strong, but now it is the football club which carries on the name, the parent company having left Birkenhead in the 1990s.

Not so resilient was **Kirkby Town**, a club formed to represent the new town of Kirkby in 1962. Had the Kirkby Sports Centre been more suited to football they might have stayed there longer than one season. Instead, they moved to an even larger, and desperately bleak, council-built stadium on **Simonswood Lane**, Northwood, in 1964, where a 432 seat stand (*above*) was built, along with earth banking reckoned optimistically to hold 10,000 standing spectators.

This original Kirkby club was replaced by another of the same name in 1984, which in 1988 was renamed Knowsley United and relocated to Alt Park, former ground of Huyton RLFC, where they limped on until 1997. The Simonswood Lane site, meanwhile, is now home to a David Lloyd sports centre and Liverpool FC's Academy.

▲ Based, despite their name, on **St Anthony's Road**, Blundellsands, **Waterloo Rugby Club** were formed in 1882 by ex-pupils of Merchant Taylors' School. They first played on the Serpentine, Blundellsands, then from 1906 at Haig Road, Waterloo, the former ground of the Northern Cricket Club (*see page 118*).

The current ground, originally called the Memorial Ground – to honour the 51 club members killed during the First World War – opened in March 1921.

Just to prepare the new ground required an immense effort

Members raised £10,000, worked all hours to level what had been a nine hole golf course, and helped to build the core of the current pavilion, seen here.

Perhaps for this reason, to this day the pavilion is one of the best preserved in senior rugby; its open fire, wood panelled dressing rooms (*right*), and displays of memorabilia providing a glowing example of the ethos of suburban rugby before the advent of professionalism in 1998.

◀ Players from **Waterloo** emerge from the 1920s pavilion in their familiar colours of myrtle green, white and scarlet, for a National League One match in 2006.

In common with many a rugby club at their level (one division below the Premiership), Waterloo have worked hard to adapt to the new era of professionalism, and were indeed saved by the sale of their second pitch in 2001. This injection of funds also allowed them to replace their timber stand with a 499 seat, concrete and steel structure (*below left*), opened in 2003 on the ground's north side. (The houses built on the former second team pitch can be seen behind this stand.)

In Waterloo's heyday between the war crowds of up to 10,000 would fill St Anthony's Road. Nowadays gates of 600–2,000 are more typical, with the capacity limited to 6,000.

But Waterloo is more than a spectator venue. In a residential area well served by independent, rugby playing schools, Waterloo forms a genuine hub of community activity. The club runs four senior teams, a women's team, a Colts team, and runs weekly sessions for under-16s. Its bars and lounges are also regularly hired for functions. So although financial survival remains an ever present challenge, here is club sport in its absolute essence.

▲ High quality sports architecture from the 1960s is surprisingly rare in Britain, much of it in the public sector having fallen into disrepair (and disrepute). But in the private sector, the **University of Liverpool** clubhouse and pavilion at the **Geoffrey Hughes Memorial Ground** on Mather Avenue, Allerton, is quite outstanding, and even a classic of its type.

The ground itself was laid out on land once attached to Wyncote House – of which only a delightful copse and pond now survive – and donated to the University by the shipowner T Harrison Hughes, in memory of his brother, Geoffrey, who was killed in action at Arras in August 1918. An earlier pavilion by the Mather Avenue gate *(shown opposite)* was built in 1922.

The modern buildings, built at a cost of £101,000 and completed in October 1962, were designed by Gerald Beech, a lecturer in architecture at the University, in association with Geoffrey Holland.

Such was its measured detail and carefully planned disposition, that the complex won a Class One Award from the Civic Trust in 1963 and is now listed Grade II.

▶ Described in the *Architects' Journal* of March 1963 as 'a building on which rather more than the usual amount of thought and imagination has been spent,' the clubhouse and pavilion at the **Geoffrey Hughes Memorial Ground** is that rare phenomenon; a 1960s design that not only retains its original spark and sense of modernism, but has also, thankfully, been little altered.

Every aspect of the design evokes the period, most notably its strong linear emphasis, glazed curtain walls, timber handrails and white rendered facing walls, set off by the black horizontals of the concrete floor and roof slabs.

In plan the range of buildings also has exceptional visual appeal.

There are four elements. The largest is the two storey changing room block, which backs onto the tree-lined pond and is clad at first floor level in brick, with narrow ceiling level windows and a rectangular, raised skylight which houses the ventilation plant.

This block is linked by a two-level walkway to the main, four storey clubhouse, square in plan, whose glazed walls offer views from two bar and social areas, to both

sides of the sports ground. The top floor serves as a viewing balcony.

From here the two-level walkway continues, linking to a two storey pavilion with another viewing balcony, originally designed to serve the cricket pitch on the north side, and store rooms below.

The final element is a long promenade, continuing the axis of the walkways and stretching out to the far end of the athletics track. Uncovered and finished in bare concrete, this offers views of both the track to the south, and the rugby and cricket pitches to the north, and also subtly bridges the fall in level between the two sides.

Admittedly this promenade, and certain other elements, have worn less well than others. Nor do the buildings meet all the demands of modern sport. A section of the grounds has also come under pressure from the neighbouring supermarket, which adjoins two synthetic pitches added on the Mather Avenue side in the 1990s.

But overall the buildings' quality is such that their conservation must rate of the highest importance, in both a local and national context, and in terms of both sport and of post war architecture generally.

Chapter Eleven

Cricket

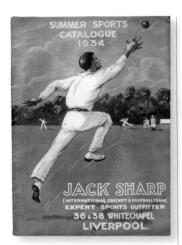

Before opening a sports outfitters, Jack Sharp (1878–1938) was one of Britain's greatest all-rounders. He won the County Championship with Lancashire in 1904 and a Cup Final medal with Everton two years later. He also represented England at both cricket and football. But while Sharp and his business rival Frank Sugg (*see page 4*) catered for cricketers with means, many a local boy learnt his craft on the streets, as seen (*right*) in the early 20th century.

Football may dominate the sporting agenda in modern day Liverpool, but the first team sport to have been played in the region was cricket.

Indeed Merseyside may claim to have two of the oldest cricket pavilions still in use anywhere in Britain: at Birkenhead Park, dating from c.1849 (*see page 48*), and, in first class cricket, at Aigburth, dating from 1881 (*page 114*).

We have already noted that the earliest record of cricket in Liverpool was on the grounds of the Mersey Bowmen, formed in 1781 in Cazneau Street. At that time the game was mainly confined to the south of England.

That it spread to Liverpool is credited to Banastre Tarleton. Born into a family enriched by the sugar trade, Tarleton – who gained a reputation as a ruthless colonel in the American War of Independence and who, as a Liverpool MP, lobbied hard against the abolition of slavery – had been present at the fashionable Star and Garter Inn, Pall Mall, in 1787, when the Marylebone Cricket Club was formed.

On Mersey's banks a town there lies,
Where may be found immense supplies,
Of youths both young and active:
Who like their business passing well,
And yet, in truth historians tell,
Find pleasure more attractive.

Lines on the formation of the
Liverpool Cricket Club
Liverpool Mercury 18 October 1811

By 1807 Liverpool's cricketers – like Tarleton, all members of the merchant classes – had formed the Mosslake Fields Cricket Society. As the name suggests, Mosslake Fields was then open, boggy ground, on the outskirts of the town, bordering William Roscoe's Botanical Gardens (opened on Myrtle Street in 1802), and extending from what is now Abercromby Square to Crown Street and Smithdown Lane.

According to one account the players used a cow house as a pavilion and drank milk to refresh themselves.

The Society's rules indicate clearly that this was an elite club.

To enrol cost seven shillings, and members were expected to gather at Mosslake Fields during the season at no later than 6am every Monday, Wednesday and Friday. Non-attendance or lateness was subject to a system of fines, and could only be excused by sickness or by business commitments.

Although no documentary evidence exists, it is generally accepted that the Mosslake Society evolved into the Liverpool Cricket Club, which was formally established in 1811 and played on the same ground.

Or at least it did for its first eight years. The march of the bricks and mortar brigade would force the Liverpool club to move four times over the next 70 years, each time a little further from the town's expanding borders.

In 1820, following the development of Abercromby Square, the club moved a short distance to Rectors Field (on what is now Falkner Street). It was here that the first matches involving outside opposition were played, against clubs representing Cheshire and Manchester.

By this time other local teams were forming. For example in 1817 the *Liverpool Mercury* reported on matches between Union and North Liverpool, while Liverpool CC also played a club called North Shore at their ground near the Waterloo Hotel. This was followed in the 1820s by teams such as Phoenix, Toxteth and Britannia.

Meanwhile in 1829, housing developments forced Liverpool CC to move again, to the then rural area of Edge Hill, where they laid out a ground on Wavertree Road and set up headquarters in the Half-way House Inn, where there were tea gardens and a skittle alley.

Again, this proved only a short term solution. After the opening of the Manchester to Liverpool railway in 1830, and, just south of their ground, of Edge Hill Station six years later, Liverpool CC found themselves homeless in 1845.

Their fourth ground lay west of the new station and was opened in May 1847. It was here that Liverpool staged its inaugural first class match, Lancashire v. Surrey, in August 1866.

Cricket was now the most popular sport in Britain, no longer the preserve of the leisured classes. Before 1850 no more than 20 clubs existed in Liverpool. By 1867, as more working men attained the right to Saturday half-holidays, this figure had tripled.

Even so, as described in earlier chapters, there was still a shortage of pitches. Apart from Liverpool's Edge Hill ground, the only other bespoke ground close to the town centre was in Princes Park, and that was barred from public use. This shortage was partly remedied by the opening of Wavertree Park, almost directly opposite Edge Hill, in 1856. But demand soon outstripped supply. As a letter to

the *Liverpool Mercury* of July 1863 made clear, Wavertree Park 'is a great boon to those within easy walking distance of it, but to me and hundreds besides, at the north end of the town, it is only a place to think of, and to envy those who are fortunately situated.

'I have been, with several others, at the expense of procuring the requisites for the game of cricket, flattering ourselves that there would be room for us in Wavertree Park; but we were only doomed to disappoint, for by the time we can reach the park in the evening every place is already taken up, and it is only at the risk of getting crippled that you can play there... We have heard now for a considerable time of a contemplated park in the north end, but I am afraid, as also are many others, that this is all talk.'

Stanley Park's opening in 1870 partially answered this demand in the north of the town. But for Liverpool CC the continuing development of Edge Hill Station and a gas works rendered them homeless again in 1877, and after four years playing at other grounds (Croxteth Hall, Childwall, Dingle and Birkenhead Park), in 1881 the club finally settled at Aigburth, far from the reach of developers.

Liverpool was now a major centre of Lancashire club cricket, even if it failed to attract more than a handful of county matches each season from its more powerful rival at Old Trafford, Manchester.

Liverpool clubs also struck rigidly to their amateur ethos, declining to compete for cups or trophies, despite the fact that they played each other on a regular basis. However, in 1892 Liverpool newspapers began to treat their games as if they were indeed part of an organised league. The

newspapers named this league the Liverpool Competition.

Its eleven *de facto* members were Liverpool, Birkenhead Park, Bootle, Formby, Huyton, New Brighton, Northern, Ormskirk, Oxton, Rock Ferry and Sefton.

Over the years the composition of this grouping would change. Neston joined in 1908. Hightown and Southport & Birkdale entered in 1919, while Wallasey took the place of Rock Ferry. Broughton Hall were invited to join in 1923, as were Preston in 1947, later replaced by St Helen's Rec in 1953.

Yet only in 1949 would the organisers concede that the Liverpool Competition was in effect a league. Fixtures became standardised and the published league table was finally acknowledged as being official.

A further break with tradition followed in 1999 when the 24 members split into two divisions, and in the process introduced promotion and relegation for the first time in almost two centuries of local cricket.

But make no mistake. For all its modern sponsorship deals and status as one of English cricket's designated Premier Leagues, the Liverpool Competition is steeped in tradition. Not all its clubs possess grounds or pavilions of historic interest. Attendances at games have plummeted since the 1950s, making survival a constant challenge. But of the Competition's 28 member clubs in 2007, no fewer than 18 can trace their origins back to before 1872; that is, before the establishment of Association football in Liverpool.

The proverbial sound of leather on willow is as much a part of Britain's urban heritage as it is of the village greens of popular imagination.

When Liverpool's Edge Hill ground from 1847–77 was redeveloped, five streets on the site were named after Australian cricketers. Only two would survive subsequent expansion of the railway. Charles Bannerman, though born in London, was the first player ever to score a test century, in 1877. Sydney-born Fred 'The Demon' Spofforth, after whom both a street and pub (*below*) were named, was the most feared bowler of his generation. He later settled in London and became a successful tea merchant.

▲ Had the **Aigburth** ground of **Liverpool Cricket Club** become a full-fledged county ground, as is Old Trafford, no doubt it would have lost many of its original features, such as this fine, if rusting turnstile (sadly with no markings to identify its manufacturer).

Equally, the pavilion would not have survived so intact. Opened in 1881 and designed by Thomas Harnett Harrison, it is not only one of the most substantial club pavilions in Britain, but also the oldest at any first class venue; older, for example, than Trent Bridge (1886) and Lord's (1890).

A measure of Liverpool CC's wealth is that it spent £2,000 to purchase the site, plus £21,000 on the pavilion and ground layout, carried out by Cubitts, one of the leading contractors of the day.

▲ Looking out over the Mersey at the point where the river widens and the suburbs stretch southwards towards Garston and Speke, **Aigburth** has always been more than a cricket ground.

Laid out on 20 acres, divided almost in half by a commuter railway line running north to south, the lower area closest to the river features two rugby pitches. **Liverpool Rugby Club** played on these from 1889–1963 (see page 13), while additional rugby pitches beyond these were sold for housing in the 1990s to help the club's finances.

The upper ground is dominated by the cricket pitch, which, with a square for 24 wickets, is second in size only to the Oval in London.

On each side of the pitch are two **bowling greens**, one of which can be seen above, beyond the gate. The other, reserved for ladies on the far side of the main pavilion, is overlooked by the former Ladies Pavilion, built c.1900 and now leased out as a children's nursery.

Other facilities include three grass **hockey** pitches, five **squash** courts and nine **tennis** courts (six grass). From 1882–1928 Aigburth alternated with the Northern Tennis Club in Manchester as the venue for the annual **Northern Tournament**, an event which first brought local protegé Lottie Dod to the public's attention.

Aigburth also has a place in **football** history. In February 1883, a year before Everton moved to Anfield, the ground staged the city's first ever international, England v. Ireland, watched by 2,500 but with no local players selected.

Aigburth was also once a regular venue for the game of **quoits**, now played only once every two years against the Childwall Quoiting Club (see page 16).

▲ In cricketing parlance **Aigburth** is ranked as 'an out ground' – that is, in common with Blackpool, but formerly also with Lytham and Southport & Birkdale, it stages only one or two first class Lancashire matches per season (down from three until the 1960s). Frustrating though this is for local cricket lovers, the result is that the pavilion remains remarkably unaltered.

Conversely, the lack of income from major games – since Liverpool CC's club matches seldom draw the crowds they used to – places tremendous pressure on the club to maintain what is a substantial structure with a warren of rooms, corridors and bars.

At the heart of the club are two lounges, both named after former players who won Victoria Crosses during the First World War: Dr Noel Chevasse, a former Olympic runner and one of only three British soldiers to have won the Victoria Cross twice, and Eric Dougall.

Aigburth today holds a maximum of 5,000 spectators, though this has rarely been tested in modern times. The ground's all time record was 7,633, for the visit of the West Indies in 1984.

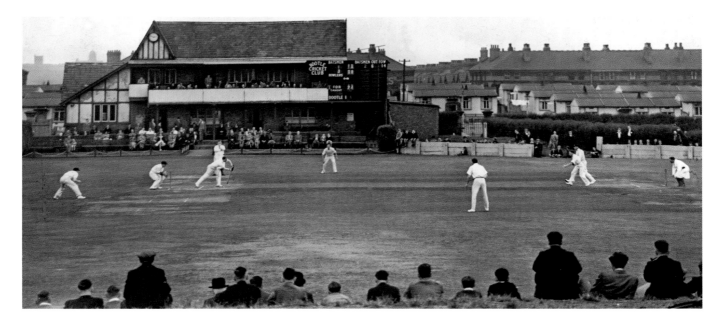

▲ Founded in 1833, **Bootle** is the city's second oldest cricket club and, since 1999, the most successful one in the Liverpool Competition's Premier League.

Bootle moved to their current ground (seen here from **Hawthorne Road** in 1950) in 1884, raising £600 for the pavilion by staging a bazaar at Bootle Town Hall. The new ground occupied one of four quadrants of open space, the other three of which were landscaped to form South Park. To the north lies Balliol Road, site of Bootle Baths, opened in 1888 (see page 174).

Bootle at this time still retained a strong, separate identity from its southern neighbour, Liverpool. The town's population had rocketed, resulting in the cricket club's former ground in Irlam Road being sold as land values increased. (A disused fire station now occupies the site).

In 1868 Irlam Road staged two matches against the first Australian cricketers to visit Britain, a team

of 'aboriginals', who not only beat Bootle but put on displays of mock battles, backwards running and cricket ball dodging. One spectator was injured by a stray boomerang.

Had fate decreed otherwise, Hawthorne Road might have become a major venue. In its early years it was shared by **Bootle FC** (formed 1878), who played on a pitch sited on what is now housing on Wadham Road (to the left of

the pavilion seen above). For over a decade Bootle were Everton's main rivals, with one encounter, on Boxing Day 1889, drawing an estimated 20,000 to the ground. Bootle even competed in the Second Division in 1892–93.

But they could not sustain the effort and after they disbanded in August 1893, the way was clear for the newly formed Liverpool to become the city's second club.

Ironically, Hawthorne Road would host the first ever derby match between Everton and Liverpool, in the final of the Liverpool Senior Cup (won 1–0 by the Reds and watched by 10,000), on 22 April 1893.

Had the pavilion survived, today it would be the oldest structure ever to have hosted League football. Instead, in 2002 it was demolished, and a new pavilion (below) built on Wadham Road.

▲ As these three examples demonstrate, British cricketers have always favoured a conservative, vernacular style for their pavilions.

Above is the pavilion of **Huyton Cricket Club**, on Huyton Lane, founder members, as were Bootle, of the Liverpool Competition.

The club itself was formed in 1860, under the chairmanship of Alexander Eccles, a cotton broker who typified the ethos of Victorian sporting patrons. Its pavilion dates from 1875, and although enlarged since, its core is one of the oldest surviving structures in cricket.

Behind the pavilion is a bowling green. It is common for cricket clubs to feature greens, partly to ensure that older members who can no longer keep their place in the team may extend their sporting life without moving to another club.

In a similar vein but in a rather more affluent area, another founder member of the Liverpool Competition is **Formby Cricket Club**, established in 1865.

Since building this well tended pavilion in the early 20th century (*above right*), Formby have expanded their activities to include

squash, with an all-weather hockey pitch now occupying a corner of the site. Adjoining the cricket pitch to the west is the Formby Lawn Tennis Club, while to the north is the Freshfield Bowling Club.

As may be noted, the most common pavilion feature of all is the rooftop gable.

At the pavilion of **Merchant Taylors' School**, Crosby (*right*), opened in 1912, this gable has been heightened to accommodate a scoreboard, presented in memory of Vernon Robinson, a former captain of rugby and cricket, killed in 1942 while serving as a pilot.

There is an intriguing tale concerning another former rugby playing pupil at Merchant Taylors'.

Arthur Witty, the son of a prominent shipping agent based in Spain, was one of the earliest members of the newly formed FC Barcelona in 1899, helping the club both as a player and by importing balls, whistles plus, of course, Brodie patented goal nets.

One theory has it that the reason why Barcelona adopted blue and red as their colours was because those had also been the colours of

Merchant Taylors' rugby XV during Witty's time there. A cap from the period has been traced to back this up, but alas it would seem that other explanations for Barca's choice of colours bear more weight.

Meanwhile the school has also supplied many a fine player to the neighbouring Waterloo Rugby Club (*see page 108*) and to the Northern Cricket Club (*next page*).

▶ April 13 1907, and members of the **Northern Cricket Club** pose with their wives at the newly opened **Moor Park** ground, Crosby.

Fifty years later, to the day, the scene was repeated (*below right*), as, hopefully, will be the case on April 13 2007 (as this book went to press).

The attire may change. The number of women involved has certainly increased. But the social function of the Northern remains unaltered, with the pavilion forming the very core of the club's activities.

Founder members of the Liverpool Competition, Northern formed in 1859, at a ground on Rawson Road, Seaforth, then a small seaside town that was attracting an ever growing number of middle class residents.

In addition to cricket, Rawson Road catered for bowls and for archery, which was then the only sport deemed suitable for women. But even in the suburbs land was at a premium, and so in 1879 the club moved to new grounds in Waterloo, where, as was the fashion, tennis superceded archery.

Unbeknown to the club these grounds were sold to a property developer in 1906, who demanded such a high rent that Northern took the plunge and finally purchased land of their own, at Moor Park.

No wonder they posed with such pride.

▲ A century later and the pavilion may have lost its balcony and had its verandah enclosed, but of all the clubs in the Liverpool Competition, **Northern** might claim to be in the finest fettle. Partly this is a result of a merger with Waterloo Cricket Club in the 1970s and the subsequent sale of Waterloo's ground, which enabled Northern to purchase nine extra acres of farmland adjoining **Moor Park** (viewed above in 2005).

Northern now has at its disposal two bowling greens, five squash courts, a synthetic hockey pitch, and three cricket pitches.

With some 1,000 members overall, this allows the club to field no fewer than 39 teams in the four different sports catered for, from under-11s to veterans.

Compared with their inner city counterparts, it is true that Northern occupy an idyllic location. But to adapt a phrase, 'it is just not cricket', or at least, not cricket alone, that keeps Northern, or any of the clubs in this chapter going, well into their second century of existence. Dedication and voluntary effort, in 2007 as much as in 1907, still rank highest of all.

Chapter Twelve

Bowls

The St Anne Street firm of EA Clare Ltd manufactures accessories for bowls as well as billiards (*see Chapter Seven*). Here a workman finishes off a bowl made from synthetic, or composite materials, marketed under the trade name Drake's Pride (which Clare took over from an older Liverpool manufacturer called Darlington's, established in 1820). Clare is now one of only three companies in the world making licensed bowls, the others being in Glasgow and Melbourne.

Bowls is Britain's longest established sport and may even be described in historical terms as our national game. There are greens in Southampton and Chesterfield that claim to have been established in the 13th century, and many more that date from the 16th century onwards.

Everyone knows the tale of Sir Francis Drake, bowling as the Armada approached in 1588. But Drake was not alone. Bowling was popular at every level of society, despite a series of banning orders which sought to dissuade the lower orders from playing, when they should have been practising archery. (The gentry were of course not prevented, as long they bowled within their own properties.)

There are various early references to bowls in Liverpool.

As noted in Chapter One, a bye-law adopted by the Common Council in 1541 declared that 'noe servaunte nor apprentice playe at cardes, dice bowlis and other unlawful games invented or to be inventyd'. But as the Liverpool Town Books reveal, this edict appears to have had little effect, as a constant stream of people were hauled before the Portmoot, either for playing bowls or for gambling.

However, from the 18th century onwards a more liberal attitude, and a growing population resulted in a number of bowling greens appearing openly in the town.

The earliest recorded green appears on WS Sherwood's map of 1725, next to an alms house on Hope Street, close to Duke Street. By 1785, according to Eye's town plan, there were four more greens. Two were on the river front, approximately where Vulcan Street and Oil Street are now sited. Two others were on Mount Pleasant; one by Clarence Street (perhaps explaining the presence of Green Lane in that area), the other on the corner of Hope Street, where the Everyman Theatre now stands.

This latter green stood next to the Bowling Green Tavern, birthplace in 1753 of William Roscoe, the prominent politician, art collector and botanist.

More greens existed on the town approaches. By 1835 there was a green attached to the Derby Arms, on Irlam Road, close to the Coffee House Bridge over the Leeds and Liverpool Canal. (St Mary's C of E school now occupies the site.)

There were also greens at the Strawberry Gardens on Boundary Lane and at the Zoological Gardens on West Derby Road (where the Boaler Street industrial estate now stands). Bowling, by the mid 19th century, was not only respectable but profitable also.

As the pace of urbanisation increased, so too did the provision of greens. Indeed they were ideally suited in shape and scale to the emerging street pattern. Bowls took up less room than cricket, required little equipment, and if it failed to pay its way the green was easily sold for housing.

Between 1870 and 1914 greens proliferated in Liverpool: attached to pubs (such as the Sandon Hotel, by Anfield, and at Cabbage Hall on Breck Road); attached to clubs (such as Aigburth People's Hall, and the Woolton Village Club), and as part of private member clubs, several of which are featured in this chapter.

The Edwardian period then saw the laying out of bowling greens

in almost every public park, while the Liverpool Shipping League, formed in 1912, grew to have 28 affiliated teams, representing such companies as Furness & Withy, Lamport & Holt, and Coastlines.

Since the Second World War, the popularity of bowls has declined,. and numerous greens have been been lost. The one at Cabbage Hall was one of the most recent,

converted, as is common, into a beer garden. In one district where there were 14 greens in 1890, by 2006 only six survived. Meanwhile several park greens have been returned to nature as maintenance and security costs have risen and demand fallen. The Shipping League disbanded in 2006.

Yet the indicators are not all gloomy. The region still has

some 300 bowling clubs of one sort or another, with a combined membership of at least 10,000 individuals. Indoor clubs are in particular more popular than ever, suggesting that bowls, despite its reputation as 'old men's marbles', is in fact adapting well to modern demands, and is still very much a part of the local sporting scene on Merseyside.

Bowling on Great George Square between the wars, with not a car in sight and the Anglican cathedral still in mid-construction (it was not finished until 1978). The square is one of the few green spaces in the city centre to have survived two centuries of development, not to mention heavy bombing during the war. It is still an open space, now part of the Chinese quarter.

No one is certain how the Olympic Bowling Club on Park Vale Road, Orrell Park, got its name. But the most feasible explanation is that in 1892, the year of the club's foundation, the Liverpool Gymnasium staged an Olympic Festival at its headquarters on Myrtle Street, a revival of the earlier series of festivals held in Liverpool during the 1860s (*see page 12*). It is possible that some of the founder members were also active in the Gymnasium. But it could also be that the city was undergoing a brief bout of Olympic fever, at a time when the modern games were still four years from being revived in Athens.

▲ You could live your entire life in the Orrell Park district of Liverpool without ever knowing that the **Olympic Bowling Club** existed. And the same is true of many of the city's bowling clubs. Tucked away down back streets or hidden behind walls and hedges, bowling greens are often discreet to the point of invisibility. The only outward sign of the Olympic's presence is a single gate at the end of a cul-de-sac.

Otherwise the club is hemmed in by terraced housing and by a Roman Catholic church.

As is also true of many a bowling club, its clubhouse is of modest proportions, with a mixture of domestic styles accrued over the years. Seen here on the occasion of the Closing of the Green match in 2006, the original 1892 section can be seen on the left, built, it

is thought, by one of the founder members, Thomas Spencer, a local builder and brickmaker.

On the right is a later 20th century extension, housing a billiard room and function suite.

In common with all bowling clubs on Merseyside, the Olympic is a crown green club. That is, its green rises slightly in the centre and games are played in any direction (as opposed to flat green bowling, which predominates south of Birmingham and in Scotland, and is played in strictly divided rinks). It may also be noted that crown green players dress as they please, whereas flat green bowlers always conform to a mainly white dress code.

But these less rigid customs should not be equated with a casual attitude.

The Olympic is a strict members club. It was formed by local tradesmen and professional men with a capital of 600 one pound shares, with a constitution which makes it impossible for any one individual to gain a majority.

Until 1960 matches were held only amongst the members, although as a concession members could invite one guest to the annual hot-pot dinner. Since then, matches against outside opposition have been permitted, but the club still refuses to play in a league.

Another quirk was that before 1960 the Olympic would not serve beer in pint glasses. When this ruling was challenged by one particular member he was told politely but firmly by the steward that the Labour Club was further along the road.

OLYMPIC
BOWLING CLUB
❋ Founded·1892. ❋

YEAR	PRESIDENT	YEAR	PRESIDENT
1892	WILLIAM ADAMS	1940	DAN DAVIES
1893	FRED⁵ W.WHEATLEY	1941	P.C.THOMPSON
1894	FRED⁵ W.WHEATLEY	1942	RICHARD SPENCER
1895	FRED⁵ W.WHEATLEY	1943	RICHARD SPENCER
1896	CHA⁵ H.C.SKAFTE	1944	RICHARD SPENCER
1897	THOMAS B.MARSDEN	1945	DAN DAVIES
1898	THOMAS B.MARSDEN	1946	P.C.THOMPSON
1899	ROB⁵ W.BYRNES	1947	F.MOLYNEUX
1900	ROB⁵ W.BYRNES	1948	JOHN LAWSON
1901	JAMES Y.PATTERSON	1949	COLIN SMITH
1902	ALBERT GREAVES	1950	W.R.MARSH
1903	ARCH⁵ BROWN	1951	COLIN SMITH
1904	ARCH⁵ BROWN	1952	RICHARD SPENCER
1905	ARCH⁵ BROWN	1953	P.C.THOMPSON
1906	T.EATON JONES	1954	JOHN T.HUGHES
1907	GEORGE A.CASSADY	1955	JOHN T.HUGHES
1908	THOMAS SPENCER	1956	LESLIE A.MOORE
1909	JOHN S.THOMPSON	1957	STANLEY J.ROCKLIFF
1910	ANGUS HOLDEN	1957	RICHARD D.ROBERTS
1911	WILLIAM LOCKIER	1958	JOHN T.HUGHES
1912	BEN⁵ KELLY	1959	S.Y.BARBER
1913	T.EATON JONES	1960	ROBERT DRAPER

▲ These delightful stained glass panels on the entrance doors of the **Olympic Bowling Club** almost certainly date from the club's creation in 1892, and tell us much about the ethos of the founding members. Here was a group of local trademen aspiring to the ambience of a gentlemen's club, and at the same time emphasising that their game, unlike the newly popular sports of football and lawn tennis, was rooted in centuries of history and tradition.

Some of these traditions clung on perhaps too long. For example it was only in 1963 that members voted to allow women to enter the club, and even then this concession was limited to Sunday nights. In 1980 they voted again to extend the concession to Saturday nights.

Another change in the rules also now allows the club to host mixed doubles matches.

Rather more endearing is the tradition by which a bowls match is referred to as a 'main'. Hence the first match of the season will be called 'The Opening of the Green Main', or there might also be a 'President's Main'.

An archaic word, originally applied to cockfights (see page 10), 'main' has for some reason survived in the Merseyside region, but seemingly nowhere else within the world of bowling.

▲ Members of the **Richmond Bowling Club** on Richmond Park (just north of Newsham Park), pose in 1903 with their wives – every one of them wearing a bonnet – and children, to celebrate the tenth anniversary of the club's inauguration. The club, which still thrives, was formed after bowlers fell out with their landlords at the Cabbage Hall pub in 1892 (the same year as the dispute at nearby Anfield, involving Everton football club). Richmond's first president was a Mr Affleck, known locally as the 'genial bookie'.

The club's apparent willingness to involve women was in contrast to the **Liverpool Bowling Club** (*right*), set up in 1902 on Church Road, Wavertree, by six merchants. They issued 2,000 shares at one pound each, but after spending £1,588 to buy the plot, £750 on the pavilion (still extant), and £284

on the green, had to take out a mortgage to meet the excess.

Membership, costing one guinea, was restricted to 100 individuals.

'The promoters of the Liverpool Bowling Club are to be heartily congratulated upon the result of their labours,' gushed one local reporter. 'They have succeeded in securing a splendid piece of land in one of the most delightful avenues within the city boundaries... They have had the common sense to keep the fine old trees which have stood for a century or more and which will afford a comforting shade... The pavilion is a pretty and spacious structure... baskets of flowers hang in front, and the broad platform has ample chair accommodation for non players and lady friends.'

In the bowl house, 'two new full-sized billiard tables, with the necessary appointments, occupy

one half, while the other portion is allotted to card tables and other amusements, a piano being a prominent feature...'

It was also noted that players at the early 'mains' wore galoshes to protect the newly laid turf, and that the club was already so popular

that four 'hands' were employed 'to look after affairs'.

Over a century later and ladies are now admitted as playing members to the club, while the original billiard tables (Ashcrofts, naturally), are said to be still in fine fettle.

▲ Funded by a local businessman, socialite and big game hunter, William Dodge James in 1885, **Woolton Village Club**, on Allerton Road (*top left*), was set up as a place where, according to James, men could meet 'without any distinctions of creed, social standing or political parties'. He hardly needed to add that women were, of course, excluded.

Although numerous wealthy villagers also subscribed, the main membership was agricultural workers, and later also workers from the local quarry. The original bowling green and billiards room are still in regular use, and since 2000 the club has been owned and run by its members.

Calderstones Ladies BC (*above*) are a more casual group of bowlers,

based in Calderstones Park, where they play on one of the 18 greens still maintained by the Council's Parks and Environment service.

West Derby BC, who formed in 1884, moved to their current home, a converted house and orchard on Haymans Green, in 1941. Their storeroom (*top right*), once the orchard's produce shed, is known as Number Ten, after the

number on the second-hand door that was fitted in the 1980s.

Finally an example of one of the new generation of artificial greens, at the **Elaine Norris Sports Centre** Vauxhall Road (*above*), designed by the Halsall Lloyd Partnership and opened in 1998. Such greens are disliked by traditionalists, but have the advantage of low maintenance costs and all year availability.

Chapter Thirteen

Baseball

Kirkdale-born Louis Page captains the English baseball team at the Police Athletics Ground, Fairfield, in the 1920s. Better known as a winger for Burnley and England, Page was one of many footballers to play baseball in the summer. Note the use of a flat bat in the English version of the game.

While baseball may never have caught on fully in Britain, it holds a special place in the sporting heritage of Liverpool.

Baseball, it is often stated, derived from the old English game of rounders, whose first modern rules were published in the *Boys Own Book* of 1828. But the issue is hardly clear cut, for the name baseball was already in use by then. Jane Austen referred to it in *Northanger Abbey* (1803), while the game of 'base' mentioned in Shakespeare's *Cymbeline* and witnessed in London in 1770 by Joseph Strutt, shared certain similarities with baseball, even if no ball was involved.

That said, it was Liverpool's fate, presumably as the first port of call for transatlantic steamers, to be the location for the first ever American-style baseball matches played in Britain, between teams from Boston and Philadelphia, on 30–31 July 1874 (a mere three years after the formation of America's first major baseball league).

Played at Edge Hill, then home to Liverpool Cricket Club, a small crowd in poor weather saw what

The Athletics Ground at Fairfield was the scene of an earlier triumph for Liverpool when, in 1888, a local team called Union beat one called Crescent to win the National Challenge Shield. Over 5,000 spectators saw the match. Again, note how much flatter is the bat used, compared with modern day rounders.

The Graphic described as 'very much like the simple game of rounders'. But it must have inspired someone because three weeks later at the Cattle Market Inn, Stanley, a well attended charity baseball match took place between youths from the *Indefatigable* (a training ship) and the Orphan Boys' Asylum. They put on a polo match too.

But the game that appeared to catch on most in the aftermath of these matches turned out not to be baseball, but rounders, which by the 1880s was thriving in Liverpool. One factor may well have been the shortage of cricket pitches, since rounders can be played on almost any surface. Also, as rounders requires less equipment it was more affordable.

Two Liverpool leagues emerged, featuring ten senior and twelve junior teams, with crowds of 3–5,000 being common, mostly in Newsham Park, Sefton Park and Stanley Park. 'The extraordinary

hold which this game has on many thousands in and around the neighbourhood is marvellous,' noted the *Liverpool Review* in 1888, 'and that it is rapidly spreading to other districts is not astonishing.' The report went on to describe the players sporting 'loud jerseys' and 'gaudy caps with tassels'.

In March 1889 the Americans returned, and this time a crowd of 9,000 gathered at Shiel Park to see the pick of local rounders players, including Lancashire cricketer and Everton footballer Frank Sugg (*see page* 4), take on a strong visiting contingent led by baseball star AG Spalding. Two matches were played, one baseball and one rounders, with each team winning at their own game.

But it would be the American game that ultimately won out.

Soon after the Spalding tour, four football clubs (Derby, Preston, Stoke and Aston Villa, all members of the recently formed

Football League) were persuaded to set up the grandly titled National Baseball League, if only to keep their players fit and to earn extra income during the summer. (Derby even called their new ground the Baseball Ground.)

Meanwhile, also in 1889, the National Rounders Association was set up in Liverpool. But its members were clearly leaning towards the American game, and in March 1892, at the Oddfellows Hall, St Anne Street, they opted to establish their own competition, the English Baseball League, because 'the old game of rounders had no affinity with the pastime played at present'.

Not all the American rules were adopted, however. Rather, a hybrid form of English or British baseball emerged: that is, with a flatter bat, as used then in rounders; each run between bases was scored – so that a home run was worth four (rather than one, as in America); and as in cricket, each team had eleven players (compared with nine in America) and all eleven had to bat to complete an innings. Also, only two innings each were played, compared with nine in America.

As the 1890s wore on, baseball clubs were formed in the north east, in south Wales, as well as in Liverpool. Even so, the sport remained a minority interest. As the Football Echo stated bluntly in September 1892, when players drifted away from their baseball duties before the season's end, 'football has ignominiously routed every summer pastime'.

Certainly none of the Liverpool baseball clubs could afford their own grounds. Instead they used such parks as Walton Hall Park and the Wavertree Playground, or rented the Police Athletics Ground on Prescot Road, and the

North Western Ground, Green Lane, Tuebrook, which in 1922 became the regular venue for the newly established English Baseball Association Cup. A Liverpool club called Crystal Palace won this trophy on six occasions.

Liverpool also hosted regular internationals against Wales, while there are records of a club called Liverpool Amateurs playing against a team of Japanese sailors in July 1933.

A week before that Liverpool was again to the fore when a radical reorganisation of the sport was effected at a meeting of various local factions held at the Law Association Rooms in Cook Street. At that meeting John Moores, the founder of Littlewoods Pools (*see page 88*), made the clubs an offer many of them could hardly refuse.

Anxious to establish a regular fixture list that could be used on pools coupons during football's close season, Moores announced that he was setting up a National Baseball Association. Any club joining would be given £100, but they would have to switch to American rules. Indeed Moores had already signed up several US and Canadian players in advance.

Seven clubs took the bait, and on August 21, at Priory Road (possibly in Stanley Park), Liverpool Amateurs and Oakfield Social became the first English teams to play an American-rules match in Britain.

An exhibition match featuring American players followed two days later at the Littlewoods Sports Ground on Picton Road, where a public address system was used to explain the rules to onlookers.

The following year John Moores, always the arch publicist, threw the first pitch to launch »

▲ One of numerous attempts to convert the British public to such American favourites as ice hockey, basketball and gridiron, was this visit of the **Chicago White Sox and New York Giants** to **Goodison Park** in October 1924, part of a tour which also took in a match at Chelsea's Stamford Bridge.

On the left, in front of the Bullens Road paddock, is Chicago's Bibb Falk, talking to the US Consul in Liverpool. The Giants were led by Frankie Frisch (in the stripes).

But while the games attracted reasonable crowds, it was clear that the majority of onlookers were bemused, particularly as Goodison's pitch proved far too small to contain the action.

'These fellows have no compunction about them at all,' reported the *Liverpool Echo*.

'They fling the five ounce white ball about as though they want to kill something.' Several times spectators were forced to scatter as balls zipped into the stands, and on one occasion the club's nameplate, high up on the roof of the Goodison Road Stand, was hit.

Great play was also made of the monetary might of these missionaries from 'the golden land'.

Willie Kamm of the White Sox was described as 'a $100,000 man', at a time when Britain's most expensive footballer had cost less than a quarter of that, while the Giants squad had recently shared £74,000 worth of receipts from their World Series matches against the Washington Senators. English footballers' wages at that time were capped at just £8 per week.

The *Echo* reporter also noted how the players made a tremendous din. 'What they were yelling neither I nor anyone else could make out, but it gave the crowd much encouragement.

'That, by the way, is a point worth considering – the initiation of applause by the entertainers themselves. It holds possibilities.'

As to the score, 'A stentor in the uniform of the Giants informed us at the close that the "White Sarks" had won. How they managed it, I don't know. Perhaps they hit the greatest number of spectators. But it was some game, baby, believe me.'

▶ One aspect of baseball that continually amused onlookers was the constant banter of the players, captured here in the *Liverpool Echo* of 1934 by cartoonist **George Green**. Apparently Green, whose work first appeared in the newspaper in 1925, would watch matches through field glasses and then draw rough sketches of each individual as if naked, before finally applying the appropriate kits. He was best known for his longrunning *Echo* series called *The Back Entry Diddlers*, based on a scratch team of street urchins he saw playing football in Vauxhall.

the NBA at the Wavertree Playground, home of the Liverpool Giants. Twenty teams competed initially, to be joined in 1935 by more teams from Blackpool and the Manchester area and in 1936 from Hull, Bradford, Halifax, Oldham, Rochdale and Leeds. Interest was further roused when the newly formed Liverpool Caledonians signed up one of the leading footballers of the day, the prolific Everton striker, Bill 'Dixie' Dean. Dean had earlier played English baseball for Blundellsands, having been introduced to the game a few years earlier by his fellow England international Louis Page (himself one of four footballing brothers to play the game). Other footballers to join the fray included Liverpool's Lance Carr, Berry Niewenhuys and Alf Hanson, Tranmere's Bertt Gray.

With continued backing from Moores, by 1938 the National Baseball Association had nearly 800 teams. Moreover, the standard was improving, as shown that year when a 6,000 crowd at Wavertree Playground saw an England selection beat a US team 3–0, one of four victories in a five test series.

Had the Second World War not interrupted this growth, the story of American baseball in Britain might have been quite different.

Instead, the impetus was lost and although a series of wartime matches featuring US servicemen took place at Goodison Park, the post war period saw the domestic game return to relative anonymity in local parks, where it remains today.

English baseball, meanwhile, is all but defunct, with the last international match having been played, against Wales, at Breck Park, Liverpool, in 1988.

Since 1945 the principal torchbearers for baseball in Liverpool have been the **Trojans**, seen here in 1948 at Everton's training ground at **Bellefield**. (Everton's manager at the time, Theo Kelly, was a keen baseball man and even fielded an Everton team in the local league.)

The Trojans formed in 1946 when Norman Wells and other fellow ex-servicemen challenged an existing team called the Liverpool Robins to a game. Despite being trounced they persevered, adopting the name of Trojan, a brand of locally brewed Higson's mild, on tap at their regular haunt, the Halton Castle pub, West Derby.

As the Halton Trojans the club went on to play in the last baseball match ever staged at Goodison Park, a Lancashire Cup Final against Formby Cardinals, in 1948.

Ten years later, finding it hard to recruit local players, the Trojans disbanded. But they reformed in 1964 as the Liverpool Trojans, and since then have won the British Championship on three occasions, and the North-West League on nine consecutive occasions between 1976–84, and again in 1991.

Now based at Bootle Stadium (*left*), the club currently plays in the National League North, while in the Premier Division North can be found the area's one other surviving baseball team, Halton Jaguars.

Chapter Fourteen

Golf

A reflection of golf's importance on Merseyside is a series of painted windows at the Church of St Nicholas, Wallasey, installed by the Lancaster firm of Shrigley and Hunt in 1926 to honour the support of golfers for the local cottage hospital.

Of all the ball games that may be described as 'Made in Britain', none is more rooted to the landscape than golf.

A game of golf is not only an attempt to beat an opponent. It is also a battle against topography and the elements.

First recorded in Scotland in 1457, golf has been played on the Fife coast at St Andrew's since at least 1552, spreading to England, courtesy of James I, by the early 17th century. By 1800 only seven clubs were known to be in existence. By 1900 that figure had risen to around a thousand, of which at least five of the most influential were in the Merseyside region. Today there are some 40 clubs in the area.

There are two reasons why golf has become so central to life on Merseyside. Firstly, the topography of the Liverpool coast (north of the city), and of the Wirral peninsula (across the Mersey), are both extremely similar to the original east Scottish 'links' – that is, the sandy, undulating grassy areas that lie on the margins between the shoreline and the inland.

Secondly, as a busy port and trading centre, Liverpool had the highest concentration of Scots outside London. By 1861 over 17,000 Liverpudlians were Scottish born, representing four per cent of the total. Moreover, unlike their Irish counterparts, they were predominantly middle class, and therefore wealthy enough to indulge in what was, before the modern era, an expensive hobby.

One early account suggests that golf was first played on Merseyside on farmland at West Kirby, on the Wirral, in around 1852.

However the earliest attempt to put golf on an organised footing came in 1869, when a Scottish businessman, James Muir Dowie, organised a meeting of seven individuals at the Royal Hotel, to establish a club on the racecourse of the Liverpool Hunt Club, Hoylake (just north of West Kirkby), where racing had taken place since 1831.

Their first round of what the *Liverpool Courier* described as 'the Scotch national game' took place on 7 June 1869, on the same day as an informal race meeting. Twenty

This distinctive gatepost, one of two, stands outside the clubhouse of the Royal Liverpool Golf Club, Hoylake, and is a relic from the course's days as a racecourse, where it marked the entrance to the winner's enclosure. It is thought to date from between 1847 and 1876. Also on display in the clubhouse is the 1847 racecourse bell (*see page 6*).

one players took part, with play starting and finishing at the Royal Hotel on Stanley Road, which now became the club's headquarters. Realising that here was a game with tremendous commercial potential, playable all year round, the hotel's proprietor and lessee of the racecourse, John Ball, became an instant convert, and it would not be long before the golfers' interests took precedence over those of the Hunt Club.

Within its first twelve years membership of the Liverpool Golf Club rose to over 500, and they were not happy with having to climb rails or share the course with horses and common racegoers. After 1876, however, it would seem that they had the place more or less to themselves.

In its early years the golf course was still an essentially natural

landscape. The local rabbit population kept the grass short, while the holes were marked only with feathers. Hazards, such as hollows or ditches, were natural formations, and basic maintenance was carried out by the resident professional player.

It was not until the 1880s that Britain's first 'designed' courses started to take shape. Initially, these changes were shaped by professional players, such as Tom Morris Senior at Prestwick and Willie Park from Musselburgh.

They were joined in the 1890s by a new generation of course architects, who introduced such strategic features as bunkers, trees and artificial contours to enhance the game, but also to take into account the introduction of the »

▲ A crowd gathers at the 16th hole of the **Royal Liverpool Golf Club, Hoylake**, to see Cheshire veteran Henry Cotton in action at the 1956 British Open Championships.

At the final 18th hole, an even greater crowd, estimated at 8,000, saw the Australian Peter Thompson confirm his third Open in a row.

By comparison, when Hoylake staged the 2006 Open, there were 230,000 spectators present, the largest number ever recorded at an English course. Not surprisingly the event had a major economic impact, generating an estimated £60–70 million for the local economy. It will be similar when the Open returns to Merseyside, to the Royal Birkdale course, in 2008.

The Open has been held at Hoylake eleven times since 1897.

▲ Viewed from the south, the **Royal Liverpool Golf Club, Hoylake** is a classic links course, jutting out into the Dee estuary. Uniquely at Hoylake, 'cops' (that is, raised turf dykes that once served as field boundaries) have been integrated into the course to form barriers on either side of the fairways.

Another Hoylake characteristic is its triangular shape, which exposes golfers to wind in all directions.

Originally laid out on Hoylake racecourse in 1869 with only nine holes, the current course dates from a redesign by the eminent golf course architect Harry Colt, during the 1920s.

To the right is **Hoylake Municipal Golf Course**, laid out by James Braid in the 1930s, and used as a practice course for the 2006 Open.

》 rubber-core Hesketh ball in 1902, which travelled further and therefore required longer holes.

Demand for golf spread rapidly, as growing numbers of middle class families moved from their previous enclaves in places like Bootle and Seaforth, squeezed out by dock developments and the spread of dense working class housing. In this respect the opening of the railway between Liverpool and Southport in 1848 proved crucial, cutting as it did through coastal areas that offered conditions more suited to golf than to agriculture.

On the edge of Blundellsands the West Lancashire Golf Club was established in 1873. Formby followed in 1884, Hesketh a year later, and Birkdale in 1889, leading the *Southport Visitor* to comment in 1904 that 'landowners of the Liverpool district have united in offering facilities for golf, rightly recognising a golf club as a nucleus of a residential estate'.

Golf courses also started to appear in inland areas, such as at West Derby (opened in 1896), Woolton (1900) and Childwall (1912). Woolton is an example – typical in the context of English golf – of a club that took over an existing estate, Doe Park (a former deer park), converting the Georgian mansion at its centre into their clubhouse in 1906.

Links courses offered no such opportunities. Instead, as the coastal clubs grew wealthier and their members demanded a higher level of service, a more substantial form of purpose-built clubhouse emerged from the 1890s onwards.

As several examples in this chapter show, these clubhouses had extensive bars, dining rooms and billiard rooms, and in some cases, such as at Formby, even overnight accommodation for visitors. To service these facilities the clubhouses also had servants' quarters and a hierarchy that reflected the members' own domestic situations. For example the club professional, who had his own workshop, was expected to make and repair clubs for the members, sell equipment and generally look to the members' needs, on and off the course.

Inevitably some of the early clubs and courses have fallen by the wayside. But the majority have become more popular than ever.

Indeed new courses have opened at Lee Park (in 1950), and at Formby Hall and Mossock Hall (in 1996), while a network of municipal courses also survives from the early 20th century.

Merseyside clubs are also known for their artisan clubs; that is, clubs formed for local people who are allowed to play without charge, in return for duties performed (*see page 136*).

Merseyside can, as a result, be rightly considered a hotbed of modern British golf, with more championship courses than any other region. It has two of the four courses that regularly stage the British Open; the Royal Liverpool and Royal Birkdale. In addition, Royal Birkdale and Southport & Ainsdale have each hosted the Ryder Cup twice, while the British Amateur Championships and the Walker Cup also have their origins at Royal Liverpool.

When historians consider the legacy of Liverpool's merchant classes, it is to the docks, the public institutions and to the Georgian terraces that they tend to look first for evidence.

Perhaps it is time to recognise that the golf courses of the region are as much part of this legacy too.

▲ Designed by the Liverpool architects Woolfall and Eccles and costing £6,500 when it opened in 1895, the clubhouse of the **Royal Liverpool Golf Club** at Hoylake is today a rambling agglomeration of extensions and styles, built up over the years with apparently little concern for outward appearances, but with a sumptuous interior.

The prominent double clock face commemorates John Ball, the club's greatest player. His father, also John Ball, ran the Royal Hotel (no longer extant), where the club established its first headquarters in 1869. (However it should be noted that the club's name derives not from this hotel but from its royal charter, granted in 1871 by the Duke of Connaught.)

In 1890, at Prestwick, John Ball Junior (*left*) became the first Englishman to win the Open, a competition that since its inception in 1860 had been held at Scottish courses only. Sandwich became the first English hosts in 1894, with Royal Liverpool, its new pavilion in place, following suit in 1897.

That year's Open – the first of eleven staged at the course – was won by a Royal Liverpool member, Harold Hilton (*right*), the only time a member of the host club has ever won the competition.

Born in West Kirby, Hilton was also the first Englishman to win

the US Amateur Championship, in 1911, and the first editor of the magazine *Golf Monthly*.

Both plaques shown here are displayed in the clubhouse, along with many other golfing treasures and artefacts, including the 1847 Liverpool Hunt Club bell (*see page 6*) and various sets of early golf clubs (*page 184*).

The so-called 'golf line' between Liverpool Central station and Southport links the highest concentration of golf courses in Britain. From Hall Road station in the south, ten courses are within close proximity to the line, including six classed as championship courses (marked below with an asterisk):

1. West Lancashire* (est. 1873)
2. Formby* (1884) and Formby Ladies (1896)
3. Formby Hall (1996)
4. Southport & Ainsdale* (1907)
5. Hillside* (1923)
6. Royal Birkdale* (1896)
7. Southport Old Links (1926)
8. Southport Municipal (1911)
9. Hesketh* (1902)

Shown in light brown are four former courses (from south to north): Banking and Insurance (1908–41), now partly an airfield; Grosvenor, Blundell and Hillside (1906–25); Blundell (1911–35), and the first Birkdale course (1889–96).

▲ Viewed from the south, the **West Lancashire Golf Club** acts as a green buffer to the expansion of Liverpool's suburbs. In the foreground are the northernmost houses of Blundellsands, with the first station on the 'golf line' – Hall Road – a short walk from the West Lancs clubhouse (*see page 141*).

Prior to World War Two there was a separate West Lancashire Ladies course, while the men's course had a number of inland holes to the east of the railway. But demand for housing led to both courses being concentrated on the present coastal location.

Signs forbidding ball games are common in public open spaces, but on Crosby beach (*right*), just south of Blundellsands, the restriction is rather more specific.

On this hole
Dr. FRANK STABLEFORD
DEVISED HIS
POINTS SCORING SYSTEM
THE FIRST STABLEFORD COMPETITION
WAS PLAYED AT WALLASEY
ON 16th MAY 1932

▲ For the average golfer, the name **Frank Stableford** is revered, especially on windy courses such as **Wallasey**, where many players struggle to complete the course without scoring well over par (that is, the number of shots deemed to be the standard of proficiency).

A local doctor, Stableford was a flamboyant character who wore colourful bow ties and drove a yellow Rolls Royce. In 1931, at the age of 61, he was playing on the second hole at Wallasey when he realised a different scoring system would give ordinary golfers more incentive to keep on playing.

The great golf writer Henry Longhurst said, 'I doubt whether any single man did more to increase the pleasure of the more humble club golfer.'

Alas Stableford suffered from blindness in his later years and shot himself with a pistol in 1959.

Wallasey, meanwhile, has become almost a place of pilgrimage for those he helped.

▲ Another buffer to development is the **Wallasey Golf Club**, viewed here from the south west, with New Brighton in the distance, and the Liverpool docks on the far side of the Mersey. Wallasey (*see also page 136*) is one of 15 courses on the Wirral peninsula. In the foreground is **Leasowe Golf Course**. The Royal Liverpool course at Hoylake lie two miles south.

As can be understood from this view, the Wallasey course has been described as the 'diamond in the dunes'. In typical links style, the fairways have been created out of the dunes to create a course that rewards players who drive straight, but penalises those that stray with their shots. The view also demonstrates how golf courses help in countering coastal erosion.

In addition to golf, this corner of the peninsula once had two large open air swimming pools. The site of the Derby Pool, opened in 1932 (*see page 180*) is now occupied by a pub of the same name (the white building in the top left corner of the golf course). The New Brighton Bathing Pool (*page 181*) was further up the coast, close to Perch Rock lighthouse (top centre).

▲ Across the road from the Church of St Nicholas (*see also page 130*) is the clubhouse of **Wallasey Golf Club**, completed in 1892, a year after the club was formed by members of the Royal Liverpool, many of them Liverpool-based businessmen who wanted a course that was easier to reach than Hoylake, further to the south.

The terrain in front of the clubhouse, overlooking the estuary to the west, illustrates perfectly how course designers adapted sandy coastal areas to the sport, with dunes fashioned to form bunkers in strategic locations.

The first designer associated with Wallasey was Tom Morris Senior, a four times winner of the Open, from St Andrew's. But this early course proved vulnerable to drifting sand, and it required improvements to the coastal defences before it could be further developed; first in 1929, on the advice of James Braid (another Scot, who won the Open five times), followed in 1936 by a second redesign by Fred Hawtree and JH Taylor (another five times Open winner). This same duo also redesigned Royal Birkdale, in 1932.

All this expertise, combined with the course's proximity to Hoylake, has brought many a great golfer to Wallasey, not least on the four occasions it has served as a qualifying course for the Open.

▶ One characteristic of the golfing scene on Merseyside is the number of so-called artisan clubs, such as the **Wallasey Artisan Golf Club**, whose clubhouse is shown here.

Although during the earliest days of golf, from the 16th to the 19th centuries, the game remained largely the preserve of wealthy individuals, it was nevertheless played on publicly accessible links, commons and heathland. In order to protect non-players from flying balls, a 'fore-caddy' would walk ahead of the play, warning of the danger. Hence the cry of 'fore!'

(The term caddy itself was an adaptation of the French 'cadet', meaning boy, used in Scotland to refer to porters and water carriers.)

One such common used for golf was the Warren, at Hoylake. Although owned by Lord Stanley it was used as a hunting ground by local fishermen, who would earn extra income as caddies.

However in 1895, when the Royal Liverpool Golf Club began to fence off the Warren, the fishermen responded by removing balls and blocking the golfers' paths.

Eventually, at a meeting with the Royal Liverpool captain, a deal was struck whereby the fishermen and any other artisans from the parish of Hoylake were permitted to play golf on the Warren at certain times, in return for carrying out maintenance duties on the course. Thus was born the **Royal Liverpool Village Play**, a golf club with its own members and separate clubhouse.

In 1905 a similar situation at Wallasey resulted in the formation of the **Wallasey Villages Golf Club**.

As other similar clubs sprang up around Britain, in 1921 they were formally brought together under the auspices of the Artisan Golfers Assocation, set up by the politician,

philanthropist and publisher of the *News of the World*, Lord Riddell, and the former golf professional, turned course designer, JH Taylor (who had started out as a greenkeeper at England's oldest surviving links course, at Westward Ho! in Devon).

Both were concerned that in a land supposedly 'fit for heroes' working class men should find both work and recreation through golf.

By 1927 the Artisan Golfers Association had over 15,000 members, and although numbers have fallen, with some 90 affiliated clubs and 3,000 members listed in 2006, the movement still plays a vital role, particularly on Merseyside, the only region in Britain to have its own league.

Indeed, aside from the Wirral, every golf course along the Liverpool coast, with the exception of Hillside, has an artisan club.

Of these, the oldest is the West Lancashire, formed out of the Crosby Comrades Club in 1921.

Today, artisan clubs not only help to maintain their host course. They also carry out stewarding duties for their parent club during major tournaments, of which there are

many on Merseyside. The clubs are also entirely self-sufficient, paying for their golfing activities from members' subscriptions.

Below is the exterior of the Wallasey Artisans Club, which until the late 1990s had served as the Ladies' Clubhouse.

This elegant trophy was made by Les Sadler, a long-standing member of the Wallasey Artisans Club, for their annual Christmas competition. It exemplifies the versatile and independent nature of the artisan movement. Members often build their own clubhouses, make their trophies and organise their own competitions. When Sadler made this trophy in 1980, his club was based in an old caddy shack on the course.

▶ Designed by architects Haigh, Marmon and Thompson in 1901, with a clock tower added in 1909 and a west wing extended in 1998, the clubhouse of the **Formby Golf Club** on Golf Road, Formby, is one of several, substantial early 20th century clubhouses on the Liverpool coast, each reflecting the growing wealth and social status of their members. The club had been in existence for just 16 years when the clubhouse was built, to replace an earlier, rudimentary clubhouse that had burnt down in 1899.

By 1900 Formby had enrolled 500 members and, uniquely, had been joined by a separate Ladies Club (formed in 1896), with its own clubhouse and course in the middle of the men's course.

Both Formby courses are characterised by their sandhills and pine woods.

In a similar vein is the pristine Tudoresque clubhouse of the **Hesketh Golf Club** (*right*), on Cockle Dick's Lane, Southport, the northernmost club on the golf coast. Hesketh formed in 1885 and moved to its present site in 1902. Its clubhouse, designed by GE Gregson, was placed on a sandhill to provide elevated views to the course's inland section on the east, and to the west, the seaward section towards the Ribble Estuary.

On Hesketh's southern edge lies the Southport Municipal Golf Course. On its northern flank is the Hesketh Out Marsh nature reserve. The course itself, in common with the course at Formby, is also a Site of Special Scientific Interest.

But perhaps the club's most celebrated piece of flora, placed outside the clubhouse, is a fir tree, awarded to Hesketh member Arnold Bentley when he led the British golf team to a gold medal at the 1936 Olympics in Berlin.

◀ Straddling the golf line between Ainsdale and Hillside stations are two, suburban-style 1920s clubhouses. The **Hillside Golf Club** formed in 1911 but moved to its present location, immediately adjacent to the Royal Birkdale course (*see next page*), in 1923, when the central section of the clubhouse was completed. Local architects Fulchett, Lancaster & Archer chose a style that would enable its conversion into a family residence should the club fold.

Since then, as may be discerned, the building has been extended on both wings.

Hillside itself is regarded by many as the best course in Britain never to have hosted an Open.

On the eastern side of the railway line – its clubhouse less than a mile southwards – lies **Southport & Ainsdale Golf Club**, another much admired course which has hosted the Ryder Cup on two occasions, in 1933 and 1937.

Formed in 1906 the club had to vacate its first clubhouse (since converted into houses) when Liverpool Road was re-routed. The current single storey clubhouse dates from 1923, when the new course was completed to the designs of James Braid.

In both clubhouses it may be observed that their original central verandahs have been glazed in to extend the club's social areas.

▶ Although numerous golf clubs are based in buildings that have been listed for their historic value, surprisingly only one 20th century purpose-built clubhouse is listed (at Knebworth, built in 1908).

Here are two possible contenders from the 1930s, a period whose architectural style seems well suited to the needs of golf.

The nautically inspired Art Deco clubhouse at **Royal Birkdale** – the third on the course since it opened in 1896 – was designed by George Tonge (architect also of the Grade II listed Garrick Theatre, Southport), who was himself a keen golfer.

At its opening in July 1935, the contractor John Tompkinson noted that 'some of the older school are rather opposed to these new ideas,' and claimed that this was the first clubhouse of its type. Certainly the only other known Modernist examples – for example at Hayling Island and Davyhulme – were later.

In true 1930s tradition, Tonge's design allowed for two sunbathing decks and for tennis on the flat roof. But whatever the old school thought of such radical ideas, Tonge's inspiring design, combined with the redesign of the course by Hawtree and Taylor, had the desired effect. Birkdale – which gained its Royal status in 1951 – has staged the Open eight times since 1954, with a further Open scheduled there for 2008.

Away from the coast, **Childwall Golf Club** (*right*), formed in 1912 and moved to its present location on Naylors Road, Gateacre, in 1938. Its immaculate Art Deco clubhouse was the work of Alfred Shennan, otherwise known for the Forum Cinema, Lime Street, and for his robust leadership of Liverpool City Council in the late 1930s and 1940s. The Childwall course was designed by James Braid.

◀ So far we have focused mainly on private golf clubs. However there are also municipal courses at Allerton, Bootle, Bowring Park, Hoylake, Kirkby and at Southport (*left*) – the oldest of them all – where the **Southport Municipal Links** were laid out on the seafront in 1911 in an attempt to attract those tourists unable to afford the neighbouring Hesketh course.

This charming, understated clubhouse, designed by a Mr Owens, the borough engineer, was opened in May 1935, two months before Birkdale's rather grander effort. On the other hand, the municipal pavilion cost £3,900, less than half the cost of Birkdale.

Today the building is used as a restaurant by those playing on the golf links.

Finally (*below*) a rare 1960s golf clubhouse, ironically belonging to the oldest club on the Liverpool coast, the **West Lancashire Golf Club**, established in 1873 on Hall Road West, Blundellsands.

Built in 1962 at a cost of £75,000, as can be seen its design represented no less a radical departure from the norm than was Birkdale's clubhouse in 1935.

Its architects were Tripe and Wakeham of London, who used broad terraces and curtain glazing on the upper storey to provide members with the best possible vistas of the links and coastline.

Chapter Fifteen

Gymnastics

Gymnastics was one of the few 19th century sports whose proponents encouraged female participation. This etching was used to illustrate the essay which won a gold medal at the Liverpool Olympics in 1862. Written by EA Browne of London, the essay, entitled *Mens Sana in Corpore Sano*, was read out at the medal ceremony in St George's Hall.

From the greens and fairways of Merseyside we now move indoors and turn our attention to three sports in which Liverpool has a long tradition: gymnastics, boxing and swimming.

In gymnastics, the city has had recent cause to celebrate the achievements of Beth Tweddle (*see page 7*). But Liverpool has been a centre of gymnastic excellence for over 150 years.

The gymnastic movement was introduced to Britain during the early 19th century, at a time of heightened interest in all matters relating to ancient Greece and to classical notions of beauty and physical strength. At the fore was an American-born Swiss military instructor, Heinrich Clias, who arrived in London in 1822 and soon developed a following with his books and lectures.

Liverpool's earliest recorded gymnasium was set up in 1844 by Louis Huguenin (himself also a Continental emigré), on Cook Street. This was followed in the late 1850s by another, set up by one of Huguenin's pupils, John Hulley, on Bold Street, in a circular brick

building known as the Rotunda (previously used as a billiard room and not far from another favourite gentlemen's haunt, the Lyceum, a library and news room).

The costs of this new enterprise were borne by Hulley's benefactor, George McKinley. But in 1862 the pair had a disagreement, forcing Hulley to find new premises.

The man he turned to for help was Charles Melly.

As detailed in Chapter One, Melly had already championed the cause of public health by financing Liverpool's first outdoor gymnasiums (what we would now call playgrounds), in 1858. Between them, Melly and Hulley formed the Liverpool Athletics Club in 1862.

With its motto *Mens Sana in Corpore Sano*, the club organised the first Liverpool Olympic Festival in 1862, followed by five more in subsequent years (*see page 12*).

Still, these were summer events, staged outdoors. In 1864 therefore, Hulley and Melly launched a company with £10,000 worth of shares to erect a purpose built indoor gymnasium on one of

Liverpool's busiest thoroughfares, Myrtle Street. At the time, it is thought, only Edinburgh had a purpose-built gymnasium, while in London there were also plans for a large German Gymnasium next to St Pancras Station. In the end, Liverpool's opened just a few weeks before London's, in November 1865.

For 40 years or more (*see right*) the Liverpool Gymnasium formed a vital hub for British gymnastics, helping to train a generation of physical education instructors and, in the process, establish a tradition which lives on today in a network of nearly 30 private gymnasiums and eleven public Lifestyle Fitness Suites. One of these, at Park Road, where Beth Tweddle trains, may be regarded as the true successor of Myrtle Street, in terms of gymnastic excellence, if not in architectural grandeur.

Alas unlike London's German Gymnasium – recently restored – Hulley and Melly's grand edifice, no longer stands. Having ceased use in 1937, it was demolished in the 1970s, a great loss to the city's sporting heritage.

John Hulley (1832–75) was a quixotic figure, known, according to the *Liverpool Citizen* for his 'harmless eccentricities'. He appeared at the 1866 Olympian Games in London dressed as a Turk, and always insisted on the Greek title of 'Gymnasiarch'. He was also shunned by certain sectors of society because he took a salary from the Liverpool

Gymnasium (and was therefore not a true amateur), and because he introduced classes for ladies. But he was a tireless advocate of Olympianism, and might have achieved wider recognition had he not shocked the establishment by eloping with the daughter of a Liverpool shipping magnate. He then died from a chest complaint at the age of just 42.

▲ As depicted in the *Illustrated London News* – two weeks after its opening by Lord Stanley, on 6 November 1865 – the **Liverpool Gymnasium** was a more elaborate building than its London counterpart, opened a few weeks later. Designed by the Birkenhead architect Walter Scott, its final cost of £14,000 was nearly double that of the German Gymnasium at St Pancras, forcing Hulley's company to take out a mortgage of £4,000.

Still, its prospects appeared excellent. Five hundred individuals signed up for evening membership before it even opened. Fencing lessons were offered by André Durbec, a Frenchman. Jem Mace (*see page 162*) was hired as a boxing instructor. Sessions were also set aside for 'young lads', though as Lord Stanley conceded, membership was beyond the reach 'of the labouring and artisan class'.

Stanley hoped above all that the Gymnasium would help those many middle class men who were forced into sedentary occupations and whose 'utmost bodily exertion is driving a pen for hours… and handling a knife and fork at dinner'.

Among many curious visitors during the early years was the social reformer, Charles Kingsley, when he was Canon of Chester Cathedral – he later wrote a book called *Health and Education* – and Thomas Hughes, the MP and author of *Tom Brown's Schooldays*.

But despite Hulley's efforts, the Gymnasium struggled to pay its debts, and after membership peaked in 1869, in 1871 he stood down, for the reasons stated opposite. The building was then taken over by the Young Men's Christian Association in 1883.

Under their ownership and the directorship of a former Hulley apprentice, Alexander Alexander, the Gymnasium flourished once again. In 1886 Alexander formed the National Physical Recreation Society, with the intention of improving the fitness of the working classes, while a number of Gymnasium trainees went on to become instructors at various British colleges (including Irene Marsh, later to establish a Ladies Physical Training College in Southport, now part of Liverpool John Moores University).

▲ Messrs Hulley and Melly must have been delighted with this engraving of their **Liverpool Gymnasium** in the *Illustrated London News* of November 1865.

The main hall, it was stated, measured 105 x 75 feet (larger than the Philharmonic Hall), while boxing, fencing and broadsword training were catered for in a smaller, adjoining gymnasium.

There were dressing rooms and bathrooms for both sexes, a spectator gallery, and a wealth of equipment on offer. As the journal *Porcupine* remarked, 'machines for every species are here, each having their individual uses for the development of certain muscles'.

Of course by modern standards the equipment was fairly basic, consisting, as can be seen, of numerous ropes, wall bars, swings, trapezes, a horse (at the far end), and castellated climbing frames at the sides and far end. Not a mat or safety net was in sight.

On the right hand wall were dumb bells, some light enough to allow 'young lads' to take part.

The cost of all this equipment amounted to £1,900, twice what Melly had spent on supplying his four public outdoor playgrounds.

In 1867 a velocipede club formed at the Gymnasium, and in the same year it co-hosted, with Shiel Park, several events within

the Olympic Festival (*see page 14*). A second wave of Olympic Festivals followed in 1892 and 1894.

But in 1896 director Alexander Alexander parted company with the Gymnasium's owners, the YMCA, who complained that too little emphasis was being made on members' spiritual development. Without him, for the next three decades the Gymnasium went into steady decline. (A similar fate befell London's German Gymnasium, which, in view of its name, failed to re-open after the First World War.)

A new director introduced rifle shooting and even roller skating to maintain interest, until in 1937 the YMCA gladly handed over the

building to the government, who used it as a centre for issuing gas masks and ration cards. In 1951 the United Liverpool Hospitals Board purchased the premises for £17,000, before it was demolished in the 1970s to make way for a car park. The site is now occupied by the Liverpool Community College.

Meanwhile, recently discovered at the Park Road gymnasium, this fine shield (*right*) was awarded in 1884 to AE Jones, for winning the Championships at the Liverpool Gymnasium for the third year running. It is the only memento of the Gymnasium known to have survived, and is now in the keeping of the Museum of Liverpool.

▲ Gymnastics is well suited to historic buildings that offer large, open floorspace and high ceilings.

The small gymnasium of the **Lifestyles Sports Centre** at **Park Road, Toxteth**, occupies the former wash house of Steble Street Baths (*see page 171*). Built in 1874, coincidentally the building stands on the site of one of Charles Melly's open air playgrounds.

The gymnasium shown here was created in 1984, and proved so popular that in 1991 an extension was added, with a larger gym holding 450 spectators, two small swimming pools, a health suite and an outdoor synthetic pitch.

Now ranked as a Centre of Excellence, Park Road is home to the **City of Liverpool Gymnastics Club**, one of the dominant forces in

British gymnastics. The club won the British Team Championships every year between 2002 and 2006 , and also won all three age divisions at the 2006 National Championships. Apart from honing the talents of club member Beth Tweddle, several members have appeared in international events, and hope to be selected to compete at the 2008 Olympics in Beijing.

▲ Another historic building that now caters for a range of gymnastic activities is the **Grange Road West Sports Centre, Birkenhead**.

Built originally as an Army Drill Hall in 1901, the building – whose main hall is a generous 136 x 75 feet – became a popular venue for boxing in 1931, and also for badminton. Its current usage dates back to 1968, when it was taken over by Wirral Borough Council and converted into a multi-purpose community sports hall. The former officers' mess became a crèche, while the billiard room was turned into dressing rooms.

Since then the centre (*see also right*) has become best known as the home of the **Birkenhead Trampoline Club**. Formed in 1975 the club runs 19 sessions per week and has trained five full, and twelve youth internationals.

The trampoline itself is a recent addition to gymnastics, having been developed from bouncing beds used by circus tumblers in the early 20th century. As shown here, during regional championships held in 2006, it especially requires head room. A top performer can reach as high as ten metres.

Chapter Sixteen

Boys' and Girls' Clubs

For former pupils of Liverpool College, Merchant Taylors' and other educational institutions of that ilk, the old school tie exists as a metaphor for a lifelong bond. But for generations of poorer Liverpudlians, their common heritage was membership of a boys' club. This is the badge of the Shrewsbury Boys' Club – 'the Shewsy' – founded in October 1903 by Old Salopians resident in the city, with the intention of regenerating 'the slum lad'. The club, in common with several other youth organisations formed in the late 19th and early 20th centuries, is still active today.

For those who could afford it, the Liverpool Gymnasium provided a welcome outlet for physical recreation in the town centre. But for the majority of young Liverpudlians, crowded into insanitary housing and weakened by poor nutrition, indoor sporting activity was a luxury only made possible by the formation of boys' and girls' clubs.

In this chapter we focus on three buildings erected by charitable institutions and philanthropists between 1886–89. All three survive, and are thought to be the oldest of their type still extant in Britain. Moreover, two still operate as youth and community centres, while the third is expected to re-open in the near future.

No other city can claim such a rich stock of historic buildings of this specialised type; that is, part social club, part sports centre.

Before their creation and the advent of universal, publicly funded education, the care of poor children and youths was largely in the hands of Ragged Schools and such institutions as the St George's Catholic Industrial

School for Boys, on Soho Street, which tutored pupils in tailoring, knitting, clog and net-making, together with providing three basic meals a day. By the 1850s some 20 schools of this kind existed around Liverpool, albeit with no provision for sport or physical recreation as part of their agenda.

For older, male youths there was also the YMCA, which arrived in Liverpool in 1846 and built an impressive centre on Mount Pleasant in 1877 (still extant). It will be recalled that the organisation also took over the Liverpool Gymnasium in 1883.

But still there were plenty of young people untouched by these provisions; those forced either to work in unregulated occupations (not covered by the various Factory Acts which limited child employment), or simply left on the street to eke out their survival. Even as late as 1875, it was noted by one government commission, gang masters in Liverpool were still able to recruit 'any quantity' of boys as chimney sweeps, despite the practice being outlawed by previous legislation.

Indeed the sheer number of youths roaming the streets created a degree of moral panic amongst the elite, as reflected by the *Liverpool Citizen* which, in 1890, noted that precocious youngsters were not only an evil to themselves but also a cause of evil.

It was in this climate of social concern, underpinned by a fear of rowdyism, that the movement for boys' clubs emerged, with sport and recreation playing a key role in its philosophy.

Britain's first boys' club to be formed and specifically named as such was in Kennington, London, in 1872. In Liverpool the first was the Earle Road Boys' Club, set up in the mid 1880s by Dr John Watson of the Sefton Park Presbyterian Church, and in 1886 reformed at the Balfour Institute. But this had a minimum age of 16 and concentrated on education.

Two other clubs from this period were in Bootle, set up by an artillery captain, George Osborn, and at Bevington Bush, off

Opened in 1886, the Gordon Institute – thought to be Britain's oldest surviving purpose-built Boys' Club – today serves as a community centre for the Kirkdale area. The building had actually been closed in 1995, only to be revived by a local action group in 2000. A grant of £800,000 from the European Regional

Development Fund has paid for the building to be underpinned, and for the sympathetic restoration of various internal features, such as this staircase in the main lobby. Further refurbishment of the main concert hall and the building's sandstone exterior is also planned, it is hoped with assistance from the Heritage Lottery Fund.

Scotland Road. In 1885 these two clubs combined to raise funds for a purpose-built headquarters.

A member of the fundraising committee explained its objectives in a letter to the *Liverpool Daily Post* on 14 August 1885. The north end of Liverpool, it was stated, had attracted a large number of rural immigrants from across the British Isles, lured by the promise of well paid work in the docks, for which no qualifications or character references were necessary. But they soon found that they could only get one or two days' work a week, leaving them unable to provide for their families. In particular, youths in the 14–23 age group were left to seek amusement in pubs or 'loaf in the streets'.

As it transpired, the committee soon found itself an exceptionally generous benefactor.

William Cliff, a West Indies merchant and shipowner of West Derby, who wished to honour the memory of his late son, donated the bulk of the £50,000 costs of erecting and equipping the new boys' club, which was to be built on Stanley Road, Kirkdale.

Named after General Gordon, who had been killed earlier that year at Khartoum, the Gordon Institute (*see right*) set a standard against which all future boys' clubs would be measured. It also established an excellent model for the design of such buildings.

When it opened there was a large concert hall, billiards room, a library, various classrooms and a social room where boys might gather around an open hearth.

Weekly subscriptions were set at one penny; affordable for the majority, but enough also to ensure that boys did not take the facilities for granted. »

▲ Designed by Liverpool architect David Walker and built by Morrison & Sons of Wavertree, the **Gordon Institute** on Stanley Road, Kirkdale, was opened in December 1886 by the mayor, James Poole, in the presence of the first Bishop of Liverpool, Dr JC Ryle.

A marble plaque in the vestibule records the founders' motives:

This Institute has been erected by William Cliff, Merchant of Liverpool, to the memory of his eldest son, William Frater Cliff, who departed this life 18th Dec. 1853, aged 11 years. Although so young, he felt deep sympathy for poor and neglected Boys and took the greatest interest in the Ragged Schools which were then being established for their benefit.

The Institute is also intended to perpetuate the name and memory of Major General Charles Gordon RE who devoted much of his time to the benefit of destitute Lads at Gravesend where he was stationed from 1865 to 1869, superintending the construction of the new defences of the Thames and where he established a Boys Home and did other Philanthropic work.

He was killed at Khartoum, 26th Jan. 1885, aged 52 years in his heroic, but unsuccessful attempt to rescue the Egyptian Garrison which perished with him.

This Institute, erected for the benefit of the working lads of Liverpool, is therefore a suitable monument of what was so noble in youth and manhood.

It is the hope of the Donor that the members of the Institute will use it in the spirit of these examples which it commemorates; that they will profit by the Instruction and harmless recreation which it provides; and thereby form in youth, such worthy habits as may help them to live happy and useful lives, for the service of God and the good of their fellow men.

"Herein is my Father glorified that ye bear much fruit, so shall ye be my disciples."
St John XV 2

This Institute erected for the benefit of the working lads of Liverpool, is therefore a suitable monument of what was so noble in youth and manhood

A mile from the Gordon Institute is the Bankhall Girls' Institute and Girls' Evening Home on Stanley Road, Kirkdale, opened in 1889 and designed by Picton, Chamber & Bradley of Dale Street, with the aim of promoting the spiritual and temporal welfare of women and girls. Since 1974 the building has housed the Rydal Youth Centre. The murals seen here, part of a project overseen by Liverpool artist David Jacques, depict young people in north Liverpool over the last century.

» The Gordon Institute was an instant success. Within weeks it had some 2,000 members, with around 250 attending every night. Indeed so popular was it that Cliff donated a further £1,000 for a gymnasium to be added to the rear in 1888. Alexander Alexander from the Liverpool Gymnasium assisted in providing equipment.

Meanwhile the Institute also formed clubs for cricket, rounders, football and swimming, and developed a fine tradition for boxing. (Local hero Nel Tarleton was one of its amateurs, while in later years the featherweight, Dom Volante, a product of Liverpool's Little Italy, offered coaching.)

Having set the standard, two more clubs followed in 1889: the Bankhall Girls' Institute (below),

and the Florence Institute (right), both based on the lessons learnt at the Gordon.

Of course Liverpool was not alone in such provision.

In Birkenhead, the Shaftesbury Boys' Club had opened in January 1886, based in the Chester Street Mission Sunday School, while Manchester's first club opened in Hulme, just prior to the Gordon Institute, in a converted building.

But nowhere in Britain have there been found any purpose built clubs older than the Liverpool trio.

Following those early years, a number of other boys' clubs were established in the city, leading to the formation in 1911 of the Liverpool Union of Clubs for Boys and Young Men, under the direction of Frederic D'Aeth (a

former clergyman who was the first paid lecturer at the University of Liverpool's pioneering School of Social Science). When this body changed its name to the Liverpool Union of Boys' Clubs in 1916 its objectives included the commitment to 'organise and manage athletics and games' and to 'provide playing fields'.

In 1925 the LUBC joined forces with the Liverpool Holiday Camps organisation, to form the Liverpool Boys' Association, and in the same year purchased three playing fields at Fazakerley (the Geoffrey Humble ground), at Woolton (the Simpson Ground) and at Allerton (Heron Eccles Playing Fields). These latter fields, so vital a focus for the development of footballing talent in the city until recent years, were named after the chairman of the LBA, J Heron Eccles, a Liverpool businessman.

By 1946 the LBA had 114 acres of playing fields at five locations, with over 1,000 boys using the facilities every week.

But the LBA and Merseyside in general also played a central role in the development of youth activities at a national level.

For example it was during visits to the YMCA on Grange Road, Birkenhead, in 1906 and 1907, that Robert Baden Powell raised the idea of forming a national boy scouts movement. As a result, the 2nd Birkenhead Scout Group, formed in February 1908, may claim to be the oldest scout group in the world. (Birkenhead would later host the first World Scout Jamboree, in Arrowe Park in 1929.)

Also during the 1920s, in 1924 Frederic D'Aeth played a leading role in the formation of the National Association of Boys' Clubs, of which J Heron Eccles, became the first chairman.

Then in December 1929 the decision of the Liverpool and District Ramblers Federation to form the Merseyside Youth Hostel Association led to the formation of the national Youth Hostel Association the following year.

Liverpool was also at the forefront of attempts to provide for the welfare of girls.

The creation of the Bankhall Institute for Girls in 1889 has already been noted. In 1890, following a meeting between the Institute's founders and various philanthropists and social campaigners – Mrs Picton, Miss Crossfield and the young Eleanor Rathbone included – the Liverpool Union of Girls' Clubs was formed, with the aim of helping members to cope with the demands and dangers of 'modern' girlhood. The union was non-denominational and non-political, offering handicrafts, singing and drill. (Eleanor Rathbone of course went on to become a leading campaigner for women and family rights and for the study of social sciences generally.)

Importantly, the LUGC is also thought to have been the first youth organisation in Britain to provide organised games for young female workers on a large scale. In 1929 it appointed a physical training instructor, and by 1938 – by which time it had over 100 affiliated clubs – LUGC members were fielding 110 rounders teams and over 60 netball teams, using public playing fields and school playgrounds.

In 1959 the LBA and the LUGC merged into one organisation, which was renamed in 1961 as the Liverpool Union of Youth Clubs. This has since been reformed as the Merseyside Youth Association, with offices on Hanover Street.

▲ Known locally as 'the Florrie' and opened in September 1889, the **Florence Institute**, on Mill Street, Dingle, is one of Britain's finest historic community buildings, hence its Grade II listing.

Financed by Bernard Hall, a West Indies merchant and former lord mayor, as a memorial to his daughter Florence (who had died aged 22, two years earlier), the building was probably designed by Cornelius Sherlock, architect also of the Walker Art Gallery and the Picton Reading Room. However, Sherlock died in 1888 and the actual building work appears to have been overseen by one of his partners, Herbert Keef.

The Florence's design differed from the Gordon in three respects.

Whereas the Gordon had been envisaged primarily as a place of instruction and moral development, the Florrie's aims were 'to promote the welfare of poor and working boys, more especially during the critical period between the time they leave school up to the age of 21', and to provide 'a place of instruction and recreation for the poor and working boys of this parish'. Note the word recreation.

For this reason, although there was still an emphasis on Christian values and bible studies – there were four classrooms and a library – the Florence's design incorporated a large gymnasium from its inception (a lesson that all other boys' clubs over the next two decades would follow).

Secondly, it may be noted from this view of the building taken shortly after its opening, instead of adopting a symmetrical facade, as at the Gordon and Bankhall Institutes, the Florence's main entrance was offset on Mill Street, adjacent to the polygonal stair tower forming the corner with what is now Wellington Road. On the fourth floor of this tower was a balcony, with an observatory above.

Finally, the use of warm red brick and terracotta created the impression, as noted by the *Liverpool Citizen* in 1890, of a 16th century manor house; a style echoed by one of Britain's other fine clubs of this genre, the Salford Lads' Club in Manchester (b.1903) whose design is remarkably similar.

▲ The gymnasium and library of the **Florence Institute** illustrate the founders' twin aims of improving both the minds and bodies of Dingle's poorest boys. No less important was that the Institute offered boys warmth and respite from their overcrowded terraces.

As with the Gordon, the Florrie proved instantly popular, enrolling 2,000 boys in its first two years.

Although this figure fluctuated over the years, sport played a vital role. Boxing became a core activity, while cricket and football teams were formed to play at Sefton Park.

But as fashions changed and as the building showed signs of wear and tear, its upkeep proved a constant problem. Former members were repeatedly asked for funds to patch up the structure.

Worst of all, in 1999 a fire destroyed much of the roof, leading to the Institute's closure and the very real threat of demolition.

For seven years the Friends of the Florrie campaigned tirelessly for the now derelict building to be saved, a call that was finally answered by the award of £3.9 million from the Heritage Lottery Fund, to restore the fabric and

return the Institute to its role as a community centre. A further £1.7m in matching funds is needed to complete this task, and so the campaign dare not rest on its laurels. But at least the Florrie's importance is now recognised.

For this is truly a national treasure, and one of only a few remaining buildings of its type left extant in Britain.

▲ Not all Liverpool's boys' and girls' clubs had the benefit of their own, purpose built premises.

This view is from the entrance of the **Shrewsbury Boys' Club** on Portland Place, Everton, where the club occupied four converted mid Victorian terraced houses.

Known as 'the Shewsy', the club was founded in 1903 by Reverend Digby Kittermaster, a former pupil of Shrewsbury School, who sought to make 'straight-thinking honest Christian men' out of 'good hearted street ruffians'.

As a newspaper report of a club party in 1905 noted, 'The work is amidst the very poor – that could be seen by glancing round the room'. Despite there being a blizzard that night, several boys had walked to the party barefoot.

Every boy was given a mug of cocoa, and bags containing a meat pie, a bun and an orange.

The club's first premises were in a former public house on the corner of Mansfield Street, close to the open-air pool (see page 167). Old Salopians in the city were recruited as voluntary tutors, while those who could not volunteer were asked to make a financial contribution.

In 1907 these donations allowed the club to purchase the Portland Place houses, each of which was assigned a house captain, echoing the public school model.

In addition to Sunday church services the club ran classes in such subjects as joinery, geography, science, cobbling and boxing. There was an indoor gymnasium and a caged football pitch on a flat roof.

In common with many boys' clubs, during the 1960s the Shewsy started opening its doors to girls. But as the surrounding terraced houses were gradually cleared and the local population declined, the need for modern premises resulted in a move to a new complex, built in 1974 as part of St Peter's Church, on Langrove Street, where the Shewsy still operates today.

Attached to the image shown here – used in the 1950s as a Christmas card – was the caption, 'What are you doing tonight?'

That concern for the welfare of local youth remains as valid today as in 1903.

Meanwhile the old 'Shewsy' buildings at Portland Place have been converted into flats.

Drill time at the Liverpool Boys' Association's gymnasium at Crawford House, Shiel Road, in 1946. The Crawford family, famous for their biscuit factory on Binns Road, also funded the Old Swan Boys' Club, formed in 1935 and based since then in a converted Victorian house on Derby Lane.

Chapter Seventeen

Boxing

Punching above their weight – the Mersey ABC is one of over 30 amateur boxing clubs active on Merseyside, a higher concentration than in any part of Britain outside London. But although formed only in 2000 and based in an old converted cricket pavilion in Mersey Park, Rock Ferry, Mersey ABC members have already found success at national level, a success that is mirrored across the region. At the 2005 ABA championships seven local fighters reached the finals, while of the eleven members of Britain's squad for the 2006 Commonwealth Games in Melbourne, four were from Merseyside, of whom two won gold medals.

Merseyside has long been regarded as a fertile breeding ground for top boxers.

From the dockside slums of Dingle to the backstreets of Bootle and Birkenhead, from the densely populated lanes of Little Italy to the high rise council estates of Kirkby, in boys' clubs and church halls, in rooms above pubs and gyms below stairs, boxing, like football, has traditionally been seen as an escape route out of poverty. Or, at the very least, as a means of channelling the pent-up energies of generations of working class men and boys.

Even today, Merseyside is widely regarded as the capital of the British amateur fight game.

The story of boxing, or pugilism as it was known when this ancient form of ritualised combat was revived in Georgian Britain, falls into two distinct periods: the early, bare knuckle years, fought under the so-called London Rules, drawn up by Jack Broughton in 1743 and revised in 1853, followed by the modern form of boxing, fought with gloves, introduced under the Queensberry Rules in 1867.

Liverpool had a number of venues for bare knuckle fights. Known as 'milling cribs', in 1800 these were made illegal, not so much to protect participants but to stem the gambling and rowdyism which often accompanied fights.

The identity of most cribs went unrecorded, as fights took place at secret locations. But several more legitimate venues existed, such as the Union Street tavern (on the site of the present day Bank of England, in Castle Street), the Globe Tavern in Thomas Street, the Golden Lion in Dale Street, Houghton's Assembly Rooms, where crowds of over 300 were common, and the York Hotel, Williamson Square, where a purse of 100 sovereigns was fought for in 1826 between 'well known pupils of the London ring'. Entry fees, typically of two shillings, made sure that only a select group of gentlemen could attend.

Bare knuckle fights were also commonly staged as side shows at race meetings (as were cock fights), or during holiday periods on the sand banks of Wallasey Pool. Welch Leys, near Chester,

was another location, as recorded in the *Liverpool Sporting Register* of October 1825, when Ralph Boscow and Pat M'Gee fought for 35 gruelling rounds, watched by crowd of 5,000, including many of the Liverpool 'fancy' (that is, sporting gents who liked a wager).

As a 16 verse doggerel poem described (*see* opposite), the local constables at Hawarden tried belatedly to stop the fight, then arrested the wrong man while the victor, M'Gee, made his escape.

After the introduction of the Queensberry Rules, gloves became mandatory, wrestling, kicking and gouging were barred, and rounds were limited to three minutes.

Boxing was now seen as character forming. It was taught at the Liverpool Gymnasium, where the bare knuckle champion Jem Mace offered instruction.

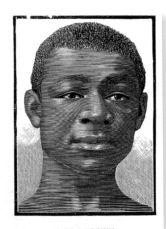

HARRY BROWN,
A Clever and Well-respected Coloured Boxer, who Hails from Liverpool.

Harry Brown – winner of the 'coloured' championship of the north in 1896 and featured in the journal *Mirror of Life* in September 1898 – was one of a number of black boxers from Liverpool denied the chance to compete for national honours, before the British Board of Boxing Control finally dropped its ban on non-white contenders in 1948. In the 1950s, Nigerians Hogan 'Kid' Bassey and Dick Tiger both settled in the city and won world titles. But Liverpool's greatest ever black boxer was Toxteth born John Conteh, holder of the world light heavyweight title from 1974–78.

Private member clubs sprang up, while the public flocked to venues such as the Gymnastic Club on Dale Street, the Adelphi Theatre – the 'Delly' – on Christian Street, and the Malakoff Music Hall in Cleveland Square.

In most towns and cities boxing would always be staged in hired premises like these; in hotels, pubs, public halls or often in boarded over swimming baths (for example, Lodge Lane Baths in Toxteth). However such was boxing's popularity in Liverpool that in 1911 a local promoter took over the Pudsey Street roller skating rink, and converted it into a bespoke 4,000 seat arena (see next page). At the time only Newcastle and London had similar establishments.

This was followed in 1932 by the construction of probably the finest purpose built boxing arena in Britain, the Liverpool Stadium (see page 158) on St Paul's Square.

Both these establishments would cement Liverpool's status as a hotbed of the sport. But even they were not always large enough to cater for public demand. Fights were also staged at the Breck Park and Stanley Greyhound Stadiums (see Chapter Ten), and more often at Anfield football ground, where in 1938 an estimated record crowd of over 40,000 saw Peter Kane secure the world flyweight title against Jackie Jurich (see page 64).

Boxing's golden era in Liverpool brought to the fore a procession of local-boys-made-good; the likes of Ike Bradley, Dom Volante and Nel Tarleton, all of whom retained their status as popular heroes long after their retirements. In the post war period they were joined by such fighters as the McAteer brothers, Billy Ellaway, Harry Scott and Johnny Cooke.

Later champions – for example Alan Rudkin and John Conteh – would emerge from the 1960s onwards.

But thereafter boxing on Merseyside entered a steady decline. Worst of all, the Liverpool Stadium finally succumbed to financial pressures in 1987.

Indeed as boxing also became taboo in political and educational circles, it seemed as if the sport might even die out completely.

And yet now, boxing is enjoying a remarkable revival.

Largely this is owing to an acceptance in official circles that boxing can, if properly taught and controlled, have a positive impact on young lives. Combined with extra funding and Council support for coaching and facilities, this has yielded a series of honours for local boxers.

At a double header staged in Stanley Park in March 1998, for example, Peter 'Choirboy' Culshaw, a product of the Huyton ABC, won the world super flyweight title, while Shea Neary, the 'Shamrock Express', based in Old Swan, won the world light welterweight title. Later that year both men defended their titles at St George's Hall. At the 2005 World Championships in China, Neil Perkins won a bronze.

Further confirmation of boxing's revival is the staging of the European Championships at Liverpool's new King's Dock Arena in 2008 (see page 163), and also the appointment of a respected Cuban coach, Mario Kindelán, to help local contenders prepare for the 2008 Olympics.

So despite the gloomy forecasts of two decades ago, boxing has fought its way back into the public arena, and looks like defending its corner well into the new century.

Extracts from **Boscow and M'Gee** (the fight in doggerel verse, to the tune of *Chevy Chace*), printed in the *Liverpool Sporting Register* October 1825:

It was in Liverpool's sea-port town,
Where lots o' the Fancy dwell,
It will be shown, two Lads of renown,
Were determined to have a mill.

Ralph Boscow, big, weighed thirteen stone,
With arms as strong as an Ox;
And M'Gee was all bone, and as hard as a stone,
And both were the Lads that could box.

Five thousand Lads stood all around,
And there was many a drag;
And many a pound, was bet on the ground,
And prigs they div'd for the swag.

The lads then peel'd upon the heath,
And up they stood to spar;
A blow that was good, and which drew the first blood,
M'Gee gave, - that son of war.

'Twas blow for blow, with horrid force.-
They struggled with all their might;
There were betting and shouts, but great were the doubts,
Which Hero would win the fight.

And so for many a round they fought,
And dealt out thund'ring blows;
Paddy's head and neck was a perfect wreck,
And shocking he look'd, God knows.

And Boscow he had got the gasps,
And often lost his pin;
He was tott'ring and weak, and great odds were at stake,
That Paddy the Battle would win.

At length in round the thirty-fifth,
Although quite out of breath,
Ralph Boscow again, struck the jugular vein, -
'Twas like a blow of Death!

The vic'try crown'd the butcher-boy,
Pat was lifeless as the tomb;
But his conduct was right, in this slaught'ring fight,
So ev'ry cove he scamper'd home!

In Hawarden town the Beakies met,
And thought to have stopt the fight;
But good Master Beak, made a sorry mistake,
And so it was "all right!"

'Twas honest Pat he thought to grab,
But he nabb'd good Mr. Rutter,
And Pat, if you please, was popt in a chaise,
And left the Beak in a sputter.

So now ye milling coves attend,
With courage bold and free,
Your glasses all fill, drink to the next mill,
And to Boscow and M'GEE!

▶ Over 70 years after its closure the old **Liverpool Stadium** on **Pudsey Street** is still revered as one of the great boxing arenas of the early 20th century. This was the venue in which Merseyside boxing enjoyed a tremendous revival after several lean decades, and where some of the city's most illustrious home-grown fighters gained their reputations. Unfortunately, however, few images of it have survived, and none of its exterior.

What is known is that the building was originally designed as stables for the Liverpool United Tramways Omnibus Company. It was then taken over by the Council in 1897, and for a short while used as a roller skating rink.

It was then converted into a 4,000 seat boxing arena in 1911 under the control of a promoter, Major Arnold Wilson. At that time there were only two purpose-built boxing venues in Britain, in London (the National Sporting Club) and in Newcastle (St James's Hall), so Wilson was taking a real gamble.

Opened in July 1911, Pudsey Street staged bouts every Thursday night, a tradition that continued until its demolition to make way for the Odeon Cinema on London Road. This programme was issued on the final night in March 1931, 18 months before its successor, the new Liverpool Stadium, opened on the other side of the city centre.

A typical Thursday night's bill at the **Pudsey Street Stadium** in 1921 illustrates the cultural mix of British boxing between the wars.

Hyman Gordon was one of a long line of Jewish fighters, while André Simeth, the Swiss champion, was challenged, and beaten, by Francis Rossi (not to be confused with the latter day rock musician), one of three Italian boxing brothers from Pontypridd.

Also to appear at Pudsey Street, defending his title twice in 1914 and 1915, was the British heavyweight from London's East End, Bombardier Billy Wells (who later featured in J Arthur Rank films, striking the famous gong).

Less successful in a title defence was the black Californian welterweight Dixie Kid, in 1913, knocked out in the eighth round by New Yorker Harry Lewis, in an epic bout which gave Pudsey Street its nickname as 'the graveyard of champions'.

But above all, Pudsey Street was home to a succession of legendary Liverpudlian fighters.

Bantamweight **Ike Bradley** (*top right*) was the first Liverpool boxer to fight there for a world title, in September 1911. On that occasion he lost on points to Digger Stanley of Hull, despite having Stanley on the canvas for 14 seconds.

Bradley fought in over 400 bouts, before becoming a 'second' at the new Liverpool Stadium. He also became a familiar presence in the city as a taxi driver.

An even greater legend in the 1920s was **Nel Tarleton** (*centre right*), a graduate of the Everton Red Triangle boxing club (which still exists). Tarleton fought in 12 title fights, including one infamous victory against his friend and fellow Liverpudlian **Dom Volante** (*lower right*) at Breck Park Stadium in

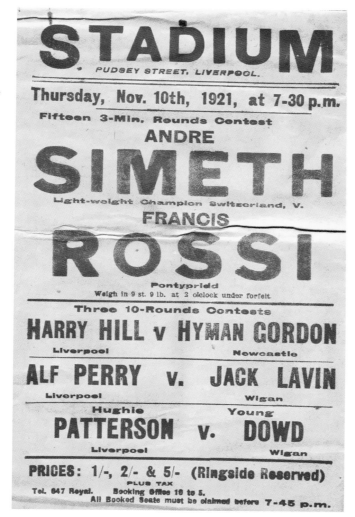

July 1928, which ended with a riot amongst the 13,000 crowd, and the referee, Bombardier Billy Wells, being badly cut by a flying seat.

Tarleton won the second of his titles at the age of 40, in 1945, a remarkable achievement for a man with only one lung.

Out of the ring Tarleton and Volante had a regular double act. Tarleton would tap dance while Volante played the mouth organ.

Volante, born in Gerard Street's Little Italy, was on the bill on Pudsey Street's final night. After retiring in 1935 he worked as an instructor aboard cruise ships, often entertaining passengers with his mouth organ. He also trained young boxers at the Gordon Institute (*see page 149*), where the Dom Volante Cup was contested for many years.

MAIN ENTRANCE TO LIVERPOOL STADIUM.

▶ Built in just three months on the site of the former graveyard of St Paul's Church, at the north end of Bixteth Street, the £15,000 **Liverpool Stadium**, successor to Pudsey Street, was the most advanced boxing arena in Britain.

(Newcastle's St James's Hall had been rebuilt in 1930, while the only other purpose-built arena, in Sunderland, closed that same year after only ten years in business. In the north west the other major venue was the King's Hall, at Belle Vue, Manchester, built in 1910 but converted into a 6,000 seat boxing arena in the 1920s).

Behind the Stadium venture was a consortium of boxing enthusiasts known as the Harmony Six, led by an official of the Amateur Boxing Association, Major J Bennett, and Arnold Wilson's successor as promoter at Pudsey Street, Johnny Best. In the programme for the opening night, architect Kenmure Kinna offered this description:

'The new Stadium, unique in conception and design, is an example of the modern style building... steel framed (of British Steel) and clothed with brickwork of a pleasing grey colour, with a large central feature faced in Terra Cotta. The roof is supported on steel trusses, and is the largest span of its kind in Liverpool, being 120 ft between supports...

'The levels of the main hall have been decided so that everyone has a clear view of the ring from any part of the building, and thus has arisen the saucer shape which was prevalent in the days of the gladiators...'

Of special note, added Kinna, was the 35,000 candle power lighting rig above the ring; its glare shielded from spectators by a suspended board showing the number of the round being fought.

Also innovative was the actual ring. Instead of 'the usual parade of buckets', wrote Kinna, sinks were plumbed in under each corner, while the ring structure was designed to be easily dismantled so that other events might take place.

In the 1950s these included circuses, religious meetings, political rallies addressed by Winston Churchill and Clement Attlee, and informal classical concerts, aimed at workers deemed unlikely to attend the Philharmonic.

But twice weekly boxing and regular wrestling nights were the staple. Even during World War Two the action hardly abated. In 1942,

80 boxing shows were staged there to maintain morale, while in 1944 there was a guest appearance by the US Army's ambassador, world heavyweight champion Joe Louis (who, as a publicity stunt during his visit, signed for Liverpool FC).

Surprisingly no official figure for the Stadium's capacity was ever recorded. But judging from newspaper reports it seems to have been in the region of 5,000.

But facts and figures cannot begin to express the atmosphere of the Stadium. In stark contrast to today's smoke-free, closely stewarded environments, here was a steamy, no-frills arena in which

the crowds were as much a part of the action as the fighters.

In one part of the arena was an aisle known as Mugs Alley, where punters would wait on the off chance of one of the boxers failing to turn up, in which case they would be expected to strip off and enter the fray at short notice.

Even for experienced boxers the Stadium was intimidating, as a result of which, like Pudsey Street, it too became known as 'the graveyard of champions' (an irony given the site's original function).

After Johnny Best's death in 1956, his son, also John, took over as managing director. He

was followed by John Moores, the Littlewoods chairman. Later, the Stadium became a rallying centre for workers at the docks and at Ford's Halewood plant during the protracted union battles of the 1970s. It also became a popular music venue, hosting concerts by Gene Vincent, David Bowie, Lou Reed and many others.

But for any boxer from the back streets, for over half a century the Liverpool Stadium was their mecca; the place in which reputations were made and broken in front of a knowing crowd of ringside experts and hardened punters, and under the glare of its unforgiving lights.

◀ Members of the **Merseyside Former Boxers' Assocation** gather on Bixteth Street on the eve of the **Liverpool Stadium**'s demolition in February 1987 – a moment of immense poignancy.

In fact the Stadium had been in steady decline for some years.

Attendances for both boxing and wrestling had started falling in the 1960s. There had been a crowd riot after a stormy night of boxing in November 1973, followed by various refurbishments in advance of what would prove to be the Stadium's last world title fight, on 5 March 1977, when John Conteh retained his light heavyweight title against Detroit's Len Hutchins.

But by then the building was also suffering from a number of structural defects.

The Liverpool Stadium's last night of boxing took place on 3 October 1985, the final bout, appropriately, featuring a local heavyweight, Noel Quarless, from the Salisbury ABC, Everton.

Following its demolition the site was used as a car park, although the actual location of the boxing ring was marked on the ground in the midst of a small public garden.

However, in 2006 development of the site into offices and shops commenced, and alas, no memorial to the boxing arena within the new development has been included.

Those former boxers and their friends and relatives identified in the 1987 photograph are as follows:

1. Jimmy Gore 2. Frank Hope 3. Mickey Flanagan 4. Vince Volante 5. Arthur Styles 6. Jimmy Melia 7. Jack Tansey 8. Les Cannon 9. Tommy Golst 10. Chuck McGowan 11. Billy Watt 12. Bernie Pugh 13. Jimmy Molloy 14. Jim Boyd 15. Gordon Ashun 16. Brian McCaffrey 17. Tommy Bailey 18. Les Dean 19. Tut Whalley 20. Harry Scott 21. Paddy Bennett 22. Tommy Moran 23. Tommy McNally 24. Jonty Pilkington 25. Billy Ellaway 26. Billy Ellaway Jnr 27. Eddie Monahan 28. Les Radcliffe 29. Johnny Holmes 30. Jim Jenkinson 31. Alf Kennedy 32. Tommy Burney 33. Teddy Snowball 34. Gerry Crummey 35. Tommy Griffiths 36. Gus Foran 37. Alf Gidman 38. Terry Riley 39. Johnny Sullivan 40. Stan Rowan 41. Terry McHale 42. Larry Parkes 43. Les McAteer 44. Billy Davies 45. Joey Singleton 46. Eric Marsden 47. George Metcalfe 48. Tony Carroll 49. Jack Saul

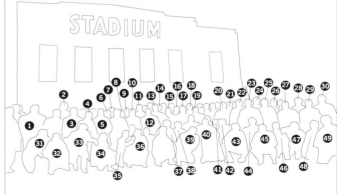

▶ For over 90 years, grave number 594 in Anfield Cemetery was completely unmarked. And yet it contained the remains of the man who is generally regarded as the father of modern scientific boxing, **James 'Jem' Mace**.

Otherwise known as the Swaffham Gypsy – he was born in Beeston, Norfolk, where there is another memorial to him – Mace was the last bare knuckle British heavyweight champion, beating Joe Goss in Purfleet in August 1866, shortly before the use of gloves became standard under the newly drawn up Queensberry rules.

On his return to Liverpool (where Mace was an instructor at the Liverpool Gymnasium and also a judge at the Olympic Festivals), a crowd of 10,000 carried him shoulder high to a civic reception.

In 1870 Mace also gained the unofficial title of world champion, after defeating Tom Allen over ten rounds in Kenner, Louisiana.

Throughout his colourful life, Mace fought hundreds of exhibition matches, including in Australia and New Zealand. He also toured Britain as a circus showman and music hall performer, and was still treading the boards and packing in audiences shortly before he died in 1910, aged 79. Yet despite his fame and all the boxers he had helped and coached over the years, only in 2003, thanks to the efforts of the **Merseyside Former Boxers' Association**, was his grave finally marked by a proper headstone.

The Association itself was set up in 1973 at the behest of former boxer Les Radcliffe, prompted by a series of interviews with old Merseyside boxers conducted by Syd Dye, boxing correspondent of the *Liverpool Echo*. Shortly after its formation it was joined by a similar group, the Wirral ex-Boxers Association. As of 2007 these two associations have a combined membership of 175 former boxers.

In recognition of boxing's special place within the cultural heritage of Merseyside, and of the region's contribution to British boxing, in June 2006 the two associations were awarded £46,000 by the Heritage Lottery Fund to develop 60 video biographies of former boxers, supplemented by a website and a mobile exhibition, scheduled to tour the region from June 2007 onwards.

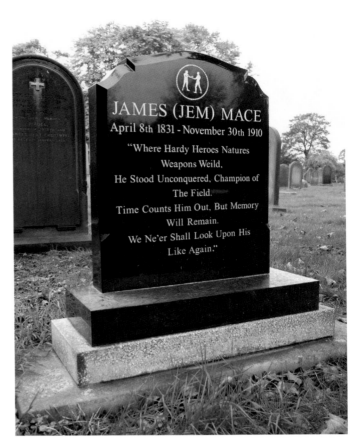

JAMES (JEM) MACE
April 8th 1831 - November 30th 1910

"Where Hardy Heroes Natures Weapons Weild,
He Stood Unconquered, Champion of The Field.
Time Counts Him Out, But Memory Will Remain.
We Ne'er Shall Look Upon His Like Again."

Another slab of masonry which bears considerable resonance for Liverpool's boxing community is the foundation stone of the Liverpool Stadium, recently rediscovered in a garage near the docks and for many years lovingly tended by James Thompson, son of the late boxer and regular at the Stadium, Dennis Thompson. It is hoped that the stone will be placed on permanent display at the new Museum of Liverpool, scheduled to open on Mann Island, close to the Pierhead, in 2010.

LIVERPOOL STADIUM
THIS STONE WAS LAID BY THE RIGHT HONOURABLE THE EARL OF LONSDALE KG
JULY 22ND 1932

▲ Former champions Tommy Bache and Alan Rudkin rescue the sign of the **Golden Gloves Amateur Boxing Club** from the demolished United Services Club in Admiral Street, Toxteth, in 1974.

Bache (*left*), a former flyweight who won a silver medal at the 1958 Empire Games, had learnt to box at the nearby Florence Institute (*see page 151*), while Rudkin, who had recently retired as British, Commonwealth and European bantamweight champion, started his career at the Golden Gloves.

The club had originally formed at the Belvedere Boys' Club (established in 1898), before moving to the Admiral Hall, Dingle, in 1950 and then to Admiral Street three years later. More recently the

Golden Gloves (and this sign) have returned to their spiritual home at the new **Belvedere Boys Club** on Miles Street (*below*), recently upgraded thanks to Sport England and in 2006 chosen as the city's first official Boxing Academy.

▲ There can surely be no stronger affirmation of boxing's status in Liverpool than the fact that the first major event to be staged at the new £146 million **Liverpool Arena** at **King's Dock** will be the European Boxing Championships in February 2008.

Apart from being a spectacular event in itself, the championships – organised over ten days by the Amateur Boxing Association in conjunction with Sport England, UK Sport and Liverpool City Council – will act as one of the Olympic qualifying competitions for the Beijing Olympics of 2008.

Commissioned by Liverpool City Council and designed by the award winning architects Wilkinson Eyre

(also known for their 'blinking eye' Millennium Bridge at Gateshead), the 9,900 seat arena – linked by a central atrium to a 1,350 seat conference centre, exhibition centre and multi-storey car park – will of course also stage a range of other high profile sporting events and music concerts.

It is by far the most ambitious sports-related building ever to have been built in the city.

But as far as Merseyside's boxing fraternity is concerned, the new King's Dock Arena is also the true successor to the Pudsey Street and Liverpool Stadiums; that is, a place where local boxers might step out proudly from their backstreet gyms and onto the world's stage.

Chapter Eighteen

Swimming

SWIM FOR HEALTH STRENGTH AND PLEASURE

LIVERPOOL CORPORATION BATHS

Since its first involvement in public baths in 1794, the local authority in Liverpool has operated a larger stock of swimming pools than any other municipality. By the 1930s when this poster was issued, it ran 16 baths, with two more due to open in 1936, plus over 20 school pools. Five were open air (four of them free of charge to children). This investment continues today with the construction of the city's first 50m pool at Wavertree.

As a city whose fortunes have depended so heavily on water-borne trade and shipping, it may seem natural that Liverpool was at the forefront of providing public facilities for swimming in the 19th and early 20th centuries.

But in fact its pioneering efforts were motivated not by a desire to promote recreation, in the modern sense, but by the desire of the merchant classes for exclusive bathing facilities, and later, by a concern for public hygiene.

Liverpool is thought to have been the first British municipality to take over and run a bath house, in 1794, and the first to build municipal swimming baths, in 1829, both located on the dock side and aimed at an elite clientele.

In the ensuing years, however, in 1842 Liverpool also became the first authority to build a public wash-house, or laundry, and in 1847 was the first to appoint both a Medical Officer of Health, in the person of Dr William Duncan, and a Borough Engineer, the Scot, James Newlands. These measures, and appointments, in turn led to the creation of a network of public swimming baths that, by 1900, was arguably the finest in Britain.

Given the squalid housing conditions that prompted this construction programme, it may seem surprising that just prior to the industrial revolution Liverpool was regarded as Lancashire's premier sea bathing resort. Indeed districts on both banks of the Mersey were even named after Georgian Britain's prototype seaside resort; that is, New Brighton on the Wirral peninsula and Brighton-le-Sands in Crosby.

Not that these resorts suited everyone. As the *Stranger's Guide to Liverpool* of 1807 noted, 'the promiscuous bathing of the sexes in this part of the river, and necessary public exposure, will not... recommend them to persons of great, real or affected delicacy.'

It is important at this juncture to draw a distinction between bathing and swimming.

For example, as early as 1701 the Liverpool Common Council had considered building an enclosed 'bagnio' on a piece of land near the old Pool inlet. This was what we might now consider a plunge pool, in which to cleanse oneself and relax, as was the Roman model, rather than to swim. The site was eventually developed as Liverpool's first dock, but the idea did not go away, and in 1756 John Naylor Wright established Liverpool's first baths at the end of the New Quay, on what became known as Bath Street.

Wright's establishment offered separate and equal facilities for both sexes. Patrons could soak in one of six private baths, could make their way down some stairs to swim in the river, or could proceed to a public plunge pool, measuring 33 x 30 feet and enclosed by high walls.

Richard Brooke described the baths as 'commodious, safe and elegant' and having 'all the advantages of the salubrity of salt water without exposing the bather to view...'

Private baths of this type were then relatively common in Britain. But what made Wright's baths different was that in 1794 the Common Council bought the leasehold for £4,000, and spent a further £1,000 on improvements.

This road sign on the wall of Princes Dock recalls the presence of John Naylor Wright's first private baths, opened in 1756. Entrance cost threepence, or five shillings for the season, which lasted from 1 May to 31 August. In 1794 the baths were taken over by the Common Council.

Not only that but when these baths were demolished in 1820 to make way for the Prince's Dock, the Corporation Surveyor, John Foster Junior, was asked to design a modern replacement. Opened in 1829, St George's Baths, also known as the Pierhead Baths (*see page 168*) were thus the first ever built and funded by a municipality.

But although public baths in name, they were still nevertheless priced at a level that ensured their exclusivity (as would be the town's other private baths, on Renshaw Street, Cases Street and Great George Street). For the vast majority of town dwellers, baths were still an unthinkable luxury.

But circumstances were about to change this dramatically.

In 1772 Liverpool's population stood at 35,000. By 1841 this had increased to 225,000. Inevitably the infrastructure failed to cope. In 1832, 1,500 people died in a cholera epidemic.

Still, councillors were loathe to intervene. Instead, famously, it was left to a housewife, Kitty Wilkinson, to establish a wash house in her back kitchen at the height of the 1832 epidemic, and in doing so, prove that hygiene was essential in fighting disease.

Her efforts soon attracted the attention of philanthropists, and of both Dr Duncan (then in private practice) and the engineer, James Newlands. The result was that in May 1842 Liverpool opened the nation's first publicly funded baths and wash house, on Frederick Street, with Wilkinson and her husband Tom as superintendents.

This was four years before the 1846 Baths and Wash-houses Act prompted other local authorities to follow suit (effectively by allowing them to borrow money in order to finance construction). »

▶ Bearing the name of William Hill, this small card is a season ticket for what is thought to be Britain's earliest known **floating baths**, launched on the River Mersey on 11 June 1816 by Thomas Colgan. (There had been floating baths in Paris since 1760 and others in Frankfurt and Vienna.)

Colgan's baths were constructed within the hull of a ship, buoyed up by air-tight chambers and moored off Prince's Parade during the summer and at Wallasey Pool in winter.

According to Samuel Cornish's *Stranger's Guide to Liverpool*, the main pool measured 80 x 27 feet, its depth increasing from 3.5 to six feet, with a continual flow of river water passing through the vessel via an iron trellis at each end.

'Gentlemen who prefer swimming in the river are allowed to go through the door on the side of the vessel which may happen to be opposite the Cheshire coast,' while for those who preferred simply to soak in privacy there was a smaller plunge bath, plus a screen so that individuals could pass from the dressing rooms into the water 'unobserved'.

Two further cabins were provided for relaxation, offering newspapers and refreshments, while on the upper deck were seats and tables affording 'a most pleasing and ever-varying prospect'.

How long Colgan's baths operated is not known, particularly once the far superior Pierhead Baths opened on terra firma in 1829 (although the floating concept remained popular in Paris for much of the 19th century).

But in 1864 a second floating bath appeared on the Mersey. This was within the hull of a converted naval frigate, the **Training Ship Indefatigable**, featured in the

Illustrated London News of June 1874 (*below*) and operated by a charity set up by shipowner, John Clint, to train the sons of sailors, destitute and orphaned boys, to become merchant seamen. It had cost £5,000 to refit the frigate, a sum donated by James Bibby.

(Three other training ships on the Mersey were the HMS Conway, launched in 1859 to train naval officers, and both the Akbar and the Clarence, used as reformatory schools for Protestant and Catholic boys respectively. Prior to 1914 the Akbar was also closely associated with the Shrewsbury Boys' Club.)

Other floating baths were built by London's Charing Cross Pier in 1875, and on the Dee at Chester in 1883. But they were expensive to maintain, vulnerable to the elements and none survive, in Britain at least (although in Paris the tradition continues with a new floating pool opened in 2006).

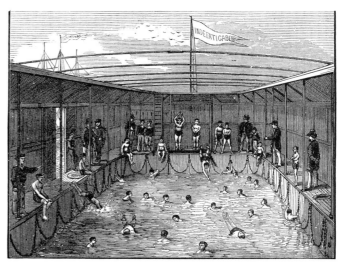

>> At this stage there was no requirement or even expectation for baths and wash-houses to include facilities for swimming. But based on the experience of the Pierhead Baths, Liverpool's next establishment did feature two small pools. This was at Paul Street, opened in 1846, and as the plans show (*see page 169*) both pools were still relatively small. They were, however, more popular than anyone anticipated.

Thus, when it came to the next baths on Cornwallis Street, opened in 1851, the newly formed Baths Committee decided to convert the space allocated for laundry facilities into a third pool instead.

As with all baths of this era, a class system was rigidly enforced.

At Cornwallis Street the 43 bathrooms were divided into three classes, each with varying degrees of comfort and hot water, while the three swimming baths were divided into Men's First and Second Class, with a third, smaller pool for females.

Apart from their size and relative comforts, the chief difference between the classes concerned water quality. Before filtration systems were introduced in the early 20th century, the water in all swimming baths was changed on a weekly basis – the so-called 'fill and empty' system.

At the start of the week the water was clean and clear. But as the week progressed it became increasingly dirty, so that the cheapest day to swim was always the last in the weekly cycle. And as the cheaper of the two pools, the second class bath was invariably the least clean.

Cornwallis Street was followed by a fourth baths building on Margaret Street in 1863, and four more, at Steble Street (1874),

▲ Apart from concerns for health, one of the prime motives for the creation of public pools in 19th century Britain was the high rate of drownings and swimming accidents in urban rivers and canals.

In Liverpool, as pictured here c.1890, the favourite place for a 'skinny dip' was a stretch of the Leeds and Liverpool Canal near the Burlington Street bridge, known to local boys as 'the hotties' or 'the scaldies' because of the discharge

of hot water from the adjoining Tate & Lyle sugar refinery.

Even after the Corporation's Baths Committee opened a safer, heated open air bath for children at Burlington Street in 1895 (*see opposite*) the canal continued to attract boys, as the heroic exploits of **James Clarke** testify.

Born in British Guyana, Clarke arrived in Liverpool in 1900 at the age of 14, and found work at the docks. Soon his prowess as a

swimmer made him a key member of the Wavertree Swimming Club, for whom he captained the water polo team. He also swam for the Bootle, Waterloo and Everton swimming clubs.

But the reason for the plaque shown here – unveiled by the Vauxhall History & Heritage Group at the Eldonian Village Hall in 2003, just by the Burlington Bridge – is that Clarke also regularly rescued boys from the canal, as well as many a dock worker and seaman from the docks and river. Eventually Clarke persuaded the authorities to allow him to teach swimming to schoolboys at the Burroughs Gardens baths. He also coached the Liverpool police's swimming and boxing teams.

Modest to the last, Clarke died in 1946. Apart from the plaque there is also a James Clarke Street, close to the site of 'the scaldies'.

Westminster Road (1877), Lodge Lane (1878) and Burroughs Gardens (1879). By now, the city's robust approach to public health provision was attracting interest from all over Britain, including from Lord Ashley's Society for the Improvement of the Condition of the Working Classes, who consulted with Newlands on how best to proceed with similar schemes in London.

In 1903 Liverpool also hosted the World Health Conference, for which a handbook was specially issued, extolling the virtues of the city's baths provision.

Liverpool was equally to the fore when it came to subsidised swimming. In the 1890s it was decided to build four small open air baths, free of charge to under 15s (*see right*). Schoolchildren were also allowed entry to other baths for one penny. Moreover, from 1900, following pressure from teachers, the Baths Committee granted free bathing to all elementary schoolboys.

The Edwardian period saw four further baths opening in the suburbs, at Lister Drive (1904), Picton Road (1906), Garston (1907) and Queens Drive (1909).

By this time bathing admissions had increased to over 1.4 million annually, more than a threefold increase since 1892. Of these, nearly 690,000 were children, swimming free of charge.

Meanwhile, as the population shifted outwards and new water filtration systems were introduced, two of the older baths – Paul Street in 1879 and the Pierhead Baths in 1906 – were demolished.

Also in this period was the gradual introduction of mixed bathing, from 1914 onwards, and, by 1924, the construction of small pools, with slipper baths, at 24

Liverpool schools, a remarkable achievement in itself.

The final phase of expansion took place in the 1930s, with the opening of identical pools in the newly created housing estates of Norris Green and Dovecot.

In the postwar period, in common with most British cities, Liverpool's older stock of pools suffered greatly from under investment and from changing social demands, leading to a succession of closures: Cornwallis Street in 1967, Margaret Street and Burroughs Gardens in 1985, Lister Drive in 1987 and Lodge Lane in 1990. Even the two showpiece baths built in 1936 failed to survive beyond the end of the century.

In their place, as the need for slipper baths and laundries receded, a new generation of multi-purpose 'sports barns' emerged, combining both wet and dry sports under the same roof. The first of these was built on Great Homer Street, Everton in 1985. But the Council also continued to build smaller pools at local schools, such as at Breckside in 1964. Interestingly, however, neither this, nor another pool built at Belle Vale in 1975, would prove durable. Both closed after less than 30 years use.

Unlike most large authorities, when competitive tendering was introduced by the government in the 1990s Liverpool retained the management of their pools. The result is that in 2007, the total number of public pools run by the city is eleven, all rebranded as Lifestyles Centres and offering a range of activities, such as fitness centres, alongside swimming.

Two new Lifestyle Centres with pools opened in 2000 as part of this new regime, at Garston and Ellergreen, followed in March

2007 by a £6 million pool and sports centre on Queen's Drive, Walton, in conjunction with Alsop High School. The Council has also, meanwhile, taken over the running of the small Newhall Pool, Fazackerley, built originally in 1890 as part of a cottage homes scheme for pauper children.

Liverpool thus has five surviving historic baths. Of these, Lister Drive and Picton Road have both been converted to other uses, as described later, leaving Steble Street, Newhall and Woolton as the only pre-1900 pools in use for swimming. All the other historic baths have been replaced, with the latest being Picton Road, where on an adjoining site Liverpool's first 50m pool is scheduled to open in 2008 (*see page 183*). Costing £15 million, of which the Council is contributing £11 million, the Picton Pools promise to set the standard for the 21st century against which all future developments will be judged.

It will therefore be fascinating to see whether Picton, and their counterparts in the Lifestyles network, serve as long, and as robustly as their Victorian and Edwardian predecessors.

▼ While in London various local authorities created open air lakes in which men and boys might cool off in summer, Liverpool created four small plunge pools.

This one, opened in June 1899 at a cost of £2,931 and with an adjoining playground, was on **Mansfield Street**. The others were at Burlington Street (near 'the scaldies', opened in 1895), Gore Street (1898) and Green Lane (March 1899). The water in each location was heated, while entry was free and, after it was realised that children were deterred by the presence of older youths, restricted to under 15s. Girls-only sessions were held one day a week at Mansfield Street.

So popular were these four baths that in 1900, 644,000 bathers were admitted, more than the combined total of all the other indoor pools. In 1923 a fifth, larger open air pool opened in Stanley Park (*see page 53*).

However during World War Two Burlington Street, Gore Street and Mansfield Street were destroyed in air raids. Green Lane closed in 1953, followed by Stanley Park in 1960. There have been no public open air pools in Liverpool since.

▶ Known variously as **St George's Baths**, **Pierhead Baths** or the **Liverpool Baths**, Britain's first publicly funded baths cost an astonishing £24,481, plus a further £19,178 when the foundations were found wanting – more in total than any other baths built in 19th century Liverpool.

Designed by John Foster Junior, architect also of Aintree's main stand, they opened on 8 June 1829 and were described on a prospectus as 'worthy of particular commendation from the casual or critical observer… The walls, rusticated, are finished upwards by a cornice surmounted by a parapet. The roof projects to form two piazzas and is supported by a colonnade of 18 columns…

'The gentlemen's baths are behind the north colonnade. The most extensive is… 45 feet by 27…

'A spacious saloon leads to the private warm baths… In the south wing are the ladies baths of which the principal is 39 feet by 27… Four private and two cold baths are annexed to this branch…

'A reservoir… containing 800 tons of water is immediately under the building, by which means an ample supply of salubrious element will be always at hand.

'The structure viewed as a whole is chaste and unique, and forms a striking, tasteful addition to the architectural beauties of the town.'

St George's Baths, Liverpool
and Cheshire Ferry Boats

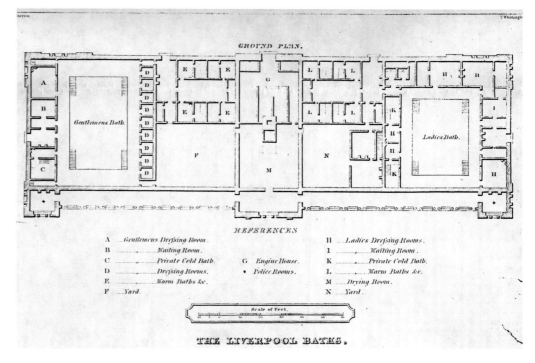

GROUND PLAN.

Gentlemens Bath.

Ladies Bath.

REFERENCES

A	Gentlemens Dressing Room.		H	Ladies Dressing Rooms.
B	Waiting Room.		I	Waiting Room.
C	Private Cold Bath.	G ...... Engine House.	K	Private Cold Bath.
D	Dressing Rooms.	● ...... Police Rooms.	L	Warm Baths &c.
E	Warm Baths &c.		M	Drying Room.
F	Yard.		N	Yard.

Scale of Feet.

THE LIVERPOOL BATHS.

◀ Photographed shortly before their demolition in 1906, the **Pierhead Baths** stood in front of what is now the Port of Liverpool building (the southernmost of the Three Graces), seen here in mid construction.

Although by then coated in grime, at their peak the baths were highly sophisticated. River water was diverted into a reservoir, then pumped into heating pans via a filtering apparatus using sand and charcoal. (Apparently the pumps would be regularly clogged by stray marbles, dropped by unemployed dockers for whom the promenade was a regular haunt.)

The Baths Committee had intended to build new baths on an adjacent site bordered by Mann Island. But war intervened in 1914 and the plans were mothballed. Thus there have been no baths in the city centre since 1906.

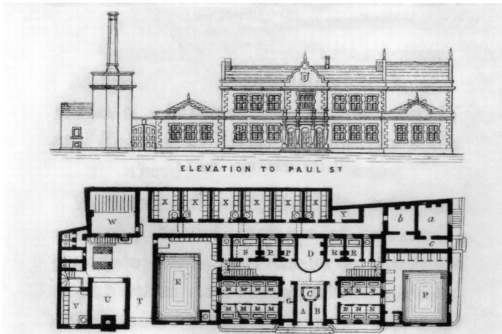

ELEVATION TO PAUL ST

◀ Designed by John Foster Junior's successor as Corporation Surveyor, Joseph Franklin, and opened in 1846, **Paul Street Baths** were Liverpool's first public baths built in a working class district.

In plan they echoed the layout of the Pierhead Baths, but at £6,500 were considerably cheaper.

Because the laundry facilities and individual slipper baths were then regarded as more important than swimming, the plunge baths were still relatively small; the larger male baths being just 27 x 17 feet and no deeper than 4 feet 9 inches.

All baths in Britain at this stage were essentially experimental, which is why so few survived into the later Victorian period. Paul Street Baths operated for only 33 years, before their demolition in 1879. But many lessons were learnt in this period, not least that plunge baths would have to be much larger to cope with demand.

Baths, Cornwallis Street, Liverpool.

◀ Opened on 5 May 1851, the **Cornwallis Street Baths** were the first in Liverpool to be built under the provisions of the 1846 Baths and Wash-houses Act, and the first in the city to have been designed by an engineer, James Newlands, rather than by an architect. The result was a model establishment that would be much copied in style and form elsewhere (at Birmingham's Woodcock Street in 1860, for example).

Newlands' original plan was to have two plunge pools, both below street level, and a large laundry, planned to cater for up to 90 washerwomen at one go. However, before it was completed the latter was converted into a third pool, making Cornwallis Street the largest swimming facility of any of its contemporaries, and also the most expensive, at nearly £28,000. Partly this was due to the expense of installing a pumping system to carry saltwater up the hill from the Mersey, via an underground pipe.

As was typical of early baths, there were no set dimensions. At Cornwallis Street the three pools measured approximately 57 x 40 feet, 42 x 27 feet and 40 x 27 feet.

It was calculated that although only about 12 per cent of bathers paid for first class facilities, they provided half the baths' income.

Along with Westminster Road (*see right*), Cornwallis Street was the city's most popular baths (despite the distinctive taste and odour of its water). It held Liverpool's first swimming gala in 1860 (a male-only affair – women were not allowed their own until 1887), and by the time it closed in 1967, a total of 16 million admissions had been recorded.

Newlands' second baths design at **Margaret Street** (*left*), opened in June 1863, after four years of lobbying by the West Derby Guardians and by residents of Everton. Its two pools were identical in size, at 67 x 34' each, and were filled with water used for condensing purposes by the nearby Aubrey Street pumping station.

As can be seen, its external dressings were not as lavish as its predecessor. Nor was its interior, hence the lower costs of £11,344.

Margaret Street was replaced by the Everton Park Sports Centre in 1985, and has since been demolished, as has Cornwallis Street, although in 2006 it was still possible to see an exposed section of the latter's basement, together with stains left over from the structure on the yellow brick wall of its neighbour, the Workshops for the Outdoor Blind (by George Redmayne, built 1870).

▲ One of the oldest operational baths in modern Britain, and certainly the oldest surviving in Liverpool, the **Steble Street Baths**, Toxteth, now forms part of the Park Road Lifestyles Sports Centre. Both its original pools, measuring approximately 52 x 38 feet, have been modernised, while its former wash-house is now a gymnasium (*see page 146*).

Named after Lieutenant Colonel RF Steble, chairman of the Baths Committee and also the Mayor at the time of its opening in April 1874, the baths had been planned as early as 1850, but a shortage of funds meant that the land was occupied for over a decade by one of Charles Melly's open air gymnasiums, or playgrounds.

Steble Street Baths was the first of four baths built in working class districts during a second phase of development in the 1870s, all designed by the Borough Engineer and costing £20–30,000 each.

The second was **Westminster Road** (*left*), Kirkdale, opened in April 1877, followed by Lodge Lane, Toxteth, in August 1878 and Burroughs Gardens, off Scotland Road, in January 1879.

Of this quartet, the Gothic-style Westminster Road was the largest, with one of its two pools measuring 100 x 34 feet, a length which made it a favourite training pool for long distance swimmers.

Although no longer in use, parts of the building remained extant in 2006. However the sign on Furness Street pointing visitors to it (*right*) has since been removed.

Steble Street's sign (*above right*) fortunately survives.

Meanwhile, Burroughs Gardens, where there were two pools, measuring 59 x 28 feet and 31 x 14 feet, was closed in 1985, while Lodge Lane, with pools measuring 75 x 32 feet and 64 x 30 feet, closed in 1990. Both have since been demolished.

▶ As subsequent amendments to the 1846 Act made it easier for local authorities to finance baths, the designs became more sophisticated. One such example of this new generation was built by the neighbouring borough of Bootle (now Sefton Metropolitan Council).

Designed by George Heaton and opened in 1888, **Bootle Baths,** Balliol Road, was faced in stone, with ashlar dressings, rather than brick, with a carriage entrance at the side for the delivery and collection of laundry. Notice also the more prominent, decorated chimney, a feature often used to draw attention to baths buildings.

For males (*below right*), the salt water pool measured 100 feet in length, and in winter was boarded over for use as a gymnasium. The female pool was only 60 feet long.

Drying racks (*below*), also now fairly standard, ensured a supply of fresh towels for hire.

Another increasingly popular feature was the provision of steam and vapour baths for relaxation.

Bootle Baths closed in 1998, but the facade has been retained and is the only baths structure in the city to be Grade II listed.

▲ The village suburb of Woolton has various claims to fame. This is where the sandstone used for the Anglican Cathedral was quarried, and where John Lennon met Paul McCartney at the local church in 1957. Woolton has a wonderful Village Club and bowling green (*see page 125*), the much loved Picture House, opened in 1927, and over one hundred listed buildings.

Yet one of Woolton's least celebrated, and unlisted gems is **Woolton Baths**, wedged artfullly into a sloping site on the corner of Quarry Street and Allerton Road.

Designed by Horton & Bridgford of Manchester (who also designed the Victoria Baths at Southport), and opened in 1893, the baths were gifted by the chemical manufacturer Holbrook Gaskell to Much Woolton Urban District Council and taken over by Liverpool Corporation when Woolton was absorbed in 1913.

The baths have a single 60 x 25 feet pool, featuring original tiles lining the water's edge (*below left*), decorated with Anthemion and Palmette motifs and believed to be manufactured by Minton's. The bath's neo-classical entrance is of course made from local sandstone.

Baths of this compact scale have great appeal, but struggle to satisfy modern demands and balance sheets. Could it be that sooner or later Woolton Baths will need all the help it can get from its friends?

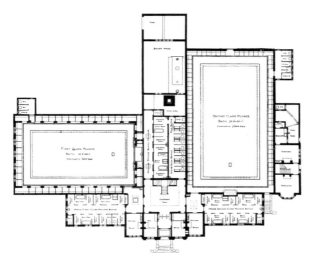

▲ All over Britain historic baths have been adapted for other uses, as pubs, gyms, flats and even as a mosque. **Lister Drive Baths**, Tuebrook, opened in May 1904, has, since 1992, housed the Lister Fisheries and Pet Centre.

Fish tanks now occupy the 60 x 30 feet first class pool (*top left*), with the arched cubicle areas housing individual tanks, while the 75 x 35 feet second class pool, still with its spectator gallery (*top right*), has been turned into retail space, as has the sumptuously tiled entrance hall (*above*). Indeed the building, its fabric otherwise barely altered, appears tailor made as a shopping emporium.

Lister Drive was the first of four Edwardian baths built by the Baths Committee under the chairmanship of William Roberts, and to the designs of Borough Engineer WR Court. Apart from their more exuberant use of materials, these new baths featured fewer slipper baths and no wash-houses. Heated water for Lister Drive was pumped in from a nearby power station.

The baths closed in 1987 and were replaced by the Peter Lloyd Lifestyles centre.

Baths and Library, Wavertree

▲ Another interesting example of the adaptive re-use of a former baths building is **Picton Road Baths**. Built alongside Wavertree Library (on the right) and opened in May 1906, the baths were promised to local residents when Liverpool Corporation absorbed the Wavertree district in 1895.

Borough Engineer WR Court was again the designer, using this time Arts and Crafts styling for the Picton Road frontage.

Internally there were two pools (75 x 35 feet and 50 x 27 feet), the smaller one being reserved for women. As at Lister Drive, the entrance hall, corridors and poolside cubicles were lined with green and cream glazed tiling and faience work, supplied by the Pilkington Tile and Pottery Company of Clifton, Lancashire (who supplied several other Edwardian baths in the north west, including Manchester's magnificent

Victoria Baths). These extra details added towards to final costs of £24,703, though by the standards of the day this still represented excellent value.

Indeed the tiling retains its sparkle today, for even though the pools were closed in 1994, the entrance block has since been converted into a One Stop Shop,

opened in December 2005 by Lord Rennard of Wavertree and funded by Liverpool's Neighbourhood Renewal Fund, the City of Liverpool and Liverpool Direct.

The two pools at the rear – due for eventual demolition – are to be replaced by the new Olympic-sized Picton Pool, due to open in 2008 (*see page 183*).

A specially commissioned piece of Pilkington faience work in the entrance hall of the former Picton Road Baths reflects the civic pride invested in Liverpool's baths.

Queen's Drive (*top*) was one of the first baths to be used during the winter months – when demand for swimming fell and heating costs were too high – as a cinema. More commonly, its main pool was also used as a dance hall (*above*), with the roof concealed by drapes. To facilitate this dual use the poolside cubicles were designed to be easily dismantled and stored away.

▲ Opened in August 1907, **Speke Road Baths**, Garston, were, like Picton Road Baths, the fulfilment of a commitment given to local people when the area was absorbed within Liverpool's boundaries in 1895. The same applied to **Queen's Drive Baths**, Walton (*top left*), opened in April 1909. Both were designed by the Borough Engineeer WR Court.

In addition to its innovative dual-usage in winter (*see left*), Queen's Drive was the first baths in Liverpool to be fitted with the newly developed continuous filtration system, thereby ending the established practice of 'fill and empty' and also, after the First World War, the distinction between first and second class bathing.

Originally it had been planned to use sea water at Queen's Drive, but when this proved impractical, sea-salt crystals were diluted in the water instead, to provide a density described proudly as 'equal to that of the Atlantic Ocean'. (Chlorination was a later innovation, in the 1930s).

Garston Baths were the smallest of Court's four designs, but gained a national reputation thanks to the **Garston Swimming Club**.

Formed in 1908 and still going strong today, the club, under Britain's leading swimming coach of the early 20th century, Bill Howcroft, provided three of the four women's relay team that won silver at the 1920 Olympics, while May Spencer held the world record in both breaststroke and backstroke. The country's leading male backstroke swimmer, Austin Rawlinson, also a Garston member, appeared in the 1924 Olympics.

Garston was replaced in 2000 by the Garston Lifestyles Centre, where the old baths' foundation stone from July 1906 is now displayed, alongside a memorial to Rawlinson, who died in 2000.

Queen's Drive was demolished in 2004 and replaced by the £6m Alsop Lifestyles Centre, jointly funded by the Big Lottery Fund and Liverpool City Council, and opened in March 2007.

▲ Two historic baths are still in use across the River Mersey.

Guinea Gap Baths, Seacombe (*above*), designed by Wallasey Urban District Council's Borough Engineer, WH Travers, and opened in April 1908, had two pools, measuring 75 x 30 feet and 75 x 27 feet, both filled with salt water from the Mersey. This in itself was not unusual. Cornwallis Street also took its water from the river.

But for reasons which have never been fully explained, the water at Guinea Gap had a rather unusual quality, even after the filtration system was updated in the 1930s. Over 200 national, European and world records were broken there, while **Wallasey Swimming Club** produced dozens of champions, including Neil McKechnie, Lilian Preece and Alan Williams.

Today only the external fabric of the building survives. After structural problems were identified in 1984 Wirral Borough Council completely gutted the building and rebuilt both pools, one of them as a lesiure pool with a beach effect, at a cost of over £2 million.

But not all those who had campaigned so hard to save the baths were entirely pleased with

the outcome, for instead of salt water the new pools were filled from the mains instead.

Also saved from closure, but by different means, was **Byrne Avenue Baths** (*top right and centre right*).

Built by Birkenhead Corporation and designed by RW Johnston, the baths opened in March 1933. The main pool, measuring 75 x 35 feet (the standard then for water polo) had a spectator gallery and was designed to stage concerts, film shows and public meetings during the winter. Even dressing rooms for performers were provided.

A second pool measured 75 x 30 feet. By 1933, however, there was no segregation of the sexes or first and second class categories.

In response to local residents who objected to the use of a tall chimney, the building used gas powered heating.

Now, ironically, local residents bear responsibility for running the baths. This is as a result of Wirral Borough Council's decision in 1996 to dispense with the building. Anxious not to lose the facility a group of volunteers set up the Byrne Avenue Recreational Trust, and this now rents the building at a peppercorn rate.

In return the Trust receives a grant of £20,000 per year from the Council, and must pay all running costs from income received from admissions, swimming lessons and other activities. But should, as is inevitable, the building require major maintenance, the Trust must seek funding from outside sources.

A handful of other baths are run on similar lines – Chester City Baths for example – as are a number of lidos. So far Byrne Avenue's trust has kept its head above water, and has increased usage appreciably. So could this be a model for other historic baths?

Modern paintwork aside, Byrne Avenue's main pool is a fine example of a 1930s reinforced concrete pool structure. Even the teak gallery seats are the originals.

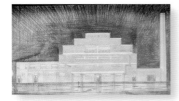

▲ By the 1920s there were 16 indoor public baths in Liverpool. But as slum clearances began in the 1930s there arose a need for new baths to serve the council estates emerging to the west of the city, and, not least, to provide employment at a time of acute work shortages.

These plans, drawn up by the City Surveyor Albert Jenkins, who also oversaw the design of Speke Airport, were for identical structures, the **William Roberts Baths**, on Utting Avenue East, Norris Green, and the **Harold Davies Baths**, on East Prescot Road, Dovecot. Both were named after members of the city's Baths Committee and cost just over £40,000 each, and both opened in 1936; the former on 29 April, the latter on 10 June.

They were first indoor baths to be built in the city for 27 years, and were far in advance of their predecessors. And yet neither survived to the end of the century.

As so often with swimming pool design, innovation proved no guarantee of longevity.

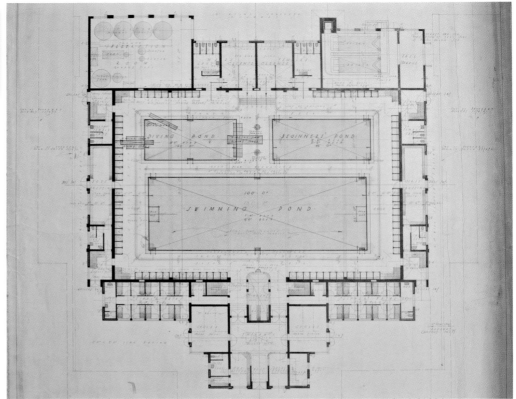

▲ The plans for both the **William Roberts Baths** and the **Harold Davies Baths** borrowed from German designs of the period, and reflected changes not only in technology but also in society.

Most radical of all was the provision of three separate but classless and non-segregated pools within the one main hall.

Yet one anomaly prevailed. The large pool measured 131 x 90 feet – an apparently arbitrary, imperial size, unrelated to any competitive swimming – while the diving pool, a mere ten feet deep, was served by a diving stage whose top board was set at 5m high, to meet international metric standards.

The third, shallow pool, 45 x 20 feet, was reserved for children, but was adjacent to the adults' pool, so that families could stay in contact.

Other innovations that would become standard were cleansing foot baths, through which all bathers had to walk before entry to the pools, and a central basket system for storing clothes, so that there could be a quicker turnover in the cubicles.

Also of note is that there was no laundry, only 20 slipper baths (because most houses on the estates had their own bathrooms), and that, for the first time in Liverpool, car parking spaces were provided for staff and visitors.

But by far the most striking element of the design was the building's superstructure.

Reinforced concrete arches were, by 1936, common in modern pools. But few were as tall and wide as these. Four giant arches spanning 90 feet dominated the main hall, which had spectator galleries at each end (not ideal for galas), and a first floor café on one side, overlooking the pools.

Natural light flooded in from three levels of clerestory windows. At night underwater electric lighting illuminated the pools, to create a theatrical effect that was in marked contrast to the baths' relatively plain, brick exteriors.

▲ Art Deco aqua temples or over-engineered follies?

At both the **Harold Davies Baths, Dovecot** (*above and left*), and at the identical William Roberts Baths, Norris Green, structural failings started to appear in the 1980s, particularly in the reinforced concrete roof structure. Meanwhile, the costs of maintaining the large expanses of flat roofing, and the baths' routine running costs both rocketed, at a time when public funds were at their most stretched.

So it was that Dovecot closed in 1988 (the site is now housing), followed by Norris Green in 1995 (a Sure Start Centre now occupies the site). Both baths were outlived by three of their Victorian and Edwardian predecessors.

◀ Undoubtedly the heyday of open air swimming in Britain was the 1930s. In Merseyside alone there were seven outdoor pools (with an eighth at Southport). These comprised the four children's baths in Liverpool, the open air pool at Stanley Park (*see page 53*), and across the Mersey, two of the new generation of lidos in New Brighton, where the local authority was desperate to keep pace with other resorts opening similar facilities.

The first of this pair to open was the **Derby Pool**, on the seafront at Harrison Drive. Designed by the Wallasey Borough Engineer G Wilkinson, it was 330 feet in length (over four times the length of a standard indoor pool of the period), with a two storey pavilion facing the bay, and sun bathing terraces on all four sides.

But even as this pool was being opened by the Earl of Derby in June 1932, as shown here, there were already advanced plans for an even larger pool less than a mile up the coast, on Marine Promenade.

Named simply the **Open Air Baths, New Brighton** (*opposite*) – the term lido was never used in the north west – this second pool, also designed by Wilkinson, was a colossal structure costing £103,000. It was opened in June 1934 with a ceremony attended by 12,000 spectators, and was one of the largest of its type ever built.

The stripped Art Deco design of Derby Pool pavilion was similar to several lidos of the period. But so too was its fate. Demolished in the 1980s, a modern pub of the same name now occupies the site. For more information on the history of lidos see *Liquid Assets*, an earlier publication in the *Played in Britain* series (*see Links*).

THE NEW BATHING POOL, NEW BRIGHTON. (17)   PHOTO. ALTIGRAPH. LTD.   G.692.

▲ New Brighton's **Open Air Baths** was one of the largest and most sophisticated lidos of the 1930s, with expansive terraces, a stunning Art Deco pavilion, which included changing rooms and six shops, and a 330 feet long D shaped pool, 225 feet at its widest. Like a beach, the pool floor sloped gradually down from deck level on the café side (*left*) to 15 feet at the opposite side where there was a diving stage and water polo section.

In its first season the baths attracted nearly one million visitors (including a record 34,560 on one particularly fine day in July 1934).

Over the years the baths became the favoured destination of holiday makers, while the Derby Pool was used more by locals. But ultimately neither could sustain their early appeal and running losses soon mounted. Moreover, the Open Air Baths suffered from having been built on shifting sands. By the 1980s annual visits were down to 30,000. Then in 1990 a storm breached the baths' foundations. An application to have the buildings listed was rejected, and in May 1990 the baths were demolished.

The site, opposite Marine Park, has lain empty since.

▶ Nowadays the sands at Crosby are best known for housing Anthony Gormley's 100 iron men statues. But visitors to Brighton-le-Sands over a longer period have also witnessed two quite contrasting examples of modern swimming pool design on the waterfront.

The original **Crosby Baths**, opened in November 1963, was typical of the period; a reinforced concrete structure with flat roofing and glazed curtain walling.

Its main pool measured 110 feet long (the new metric standard of 33m) x 42 feet, and was filled by seawater, piped in from the bay and held in a 27,000 gallon tank before chlorination.

There were 500 seats for spectators, making this the largest gala pool on Merseyside.

Unfortunately, owing to their construction and heavy running costs, few pools of this era have survived until the present day. (London's Grade II* listed Crystal Palace Sports Centre, built in 1964 is the finest.) So when the concrete at Crosby was found to have corroded from its exposure to sea air, the pool was closed in 1997.

Its replacement (*right*) could hardly be more different. Circular in plan, with a low profile steel frame and weather-resistant cladding, the £6.5 million **Crosby Leisure Centre** was Britain's first leisure complex to be financed by a PFI scheme. As is the modern way, the centre is also run by a private operator, Parkwood Leisure, contracted by Sefton Council. Internally, there are pools measuring 25 x 13m and 13 x 7m, a fitness suite and a range of facilities for indoor sports.

Yet viewed from the Crosby sands it is easy to imagine that the centre was in truth the spacecraft from which Gormley's iron men must have originally emerged.

The New Swimming Baths, Crosby   W.4308

▲ Liverpool's most recent phase of development has seen the creation of a network of centres combining wet and dry activities under the Leisure Service's own Lifestyles branding and management.

Built around the shell of an existing sports hall, the £6 million **Lifestyles Garston** centre on Long Lane (*top left*) opened in December 2000, with a standard 25 metre pool, a learner pool, fitness centre and ancillary outdoor facilities.

At Speke, the **Lifestyles Austin Rawlinson** centre (*above*), named after the former swimmer, is an extension of a 1965 building.

Both buildings are determinedly functional, in the tradition of many a post war 'sports barn'.

In contrast, the new **Picton Pools** at Wavertree (*top right and above*), due to open in 2008, promise greater aesthetic appeal. Designed by S+P Architects and housing Liverpool's first 50m pool, with 400 seats, plus a 20m training pool, the building will complement the dry sports facilities in neighbouring Wavertree Park.

The £15 million costs are being met by the City Council, with a £4 million grant from Sport England.

Chapter Nineteen

Conclusions

This collection of historic golf clubs is on display for visitors to the Royal Liverpool Golf Club at Hoylake, one of several golf clubs in the Merseyside area to own collections of artefacts and memorabilia. It is to be hoped that the proposed Museum of Liverpool will provide space so that such collections might be exhibited, temporarily or permanently, in a section dedicated to the sporting heritage of the region. Given the region's wealth of golfing history, exhibits of this nature would surely have wide appeal, both locally and internationally.

In a city where billions of pounds of both public and private finance is being invested in urban regeneration and cultural renewal, it is important that sporting heritage should not be overlooked in matters of policy and planning.

For this reason, we conclude this study with a brief series of simple, practical suggestions for safeguarding those resources which lend the sporting scene on Merseyside its distinct character.

Historic sports buildings

Buildings for sport are of course already eligible for protection under the current system of listing. Indeed several listed buildings are featured within this book.

There are, however, a number of unprotected buildings which may merit consideration, either by English Heritage or, for local listing purposes, by Liverpool City Council's Select Committee on Green, Environment and Heritage issues, and its counterparts in neighbouring authorities.

Candidates include the clubhouse and turnstile block at Waterloo Rugby Club (*see page* 108), the grandstand at Bebington Oval (*page 101*), the clubhouse of Childwall Golf Club (*page 140*), the pavilion of Liverpool CC, Aigburth (*page 114*), the clubhouse of West Lancashire Golf Club (*page 141*), and Woolton Baths (*page 173*).

Readers may have their own suggestions which should be forwarded to *Played in Britain*.

In putting forward suggestions, it is recognised that sports clubs and leisure providers have ever changing needs, and that listing has in the past been perceived by some as hampering long-term planning, whilst adding to costs.

However, as a result of reforms to the listing regime proposed in the Government's Heritage Protection White Paper of 2005, it is hoped that a new system of Heritage Protection Agreements – to be drawn up in consultation with the owners and operators of listed buildings – will lessen this burden and reduce bureaucracy.

Certainly those clubs which act as unpaid guardians of our sporting heritage need extra guidance if their historic venues and grounds are to be protected.

Maintaining historic buildings

Fortunately, no sports-related buildings on Merseyside are currently included on English Heritage's Buildings at Risk Register, while the future of the one building featured in this study that has been most at risk in recent years, the Florence Institute, now seems assured.

That said, there are concerns for the fabric of Lister Drive Baths (*see page 174*), a fine Edwardian structure whose current owners should be encouraged and assisted in their efforts towards sensitive conservation.

Equally, the successful conversion of the former Drill Hall in Birkenhead for sporting use (*page 147*) should serve as a reminder that certain historic buildings might yet enjoy a prolonged life as sports venues.

A prime candidate for consideration in this respect is the Grade II★ listed former Tate & Lyle Sugar Silo building on Regent Road, which would appear to have excellent potential for indoor sports, such as five-a-side football, tennis and rock-climbing.

Museums and collections

Apart from the private collections on view to visitors at the Royal Liverpool Golf Club, Hoylake (see opposite) and at Aintree (Chapter Three), there is at present only one museum in Liverpool specifically related to sport – the museum of Liverpool FC at Anfield (see right).

It is therefore to be hoped that a publicly accessible collection of the city's sporting treasures will form a major part of the planned Museum of Liverpool, on a scale larger than was possible in the museum's former premises.

But there is a further concern relating to sporting archives on Merseyside.

As the pages of this book confirm, the Liverpool Record Office at the Central Library is the guardian of a superb collection of sports-related archives.

But as ongoing research has repeatedly discovered, many more important artefacts and records in Merseyside have been lost through negligence or through misadventure (destroyed, for example, in pavilion fires), or sold to private collectors.

For this reason, *Played in Britain* fully endorses the current campaign by the Everton Collection Charitable Trust and the Liverpool Record Office to purchase the David France collection of Everton archives and memorabilia (see Links). This is a collection of national, as well as local importance.

The efforts of the Merseyside Former Boxers' Association to archive their history, with assistance from the Heritage Lottery Fund, is similarly to be applauded.

But there still remain other club archives that should also be transferred to public ownership, so that they may be professionally conserved, catalogued and made more widely available to researchers and educational establishments. A concerted effort in this direction will not only save archives that may be at risk, but may also save public expense in the long run.

It is further recommended that all possible support and advice be extended to the owners of the Norman Clare Collection of billiards and snooker artefacts and memorabilia (Chapter Seven). Again, this collection is of national importance and is unique to Liverpool.

Specific commemorations

There are several sports-related sites on Merseyside that merit commemoration, in the form of a simple plaque, or even a piece of commissioned public art.

These include the site of the Liverpool Gymnasium on Myrtle Street (*page 143*), the sites of the Pudsey Street boxing stadium (*page 156*) and the Liverpool Stadium (*page 158*), and the site of the Pierhead Baths (*page 168*).

Some form of recognition is also due to the Gordon Institute (*page 148*), the oldest surviving and operational Boys' Club in Britain.

Further research

Played in Liverpool has drawn information from a number of excellent studies of sport on Merseyside (see Links). However, there remain certain areas of research which we feel deserve further consideration.

Foremost amongst these are the Liverpool Olympic Festivals of the 1860s and 1890s (*page 12ff*). Known sources for this research are admittedly few and far between, but in view of the impending 2012 Olympic Games in London, a further concerted research effort should be considered a priority by one of the city's educational institutions.

Arguably as pressing is the need for a comprehensive social and historical study of the city's involvement in the mammoth football pools industry of the 20th century (Chapter Nine).

Finally, we recommend that the anomalies concerning the early history of the Grand National (Chapter Three) be reviewed by independent historians, and, if necessary, the honours board at Aintree and other official records be amended accordingly.

Visitors to the museum at Anfield inspect the European Cup, held in perpetuity by Liverpool following the club's fifth victory in the tournament in 2005, a feat matched only by Real Madrid and AC Milan. Solid silver, with a gold-plated lining, the iconic trophy was designed in Berne, Switzerland, and was first held aloft by members of Celtic's winning team in 1967. Arguably the trophy is the most valuable sporting artefect in the city, in a museum that in 2006 received 132,000 visitors; that is, second only to the Beatles Story among private museums in the city, and within the top five of all museums in the city. Such is the appeal of sporting heritage.

Links

Where no publisher listed assume self-published by organisation or author

Where no publication date listed assume published on final date within title, ie. 1860–1960 means published 1960

Abbreviations:
LRO Liverpool Record Office
nd – no date
UP – University Press

Sport General

Bale J *Landscapes of Modern Sport* Leicester UP (1994)
Cox R, Jarvie G & Vamplew W *Encyclopedia of British Sport* ABC-Clio Ltd (2000)
Cunninghan H *Leisure in the Industrial Revolution* St Martin's Press (1980)
Holt R *Sport and the British* Clarendon Press (1989)
Holt R & Mason T *Sport in Britain 1945-2000* Blackwell (2000)
Vamplew W *Pay Up and Play the Game* Cambridge UP (1988)
Wymer N *Sport in England: A History of Two Thousand Years of Games and Pastimes* George G Harrap (1949)

Liverpool General

Belchem J (ed) *Liverpool 800 Character, Culture and History* Liverpool UP (2006)
Hughes Q *Architecture and Townscape in Liverpool* Lund Humphries (1964)
Hughes Q *Liverpool – City of Architecture* Bluecoat Press (1999)
Sharples J *Liverpool – Pevsner Architectural Guide* Yale (2004)
Young P & Bellew J *Scouseology Vols 1-3* Scouse Promotions (1986–89)
sportsdevelopment.liverpool.gov.uk
www.liverpool.gov.uk
www.liverpool08.com
www.liverpoolheritageforum.org.uk
www.liverpoolhistorysociety.org.uk
www.liverpoolmuseums.org.uk
www.mersey-gateway.org
www.merseysidesport.com

Chapter 1. Played in Liverpool

Anthony D *Organic Olympism or Olympic Glory: the Roots of Modern Olympism and the Mystery of John Hulley* Journal of Olympic History (Winter 2001)
Broadbent RJ *Annals of the Liverpool Stage* (1908)
Brooke R *Liverpool as it was 1775 to 1800* Liverpool Libraries and Information Service (2003)
Brownbill J & Farrer W *The Victoria History of the County of Lancaster* University of London (1908)
Channon H *Portrait of Liverpool* Robert Hale (1970)
Davidson P *Memories of the Childwall Quoiting Club and some of its members* Henry Young (1934)
Description of The Baths and Wash-houses Owned by the Corporation of Liverpool LRO (1846)
Furlong BA *The Development of Physical Education in Liverpool 1900–18* M.Ed thesis, Liverpool University (1976)
Hope EW (ed) *Handbook for the Congress of the Royal Institute of Public Health, 1903* City of Liverpool (1903)
Jones C *The Social Survey of Merseyside* Liverpool UP (1934)
Liverpool Town Books vols 1-2 Mawdsley & Son (1853)
Melly E *Memoirs to Charles Melly* Curtis & Beamish (1889)
Midwinter E *Old Liverpool* David & Charles (1971)
Muir JR *History of Liverpool* Liverpool University (1907)
Nicholas Blundell Diaries 1702-1728 (1895)
Phillips R *The Liverpool Olympic Festivals of the 1860s* North of England Athletic Association (nd)
Picton JA *Memorials of Liverpool in two volumes* (1903)
Picton JA *Municipal Archives and Records* (1886)
Rees R *The Development of Physical Recreation in Liverpool in the 19th Century* MA Thesis, Liverpool University (1968)
Rees R *Organisation of Sport in 19th Century Liverpool* International Assoc for the History of PE and Sport (1976)
Rees R *Olympic Festivals of Mid-Victorian England* Olympic Review (1977)
Ruhl J & Keuser A *The History of the Liverpool Olympics in 19th Century England* Deutsche Sportochschule Köln (1989)
Shaw F *My Liverpool* Wolfe Publishing (1971)
Shimmin H *Low Life and Moral Improvement in Mid-Victorian England* (eds JK Walton & A Wilcox) Leicester UP (1991)
Shimmin H *Liverpool Life, articles from the Liverpool Mercury, 1856* LRO 1856
Stonehouse J *The Streets of Liverpool* (1869)
Social Survey of Merseyside Liverpool University (1933)
The Story of the GAA in Liverpool 1884-1984
Touzeau J *The Rise and Progress of Liverpool from 1551 to 1835* (1910)
Troughton T *History of Liverpool* (1810)
Wenlock Olympian Society *William Penny Brookes and the Olympic Connection* (1996)
Whale D *Lost Villages of Liverpool, part 1-3* T Stephenson & Sons (1984)

Chapter 2. River Mersey

Water Sports Centre Architects Journal, 22 September 1994
Hayward JD *Royal Mersey Yacht Club 1844-1907*
Magazines to Wallasey, 100 years of the Wallasey Yacht Club 1903-2003

Making the most of the Mersey The Environment Agency
Melville H *Redburn* (1849)
Seabird Association Handbook (2002)
Tarbuck K (ed) *Liverpool Victoria Rowing Club, 1884-1934 – Jubilee Souvenir* (1934)
www.lvrc.co.uk Liverpool Victoria Rowing Club
www.merseybasin.org.uk
www.royalmersey.co.uk Royal Mersey Yacht Club
www.spanish.btinternet.co.uk/mersey Mersey Rowing Club
www.wallasey-yacht-club.fsnet.co.uk Wallasey Yacht Club
www.liverpoolheartbeat.com/swim.html Across Mersey Swim

Chapter 3. Aintree
Bird TH *A Hundred Grand Nationals* (1937)
Blair GF *Some notes on the history of Crosby Races in the 16th, 17th and 18th Centuries* (nd)
Formby J *An account of the Liverpool Races, established in the year 1827, with observations on the conduct of the Committee formed in July 1828* LRO (1828)
Green R *Ossie Dale's Grand National Scrapbook* Marlborough/Punchtown (1992)
Green R *The Grand National* Virgin Publishing (2000)
Mason F *Heroes and Heroines of the Grand National* (1907)
National Museums & Galleries on Merseyside *Grand National, 150 years of Aintree's Steeplechase* Liverpool Museum (1989)
Pinfold J *Gallant Sport: The Authentic History of Liverpool Races and the Grand National* Parkway Press (1999)
Tyrer F *Crosby Races* (nd)
www.aintree.co.uk
www.grandnational.org.uk

Chapter 4. Birkenhead Park
Allan GA *Birkenhead Park Football Club 1871-1921*
Elston C *Birkenhead Park Cricket Club 1846-1996*
www.birkenheadparkrugby.com
www.wirral.gov.uk/er/birkpark.htm

Chapter 5. Stanley Park
Barnes T *Bootle FC: Third Time Lucky* (1988)
Heatley M & Welch I *The Great Derby Matches: Liverpool v Everton* Dial House (1996)
Inglis S *The Football Grounds of Britain* Collins Willow (1996)
Inglis S *Engineering Archie* English Heritage (2005)
Keates T *History of Everton Football Club* (1928)
Kelly S *The Kop* Mandarin (1993)
Kelly S *Shankly: It's much more important than that* Virgin (1996)
Kelly S *Liverpool 1892-1998* Hamlyn (1998)
Kennedy D *The Development of Professional Football Organisations in Merseyside 1878-1914* (PhD Thesis, Leeds University 2003)

Mason T *The Blues and the Reds* THSLC (1985)
Onslow T *The Forgotten Rivals, a history of Bootle FC 1880-93*
Onslow T *Men from the Hill Country, the development of Everton during the Reign of Victoria* Countywise (2002)
Preston T *The Early Days of Anfield* unpublished article (nd)
Richardson PE *The Development of Professional Football on Merseyside 1878-1894* Lancaster University (1983)
Rowlands J *Everton Football Club 1878-1946* Tempus (2001)
Sephton G *This is Anfield Calling!* Red Rag (1998)
We've had a ball for one hundred years 1895-1995 i-Zingari Football League (1995)
Young PM *Football on Merseyside* Stanley Paul (1963)
www.evertonfc.com Everton Football Club
www.liverpoolfc.tv Liverpool Football Club

Chapter 6. Sefton Park
Barnes C *The History and Development of Liverpool's Early Parks* MA Thesis, Loughborough University (1988)
Griffiths R *The History of the Royal and Ancient Park of Toxteth* (nd)
Twist C *A History of Liverpool Parks* Hornby (2000)
Liverpool Open Space Study, Volume 3
Cultural Heritage Assessment (2005)
Liverpool Parks Official Handbook (1934)
www.merseybowmen.org.uk Mersey Bowmen Tennis Club
www.seftonparkcc.co.uk Sefton Park Cricket Club

Chapter 7. Billiards
Clare N *Billiards and Snooker Bygones* Shire (1996)
Mitchell JR *Billiards and Snooker, a Trade History* British Sports and Allied Industries Federation (1981)
The Noble Game of Billiards Thurston (nd)
www.thurstonsnooker.co.uk
www.cuesnviews.co.uk

Chapter 8. Goal Nets
Brodie J *Patent: Improvements in or applicable to goals used in football, lacrosse or other like games (1890)*
Ward A *Ward's Soccerpedia – the Lore and Laws of the Beautiful Game* Robson Books (2006)

Chapter 9. Football Pools
Clegg B *The Man Who Made Littlewoods* Teach Yourself (1993)
Reed P (ed) *Football & Fortunes: the Inside Story of Littlewoods Football Pools* Brahm (2003)
Daily Herald Football and Pools Handbooks 1950-55
Sharpe G *Gambling on Goals - a Century of Football Betting* Mainstream (1997)
Smyth I *The Development of Baseball in Northern England, 1935-39* International Journal of the History of Sport, No 10 (1993)

Chapter 10. Stadiums and Grounds

Bishop P *The A-Z of Tranmere Rovers* (1990)
Daglish JA *Red, Black & Blue: the first 125 years of the Liverpool Football Club (Rugby Union) 1857-1982*
Fazey IH *Waterloo FC 1882-1982* (1982)
Genders R *Encyclopedia of Greyhound Racing* Pelham (1981)
Hunter G *The Story of the Bebington Oval* The Bridge, Unilever House Magazine No 112 (May 1997)
Luft HM *A History of Merchant Taylors' School Crosby* Liverpool UP (1970)
Twydell D *Lost But Not Forgotten* Yore Publications (various)
Wotherspoon D *The Mighty Mariners, the Story of Marine Association Football Club* (1997)
Groundtastic Magazine (various 1995-2006)
www.cammelllairdfc.co.uk
www.formbyfc.co.uk
www.knowsley.gov.uk
www.liv.ac.uk/sports
www.liverpoolramblers.com
www.marinefc.com
www.runtrackdir.com
www.speedwayswapshop.co.uk
www.tranmererovers.premiumtv.co.uk
www.waterloorugby.com

Chapter 11. Cricket

Ambrose D *Liverpool & District Cricketers: 1882-1947* Association of Cricket Statisticians (2002)
Bootle Cricket Club *150th Anniversary: 1833-1983*
Elston C *Birkenhead Park Cricket Club: 1846-1996* (1997)
Lorimer M & Ambrose D *Cricket Grounds of Lancashire* Association of Cricket Statisticians (2002)
Price DC *A History of Northern Cricket Club 1859-1961* (1985)
Ross AJ *Cricket and the Establishment: A Social History of Cricket in Lancashire with special reference to the Liverpool Competition 1775-1935* PhD Thesis, Ohio State Univ (1987)
Walker PN *The Liverpool Competition: A Study of the Development of Cricket on Merseyside* Countywise (1988)
www.firwoodbootle.co.uk Bootle Cricket Club
www.ldcc.org.uk Liverpool & District Cricket Competition
www.liverpoolcricketclub.co.uk
www.northernclub.co.uk

Chapter 12. Bowls

Olympic Bowling Club Centenary Brochure 1892-1992
Richmond Bowling Club Centenary Brochure 1993
West Derby Bowling Club Diamond Jubilee 1884-1959
Sefton Park Bowling Club 1884-2001
www.drakespride.co.uk
www.bowls.org British Crown Green Bowling Association

Chapter 13. Baseball

Bloyce D *John Moores and the Professional Baseball Leagues in 1930s England* Sport History Vol 21 No 1, Taylor Francis (March 2007)
Jackson P *Liverpool's Sporting Pages* Lechdale Press (1991)
www.haltonbaseballclub.org.uk

Chapter 14. Golf

Davies JV *Wallasey Golf Club 1891-1991* Grant (1991)
Davies P *Formby Ladies' Golf Club, A History* (1996)
Edwards L & Brocklehurst J *Royal Liverpool Golf Club* (1983)
Foster H *Links Along the Line* Birkdale (1996)
Foster H *Annals of the Hesketh Golf Club* 1885-2000 (2001)
Foster H *Southport & Ainsdale: The Golfers' Club 1906-2006*
Hawthorne N *English Notebooks 1804-1861* (1941)
Irlam P *A Lively Octogenarian: Hillside Golf Club 1911-91* Grant (1993)
Johnson AJD *The History of Royal Birkdale Golf Club* Springwood (1988)
Lewis P *The Dawn of Professional Golf* (1995)
Pinfold J *Hoylake Racecourse and the beginnings of the Royal Liverpool Golf Club* Boumphrey (2005)
Thomas I *Formby Golf Club 1884-1972*
www.childwallgolfclub.co.uk
www.formbygolfclub.co.uk
www.formbyladiesgolfclub.co.uk
www.heskethgolfclub.co.uk
www.hillside-golfclub.co.uk
www.royalbirkdale.com
www.royal-liverpool-golf.com
www.sandagolfclub.co.uk Southport & Ainsdale Golf Club
www.wallaseygolfclub.com
www.westlancashiregolf.co.uk

Chapter 15. Gymnastics

Alexander A *A Wayfarer's Log* John Murray (1919)
Graham P & Ueberhorst H *The Modern Olympics* Leisure Press (1976)
Prestidge J *The History of British Gymnastics* BGA (1988)
Seagrave J & Chu D (eds) *The Olympic Games in Transition* Human Kinetic (1988)
www.liverpoolgymnastics.bravehost.com City of Liverpool Gymnastics Club
www.birkenheadtrampolineclub.co.uk

Chapter 16. Boys' and Girls' Clubs

Eager W *Making of Men: the history of Boys' Clubs* London UP (1953)
Florence Institute, Dingle Conservation Plan (2004)
Florencian - Bulletin of the Dingle History Group (various)
Goodall I *Liverpool Charitable Institutions* (2003)

Papers and Correspondence of the Liverpool Boys' Association and MYA (LRO)
Shrewsbury House 75th Anniversary brochure (1978)
www.kirkdaleonline.co.uk Gordon Institute
www.liverpool2007.org.uk/rydal/rydal.htm Rydal Youth Centre
www.mya.org.uk Merseyside Youth Association
www.savetheflorrie.org.uk Florence Institute
www.shrewsbury.org.uk

Chapter 17. Boxing
Boxing Programmes Liverpool Pudsey Street Stadium
Boxing Programmes Liverpool Stadium, 1932-1984
Cooke T Little Italy Bluecoat Press (2002)
Jenkinson J & Shaw G The Lives and Times of Liverpool's Boxing Heroes Milo Books (2004)
Mace J Fifty Years a Fighter, the Life Story of Jem Mace (1998)
Mugs Alley Official Organ of the Merseyside Former Boxers' Association
www.accliverpool.com Liverpool Arena and Convention Centre
www.mfba.org.uk Merseyside & Wirral Former Boxers' Association

Chapter 18. Swimming
Baths Committee Centenary Brochure, 1952
Description of The Baths and Wash-houses Owned by the Corporation of Liverpool, 1846. LRO
Ellison P & Howe P Talk of the Wash House City of Liverpool (1997)
Kelly M Kitty Wilkinson Countrywise (2000)
Love C The Reflecting Pool of Society: Aquatic Sport, Leisure and Recreation in England c1800-1918 PhD Thesis, York University (2003)
Newlands J Report to the Council on Public Baths and Wash-houses (1856)

Woolton Swimming Club Centenary Brochure 1895-1995
www.merseyworld.com/bart Byrne Avenue Recreational Trust
www.lidos.org.uk

Periodicals and newspapers
Local: Bethell's Life in London and Liverpool Sporting Register; Bootle Times; Crosby Herald; Cox's Liverpool Annual 1922; Gore's General Advertiser; Liverpool Citizen; Liverpool Courier; Liverpool Daily Post; Liverpool Echo; Liverpool Mercury; Liverpool Review; Northern Daily Times; Porcupine; Stranger in Liverpool; The Liverpolitan; The Liverpool Athletic Times; Williamson's Liverpool Advertiser
National: Architect & Building News; Architects Journal; Athletic News; The Builder; The Daily Telegraph; The Guardian; Illustrated London News; The Independent; The Observer; The Times Digital Archives

Played in Manchester
Simon Inglis (2004)

Played in Birmingham
Steve Beauchampé & Simon Inglis (2006)

Engineering Archie – Archibald Leitch, football ground designer
Simon Inglis (2005)

Liquid Assets – the lidos and open air swimming pools of Britain
Janet Smith (2005)

The Best of Charles Buchan Football Monthly ed. Simon Inglis (2006)

A Load of Old Balls
Simon Inglis (2005)

For more information on the series see
www.playedinbritain.co.uk

Future titles
Great Lengths – the indoor swimming pools of Britain Dr Ian Gordon (2007)

Charles Buchan's Manchester United Gift Book (2007)

Charles Buchan's Arsenal Gift Book (2007)

Played at the Pub Arthur Taylor (2007)

Played in Glasgow Ged O'Brien (2008)

Uppies & Downies – Britain's traditional football games Hugh Hornby (2008)

Played on Tyne & Wear
Lynn Pearson (2009)

Bowled Over – the bowling greens of Britain Hugh Hornby (2009)

Played in London Simon Inglis (2011)

Credits

Photographs and images

Please note that where more than one photograph appears on a page, each photograph is identified by a letter, starting with 'a' in the top left hand corner of the page, or at the top, and continuing thereafter in a *clockwise* direction.

All English Heritage and National Monument Record photographs listed are either © English Heritage or © Crown Copyright. NMR. Application for the reproduction of these images should be made to the National Monuments Record, at Kemble Drive, Swindon SN2 2GZ. Tel. 01793 414600.

All maps are Ordnance Survey © Crown Copyright

English Heritage/National Monuments Record photographs

James Davies: 6abc, 8, 27ab, 30ab, 32, 34a, 41d, 46b, 48ab, 49a, 50b, 61a, 62a, 63b, 67, 72a, 75c, 76ab, 77ab, 79, 80, 81abcd, 82abc, 88a, 93, 94a, 101ac, 102b, 107c, 110, 114a, 116b, 117b, 119ab, 120, 122b, 125d, 130ab, 133abc, 135b, 136, 137abc, 138ab, 139ab, 141ab, 145, 146, 154a, 163c, 171ab, 177ac, 182b, 184; Dave MacLeod: 35, 47, 71, 73, 101b, 102c, 103a, 119c, 132, 134a, 135a; Bob Skingle: 21; Peter Williams: 140a; NMR: 39b, 43a, 172abc

Commissioned photographs

John Cocks: 15, 24a, 26, 27c, 31, 43bcd, 69b, 185; Simon Inglis: back cover cd, inside front, 1, 6d, 9, 20, 38b, 42, 43e, 44a, 45ab, 50a, 52, 53c, 54a, 59abc, 60ab, 61b, 62bc, 63a, 65a, 66, 68ac, 69a, 70ab, 78b, 83a, 94b, 102a, 103b, 104ab, 105ac, 108abc, 109ab, 111abc, 113ab, 114bc, 117a, 122a, 123ab, 125ac, 134b, 140b, 147ab, 148b, 149ab, 150, 152b, 162ab, 164b, 166b, 171c, 173abc, 174abc, 175bcd, 183ad; Simon Pendrigh: inside back cover, 115; Ray Physick: back cover ab, 16b, 46a, 106a, 125b, 129b

Archive photographs

Liverpool Post & Echo: 2, 17a, 40c, 65b, 76c, 99c, 116a, 126a, 157b, 159, 163a, 179b; Liverpool Record Office: front cover, 4, 10a, 11, 12, 13, 16a, 19a, 25, 36, 56, 57, 74, 75a, 84, 85, 86, 87, 95, 96ab, 98ab, 99bd, 112ab, 121, 124b, 126b, 142ab, 151, 152ac, 154b, 155, 157cd, 164a, 165a, 166a, 167, 168a, 169ab, 170ab, 171d, 174d, 175a, 176abc, 178ab, 179a, 180ab; National Museums Liverpool (Merseyside Maritime Museum, Stewart Bale Collection): 153b, 181b

Agency photographs

Action Images: 19b, 68b; Blom Aerofilms: 99a, 100; Colorsport: 55a; Corbis: 64b, 127; Empics: 39a, 69c; Getty Images: 7, 55b; John Grossick (Aintree Racecourse): 45c; Illustrated London News: 14, 143, 144, 165b; Bob Lilliman: 105b, 106bc, 107abd; Mary Evans Picture Library: 18; NMM/ Science & Society Picture Library: 19c, 90b, 91abc, 131; Propaganda Photo Agency: 192; © Yale Center for British Art, Paul Mellon Collection, USA/ The Bridgeman Art Library: 38a

Donated photographs

English Heritage thank the following for providing images: Tony Bagnall: 44b; Robin Baynes: 33b; Derek Carruthers: 97c; Norman Clare Collection: 78a, 83b; Clino d'Eletto: 54bc; Dr Ian Gordon: 168b, 181a, 182a; Peter Greville, Birkenhead Park FC: 49b; David Holroyd, Merchant Taylors' School: 117c; Jim Jenkinson: 156, 157a, 158, 160; Littlewoods Football Pools: 88b, 89, 90a, 92; Liverpool City Council: 183bc; Liverpool FC Museum: 58ab, 64a; Liverpool FC: 70c; Liverpool Victoria Rowing Club: 24b, 28, 29ab; Roger Lee: inside front cover; Merseyside & Wirral Former Boxers Association: 64c; Bob Martin: 177b; Northern Cricket Club: 118ab; Henry Pattinson, Childwall Quoits Club: 17b; Mrs MA Pointon: 33a; Bob Rowe: 97b; Richmond Bowling Club: 124a; Nigel Sharp, Liverpool City Council Parks & Environment Dept: 53ab, 72b, 75b; Shrewsbury Boys' Club: 148a, 153a; University of Liverpool: 191; Norman Wells, Liverpool Trojans: 128ab, 129a; Wilkinson Eyre Architects: 163b

Books

Troughton T *History of Liverpool* (1810): 10b
Young P & Bellew J *Scouseology Volumes 1-3*: 97a

Acknowledgements

English Heritage, Played in Britain and the author would like to thank the many individuals, organisations and club representatives who assisted with information and research. They are especially grateful to the Liverpool Culture Company for its sponsorship of the book, and in particular, Graham Boxer, Head of Heritage Development and Mike Doran.

Further thanks go to Louise O'Brien, Henry Owen-John, Peter Figueiredo, Graham Ives and Crispin Edwards at English Heritage North West, and to Rob Richardson and Dr René Rodgers at English Heritage Publications in Swindon.

The author and Played in Britain are especially grateful to David Stoker, David Govier, Roger Hull, Jeff Proffitt, Helena Smart and all staff at the superb Liverpool Record Office, whose assistance and knowledge have proved invaluable, particularly in the supply of images and reference material.

Special thanks also go to Colin Hunt and Tony Hall in the library and archives of the *Liverpool Post & Echo;* Jane Clarke, curator of the Aintree Racecourse Museum; Stephen Done of the Liverpool FC Museum at Anfield; Peter Clare and Mike Atherton of EA Clare & Sons Ltd; Terry Carson and Jim Jenkinson of the Merseyside and Wirral Former Boxers' Association, whose advice and knowledge was hugely helpful, and Norman Wells for access to his extensive archive of baseball material.

For additional help with research, thanks also go to Dr Katy Jones of the Liverpool Parks and Open Spaces Project; Nigel Sharp of Liverpool Parks and Environment Department; Gordon Dacre (Sport and Recreation Services, Liverpool City Council) and Dr Ian Gordon.

The following individuals were also generous with their time and knowledge: Gary Abbot (Wallasey Artisans Golf Club), Bob Allan (Lister Fisheries and Pet Centre), Terence Barraclough (Wallasey Golf Club), Jim Bibby (Liverpool Victoria Rowing Club), Joan Boyce and David Bridges (Wallasey Cricket Club), Ron Brown (Woolton local historian), Tony Brown, Tommy Calderbank (Florence Institute and the Golden Gloves ABA), Leo Carroll (Wirral Athletics Club), Rev Henry Corbett (Shrewsbury House), Martina Corrin, Barry Coyne and Stewart King (West Lancashire Golf Club), Vernon Cubbon and the late Tony Crane (Southport and Ainsdale Golf Club), Gill Cussons and John Perry (Liverpool Cricket Club), Steve Davies, Peter Ellison (Birkenhead Park CC), Chris Elston (Birkenhead Park Cricket Club), Commodore Barbara Fogg (Wallasey Yacht Club), Mark Fox (Kirkby Sports Centre), Albert Gee (Formby Artisan Golf Club), Anne Gleave (National Museums of Liverpool), Reg Green, staff at the Greenbank Sports Academy, Peter Greville (Birkenhead Park Football Club), Darren Griffiths (Everton FC), Clare Hartwell, Mike Henderson (Wirral MBC), George Higham (Cammell Laird FC), Peter Holmes (National Football Museum), Tom Jamieson, Dr Nicolas Jedynakiewicz and Phil Bastow (Royal Mersey Yacht Club), Sands Johnson (Formby Golf Club), Lynn Kane (Garston, Woolton and Speke swimming baths), Les Kellie (Olympic Bowling Club), Gary Kirby (Lifestyles Park Road, Gymnastics Centre of Excellence), Tom Law (Bootle Cricket Club), Mike Leddy (Formby Cricket Club), staff at the Merseyside Watersports Centre, Alison Lobb and Gary Burns (Mersey Bowmen Tennis Club), Jim McVie (Royal Liverpool Village Play) Hal Manby (Liverpool Bowling Club), Dr Stuart Marshall-Clarke (Sefton Park Cricket Club), Bob Martin and Les Rogerson (Byrne Avenue Recreational Trust), Joe Mather (Woolton Village Club), Group Captain Christopher Moore (Royal Liverpool Golf Club), Tony O'Hara (West Derby Bowling Club), Sheena Orton (Kirkdale Community Centre), Emma Owen and Ossie Dale (Aintree Racecourse), Henry Pattinson (Childwall Quoits Club), Dr Lynn Pearson, Reg Phillips (Liverpool John Moores University), Liam Physick, David Pool, John Winter and Gordon Robison (Northern Cricket Club), Dave Rannard (Marine Football Club), Dr John Rowlands, Martyn Senior (Hesketh Golf Club), Harry Sheppard (Richmond Bowling Club), Graham Snelling (The National Horseracing Museum), Jed Smith (Museum of Rugby, Twickenham), Rev Jeff Staples (St Nicholas Church Wallasey), John Stonard (CABE Space), Matthew Tinker (Southport Library), Dick Whammond, Sam Sidwell, Keith Warsop, Phil Watkins (Littlewoods Pools), John Watson (Sefton Park Bowling Club) and finally, the staffs at Birkenhead, Crosby, Wallasey and Woolton Libraries.

Designed by Austin-Smith Lord and completed in 2003, this £3.5 million extension to the University of Liverpool's Sports Centre on Oxford Street features an A-frame steel structure from which a catenary roof is suspended, linking with Denys Lasdun's original 1965 Sports Centre (*see page 21*). Along with the new Arena, the new 50m Picton Pool and Liverpool FC's new stadium in Stanley Park, the extension's innovative approach bodes well for sports architecture in the city for the 21st century.

▲ In the run-up to Wimbledon, tennis players need as much action on grass courts as possible. Hence in June 2002 the **Liverpool International Tennis Tournament** was inaugurated in the leafy surrounds of Calderstones Park. Some of the world's leading stars, Martina Navratilova included, have participated in the tournament, which is staged in a temporary stadium over six days and is noted for its unstuffy informality. It is also accompanied by a programme of coaching for up to 6,000 children.

In 2008, apart from the tennis tournament, Liverpool will stage the European Boxing Championships, and the finale of the Tour of Britain cycle race.

International sporting events have been staged in Liverpool since the Olympic Festivals of the 1860s. Looking ahead, over 140 years later, the challenge is to ensure that whatever the nature of the event, it is hosted, and presented in a way that truly reflects the character of the city and its people. *Played in Liverpool*, it is hoped, will help to shed light on how sporting heritage has, in its own way, helped to shape that special character.